SOCIAL SCIENCE IN NATURAL RESOURCE MANAGEMENT SYSTEMS

SOCIAL BEHAVIOR AND
NATURAL RESOURCES SERIES
Donald R. Field, Series Editor

Social Science in Natural Resource Management Systems, edited by Marc L. Miller, Richard P. Gale, and Perry J. Brown

Community and Forestry: Continuities in Natural Resources Sociology, edited by Robert G. Lee, Donald R. Field, and William R. Burch, Jr.

Economic Valuation of Natural Resources: Issues, Theory, and Applications, edited by Rebecca L. Johnson and Gary V. Johnson

SOCIAL SCIENCE IN NATURAL RESOURCE MANAGEMENT SYSTEMS

EDITED BY
MARC L. MILLER,
RICHARD P. GALE,
AND PERRY J. BROWN

Routledge
Taylor & Francis Group

NEW YORK AND LONDON

First published in paperback 2024

First published 1987 by Westview Press, Inc.

Published 2019 by Routledge
605 Third Avenue, New York, NY 10158

and by Routledge
4 Park Square, Milton Park, Abingdon, Oxon OX14 4RN

Routledge is an imprint of the Taylor & Francis Group, an informa business

© 1987, 2019, 2024 Taylor & Francis

Library of Congress Cataloging-in-Publication Data
Social science in natural resource management systems.
  (Social behavior and natural resources series)
  1. Conservation of natural resources—Government
policy—United States.   2. Natural resources—Social
aspects—United States.   I. Miller, Marc L.
II. Gale, Richard P.   III. Brown, Perry J.
IV. Series.
HC103.7.S62 1987   333.7'0973   87-23138

Publisher's Note
The publisher has gone to great lengths to ensure the quality of this reprint but points out that some imperfections in the original copies may be apparent.

ISBN 13: 978-0-367-28762-7 (hbk)
ISBN 13: 978-0-367-30308-2 (pbk)
ISBN 13: 978-0-429-30637-2 (ebk)

DOI: 10.4324/9780429306372

CONTENTS

Contents   vii

ABOUT THE SERIES

The *Social Behavior and Natural Resources Series* is about human adaptation to natural resources and the constraints these resources place upon institutions and work and play in everyday life. Natural resources, after all, are products of society. The very definition of natural resources arises from the interaction of population, culture, and the biophysical environment.

Biological and physical scientists are providing us with a clearer picture of the nature of species and habitats and the requirements of systems to function under varying management regimes dedicated to conservation and preservation. Social scientists are providing complementary information about the human species, our habitat, and how social systems respond to a wide range of resource management policies.

The integration of social with the biological and physical world is the focus of this series. The present book is about the conduct and contributions of applied social science.

It is apropos that this be the inaugural volume in the series. Resource management issues are human problems which can only be solved with social science knowledge in combination with knowledge from the other sciences. The utilization of these different types of knowledge within the resource management arena depends upon the establishment of a partnership between scientists and managers. Sound management requires agreement on what information is pertinent, how information should be collected, and how information should be employed in decision making.

Here the social sciences can help. Social scientists have a keen appreciation of the power, as well as the limitations, of science to resolve policy conflicts. This is important for understanding how managers filter the concerns of competing constituencies and their own professional cadre while managing the natural resources under their charge.

There are many applied science volumes in sociology, anthropology, and political science that deal with post-industrial society, but this volume is unique in its exclusive attention to natural resources. *Social Science in Natural Resource Management Systems* represents the beginning of a new intellectual tradition in applied social science.

Donald R. Field

PREFACE

Social Science in Natural Resource Management Systems is the result of a lucky combination of personalities, events, and opportunities. Until several years ago, we three editors had independently designed our careers at three universities in the Pacific Northwest. In this, each of us forged an association with a different natural resource management system. Thus, one of us studied the management of marine fisheries, another addressed forest policy, while the third focused on parks and recreation.

In the course of our work, we all reached the conclusion that social science was highly relevant to natural resource management. We also discovered that although natural resource science was formally pluralistic, it was predominantly a natural science enterprise. In this milieu, we began to appreciate the need for interdisciplinary research. At the same time, we felt a certain sociological deprivation in the sense that few professionals in our various natural resource arenas were trained in the social sciences. Even rarer were social scientists who were interested in cross-natural resource management system studies.

In 1983, Gale spent his sabbatical at the University of Washington and began to collaborate with Miller. In short order, the utility of a comparative approach to natural resource problems became apparent. In 1986, the First National Symposium on Social Science in Resource Management was held in Corvallis, Oregon. At this event, Donald R. Field had the idea for a series of edited volumes treating social behavior and natural resources. He brought Miller and Gale together with Brown and gave the three of us the opportunity to consolidate the thought of social scientists at the symposium.

The purpose of *Social Science in Natural Resource Management Systems* is to foster exchange among the variety of social scientists who are concerned with natural resource policy. To this end, 23 authors have cooperated to prepare 14 articles reporting on the management of forests, parks marine fisheries, wilderness, and wildlife. Drawing examples from the United States, Canada, and New Zealand, the authors consider the major aspects of the application of social science to natural resource problems.

The plan of the volume is simple. A first section illustrates the concept of a natural resource management system and introduces the role of social science. A second section is composed of six articles which identify the mandate for applied social science and examine the status of natural resource sociology. A third section is composed of four articles which illustrate direct applications of social science to natural resource management. A final section is composed of three articles which evaluate the behavior of management bureaucracies in natural resource systems.

This book is the production of many people and institutions. In particular, we express our gratitude to Becky A. Benton, Ora L. Chapman, Ruth Gainer, Christine McCartan, Andrea Montclair, and Vernon D. Ross at the Institute for Marine Studies, University of Washington; to Donette E. Pitt at the Department of Sociology, University of Oregon; and to Sherelyn R. Whittum at the Department of Resource Recreation Management, Oregon State University for administrative and word processing excellence. In addition, two special contributions must be noted. To Dr. Linda L. Iltis, who managed correspondence with authors and the publisher, in addition to overseeing production, and to Susan Stiles Gale, who technically edited the full text, we acknowledge enormous debts.

As a last point in this preface, we want to say that we have learned a great deal by preparing the articles which follow. It is our hope that this volume, and the series of which it is part, prove useful to those who promise to enhance the role and product of social science in natural resource management systems.

Marc L. Miller
Richard P. Gale
Perry J. Brown

I

OVERVIEW

OVERVIEW

1

NATURAL RESOURCE MANAGEMENT SYSTEMS

Marc L. Miller
Institute for Marine Studies
College of Ocean and Fishery Sciences
University of Washington

Richard P. Gale
Department of Sociology
University of Oregon

Perry J. Brown
Department of Resource Recreation Management
Oregon State University

For more than a century, the United States has experimented with the management of natural resources including forests, forage, soil, fisheries, wildlife, water, and minerals. No generic conception of resource conservation has emerged over this period. Instead, conservation themes have been argued in diametric ways. Throughout the Progressive Era, resource conservation entailed the regulation of extractive practices to achieve sustainable production. Yet, the theme of regulation of non-extractive (along with extractive) practices to preserve aesthetic and recreational values also has roots in the Progressive Era. From that period forward, the twin ethics of *extractive conservation* and *aesthetic conservation* have sparked controversy over natural resource policies.[1]

Increasingly, the rules of representative government are crucial to the settling of resource disputes. One modern consequence is that natural resource policy is social policy. Importantly, a complex management process has expanded the role of science in formulating resource policy. Today, managers benefit from the research and advice of a pluralistic scientific community.

Social scientists are legitimate members of the natural resource scientific community. These include professionals who have been traditionally trained in sociology, political science, economics, anthropology, psychology, law, geography and history; professionals who have been educated in natural resource fields such as forestry and wildlife management; and professionals who have backgrounds in such associated fields as outdoor recreation, ecology, leisure studies, and environmental education. All these social scientists manifest an interdisciplinary perspective on resource management. Working in universities and colleges, in federal and state government, for non-profit organizations, and in the private sector, social scientists generate impact statements, resource management plans, and a host of other applied and academic research products.

An analytical framework can clarify the application of social science to natural resource problems. This lead article presents a framework centered on the concept of a natural resource management system. A first section sociologically defines this four-part system. A second section reviews the intertwined, if sometimes cross-threaded, histories of selected natural resource management systems. Final sections argue for comparative social science research.

THE NATURAL RESOURCE MANAGEMENT SYSTEM CONCEPT

From a sociological perspective, a *natural resource management system* is composed of four interacting elements: natural resources, management bureaucracies, profit-seeking industries, and diverse publics (Gale and Miller 1985, Miller and Gale 1986). *Natural resources* such as timber, forage, fisheries, water, wildlife, and minerals fall along a renewable-nonrenewable continuum. As the events of resource management have shown, these vary considerably in the degree to which they have utilitarian, aesthetic, recreational, historical, and scientific values. *Management bureaucracies* exist in resource systems because government has proved to be requisite for resource conservation. For example, resources once assumed to be unregulated common property, such as air and fisheries, are now managed by elaborate bureaucratic entities.

Resource management bureaucracies operate at all government levels. Those at the federal level include the U.S. Forest Service (USFS), the National Park Service (NPS), the Bureau of Land Management, the National Marine Fisheries Service (NMFS), the U.S. Fish and Wildlife Service, and the Bureau of Reclamation, among others. Rarely, however, is a specific natural resource associated with a single management bureaucracy. Forests, for example, are under the jurisdiction of the NPS as well as under that of the USFS. Given that society has many ways of valuing resources, it is not surprising that bureaucracies at times compete to manage resources.

Profit-seeking industries include those which extract natural resources of direct commercial value and those which provide services and equipment to publics wanting experience with nature (e.g., the resort, hotel, service station, transportation, restaurant, recreational equipment, tourism, and guide industries). *Diverse publics* include highly organized embodiments of social movements (e.g., the Boone and Crockett Club, the Wilderness Society, Greenpeace) as well as relatively unorganized and politically inactive constituencies (e.g., consumers at large).

For convenience, we refer to natural resource management systems by resource.[2] Thus, "the forest system" conjures forest resources, management bureaucracies such as the USFS, profit-seeking industries such as the Weyerhaeuser Company and small logging companies, and diverse publics such as the Sierra Club and local hiking organizations. The "marine fisheries system" conjures fisheries resources, management bureaucracies such as the NMFS, profit-seeking industries involving commercial fishermen and fish processing companies, and diverse publics such as recreational and subsistence fishermen.

The concept of a natural resource management system offers several analytical advantages. First, it establishes all four components of systems as fair objects of social science research. Resource systems can be empirically and theoretically studied marshalling the spectrum of social science paradigms.

Second, management bureaucracies are portrayed as embedded within, rather than external to, natural resource management systems. The latter perspective, which characterized early resource managers, places agencies outside of systems as detached stewards and mediators of conflicts. With the idea that agencies are basic parts of systems, social science is pertinent not only to phenomena characterizing industries and publics, but also to bureaucratic phenomena. Further, communication, power and other social relations which connect the components of resource systems become available to inquiry.

Third, the concept of a natural resource management system illuminates the distribution and function of science in systems. Each of the three social components of systems separately produces scientific findings. Thus, natural resource social science is conducted by management bureaucracies, through organizations such as USFS Experiment Stations and NMFS Centers, by profit-seeking industries, through corporate research laboratories and trade associations, and by organized publics, through research sponsored by organizations such as the Sierra Club and the Friends of the

Earth. As a consequence, resource science provides common ground on which agencies, industries, and publics may exchange ideas and either avoid or engender controversy. (Political ideology and social morality are other grounds on which these parties debate resource policy.)

Finally, the natural resource management system concept provides a basis for comparing management experiences. As illustration, the articles included in this volume treat a variety of substantively different and compelling resource problems. In each case, the reader will find that the notion of natural resource management systems has currency in the interpretation of human behavior and processes of social change.

ORIGINS OF NATURAL RESOURCE MANAGEMENT SYSTEMS

The history of the United States reveals attitudes toward public lands and natural resources marked by six overlapping phases.[3] Clawson (1983) brackets the major period of *Acquisition* with the 1803 Louisiana Purchase and the 1867 procurement of Alaska from Russia.[4] *Disposal* begins with the 1812 establishment of the General Land Office and ends with the Taylor Grazing Act of 1934. *Reservation* starts with the Forest Reserve Act of 1891 and extends until the mid-1930s. *Custodial Management* overlaps much of this period, beginning in 1905 with the creation of the USFS and lasting until 1950. *Intensive Management* covers the period from 1950 to 1960. Finally, *Consultation and Confrontation* extends from 1960 to the present.[5]

Clawson's phases loosely correspond to the evolutionary sequence of natural resource management systems. Americans and resources were first linked through the development of profit-seeking industries (*Aquisition, Disposal*). Next, embryonic natural resource management systems expanded to include management bureaucracies (*Reservation, Custodial Management*). Finally, systems incorporated diverse publics (*Intensive Management, Consultation and Confrontation*).

Early America

American values concerning the relation between humankind and nature have undergone substantial revision since Jamestown.[6] From the Pilgrim point of view, wilderness represented all that was unholy. As Nash (1982:9) has shown, these settlers were schooled in the European and Judeo-Christian outlook on the environment before they crossed the Atlantic: "If paradise was early man's greatest good, wilderness...was his greatest evil.... Men dreamed of life without wilderness." The first Europeans to embark for the New World harbored dreams of a western earthly paradise, but they found wilderness. The Puritan response to this disappointment was to convert the wild scene to rural scenery (cf., Cronon 1983). This domestication theme persisted into the nineteenth century.[7]

Throughout the colonial era, those on the cutting edge of Western exploration endorsed a utilitarian natural resource ethic. Although this has proved to be a dominant philosophy in U.S. history, it was challenged in the late 1800s with the urban emergence of Romanticism. This movement, which Nash (1982:47) associates with "...an enthusiasm for the strange, remote, solitary, and mysterious," derived from the Continental Primitivism of Jean-Jacques Rousseau and the American Primitivism of William Byrd II and William Bartram. Over the first half of the nineteenth century, nationalists endeavored to transform New World wilderness from a cultural liability to an asset. They were assisted by the landscape art of Thomas Cole and his Hudson River School, and the popular writings of authors such as William Cullen Bryant, James Fenimore Cooper and Francis Parkman.[8] In 1832, painter-illustrator George Catlin ventured west of the Mississippi to report on Native American life. Enthralled with the match he found between cultural and environmental systems, Catlin prophetically envisioned a "nation's park containing man and beast" (Huth 1957:135).

It was not, however, the thought of Catlin which provoked a change in American attitudes toward nature, but rather the extraordinary expositions of multitalented George Perkins Marsh. In 1864, Marsh published *Man and Nature* which fully documented the profound and often unsatisfactory influence of humankind upon flora, fauna, lands, and waters. Marsh's objective was not to indict humanity, but to reform human practices. To achieve this, he addressed his volume to the general public, rather than to specialists. *Man and Nature* was an immediate success. Marsh's (1965:35, 112) call for the "restoration of disturbed harmonies" and his injunction "to put a wiser estimate on the works of creation" were enormously appealing and heralded the beginning of a conservation movement.

Progressive Era

Between 1871 and 1916, the themes of extractive conservation and aesthetic conservation shaped natural resource reform in both the public and private sectors. In 1871, Congress established an independent Commission of Fish and Fisheries, the ancestor of the National Marine Fisheries Service as well as the U.S. Fish and Wildlife Service.[9] The first federal entity to deal with the conservation of a specific natural resource was created at a time when public concern for wildlife was widespread. As Reiger (1986) has noted, the monthly newspaper, *American Sportsman*, appeared in 1871 in direct response to the commercial exploitation of wildlife. Other periodicals soon followed seeking to educate the public to the responsibilities of the sportsman. These

Miller/Gale/Brown

included *Forest and Stream* (1873), *Field and Stream* (1874, later renamed *The Field, Chicago Field*, and finally *American Field*), and *American Angler* (1881). In the mid-1870s, some one hundred sportsmen's organizations or clubs existed in the U.S., in addition to perhaps a dozen state associations and one national association. The Blooming Grove Park Association (1871) in Pennsylvania, for example, was a prime example of a private reserve with forestry, game, and fish culture programs (Reiger 1986:39,57).[10]

Scientific attention to resource conservation began with the 1870 creation of the American Fish Culturists' Association (renamed the American Fisheries Society in 1884). Throughout the 1870s, professionals in this association (as well as many sportsmen involved in the fish culture movement) stocked lakes, rivers, and bays with freshwater and saltwater species including "salmon trout" (lake trout), white fish, brook trout, German brown trout ("California trout", rainbow trout), "frost fish" (Atlantic cod), shad, black bass, and carp (Reiger 1986:55). In 1871, the worst fire in American history occurred in Peshtigo, Wisconsin. Some 1500 persons lost their lives and 1,300,000 acres were burned. This waste, along with widespread concern for the needless destruction of California redwoods,[11] North Calaveras Grove Big Trees, and other forests, contributed to the organization of the American Forestry Association in 1875.[12]

The national park, preservation, and wilderness movements also trace to the 1870s. In 1871, Ralph Waldo Emerson accepted the invitation of John Muir to visit the Yosemite Valley, which had been designated a state park in 1864.[13] Both men subsequently wrote about the grandeur of the area. In 1872, Congress created Yellowstone National Park,[14] the first such park in Western history. By the time the National Park Service was established in 1916, thirty-seven national parks and monuments were under federal control (Huth 1957:155).[15]

By the late nineteenth century, the general public viewed federal management of natural resources as an appropriate check against the extra-exploitative tendencies of a laissez-faire economy. In 1881, a Division of Forestry was established in the Department of Agriculture. Ten years later with the passage of the "Forest Reserve Act" (General Revision Act), the President of the U.S. was authorized to withdraw from the public domain lands which required watershed protection and timber preservation. In 1897, the Forest "Organic Act" placed forest reserves under the administration of the General Land Office of the Department of Interior.

Several other events in the late 1880s revealed concern about resource conservation. In 1886, sportsman-naturalist George Bird Grinnell founded the Audubon Society dedicated solely to the preservation of non-game species.[16] In announcing the new society in *Forest and Stream* (of which he was owner and editor between 1880 and 1911), Grinnell called for the end of fashion dependent on the feathers and skins of birds.[17] His plea occurred when many in America were deploring the demise of such species as the bison and passenger pigeon.[18] In 1887, Grinnell, Theodore Roosevelt, and a small group of friends formed "the first private organization to deal effectively with conservation issues on a national scope," the Boone and Crockett Club (Reiger 1986:120).[19] Using both the club and *Forest and Stream*, Grinnell crusaded successfully for causes such as the Yellowstone National Park Timberland Reserve, the first forest reserve set aside in 1891 by President Benjamin Harrison (Reiger 1986:133-141).

The 1890s also are marked by other important developments relating to natural resource conservation and management. In 1892, the Sierra Club was established with John Muir as its leader. Three years later, the American Scenic and Historic Preservation Society was founded.[20] Indeed, this was a time of transition in American life. Frederick Jackson Turner delivered in 1893 his classic essay, "The Significance of the Frontier in American History," at meetings of the American Historical Association (cf., Hofstadter and Lipset 1968). It was no doubt disturbing to many that while Turner's thesis glorified the role of the environment in producing democracy, the 1890 U.S. Census showed the continental frontier to be settled. A new paradigm was needed to order the relation between humankind and nature. A sign that things were about to change came with the 1898 appointment of Gifford Pinchot as Chief of the Division of Forestry.

One of the major accomplishments of the presidency (1901-1908) of Theodore Roosevelt during the Progressive Era was the institutionalization of the ideology of conservation. As Hays (1975:265) has argued, conservation reshaped the political system:

> The broader significance of the conservation movement
> stemmed from the role it played in the transformation of a
> decentralized, nontechnical, loosely organized society,
> where waste and inefficiency ran rampant, into a highly
> organized, technical, and centrally planned and directed
> social organization which would meet a complex world with
> efficiency.

Because of Roosevelt's long friendships with Gifford Pinchot, George Bird Grinnell, and John Muir, he understood that the twin themes of conservation--extractive conservation and aesthetic conservation--were incompatible. Yet, it was the extractive conservation ethic which prevailed in government.

In 1905, Roosevelt and Pinchot managed a reorganization of federal authority over forest resources with the creation of the U.S. Forest Service in the Department of Agriculture. Pinchot served as Chief of the Service until 1910, when he symbolically relinquished his position in protest over the Taft Administration's indifference to Secretary of Interior Richard A. Ballinger's policies favoring big business interests in federal coal leasing in Alaska.[21]

In response to careless forest practices, Pinchot implemented Prussian scientific forestry and turned the USFS into the epitome of a powerful and professional bureaucracy. Pinchot's respect for efficiency and long-term planning was the foundation of extractive conservation.[22]

In 1906, the passage of the Antiquities Act empowered the President to establish national monuments by proclamation. (The creation of national parks required separate acts of Congress.) Roosevelt created four national monuments--Devil's Tower, Petrified Forest, Montezuma Castle, El Morro--in that year. In 1908 he used the Act to designate the Grand Canyon as a national monument, forestalling commercial development in the area and further extending the reservation of federal lands.

In May of 1906, Roosevelt convened the Conference of Governors at the White House to consider a comprehensive approach to the natural resource problems of soil exhaustion, erosion, timber famine, water scarcity and the decline of wildlife. Pinchot organized the agenda to emphasize extractive conservation. Accordingly, the names of John Muir, Robert Underwood Johnson, E.A. Bowers and others who advocated protective measures in resource management were conspicuously absent from the list of non-governors invited to the conference. In spite of this imbalance, J. Horace McFarland, President of the American Civic Association and national park lobbyist, is remembered for a passionate speech reminding those present that one of America's greatest resources was "her unmatched scenery" (Huth 1957:187).

By the end of the nineteenth century, the American frontier was history. A new sympathy for the environment and an interest in preservation replaced the frontier ethic. People turned to nature for answers to spiritual, moral, and recreational questions. In describing the emergent wilderness cult, Nash (1982:157) notes:

> [A]s the antipode of civilization, of cities, and of machines,
> wilderness could be associated with the virtues these entities
> lacked. In the primitive, specifically, many Americans
> detected the qualities of innocence, purity, cleanliness, and
> morality which seemed on the verge of succumbing to
> utilitarianism and the surge of progress.

At the turn of the century, the forces of aesthetic conservation and extractive conservation found good reason to clash. Since the 1880s, the growing city of San Francisco had been intrigued by the possibility of obtaining fresh water and hydroelectric power by damming the spectacular high-walled Hetch Hetchy Valley in the nearby Sierra Nevadas. In 1890, the valley had become a wilderness preserve as part of the Yosemite National Park.[23] This precluded damming by San Francisco. To circumvent this restriction, San Francisco in 1901 initiated a series of petitions to the federal government requesting that Hetch Hetchy be granted to the city to eliminate water shortage problems.

The proposal to transform the Hetch Hetchy Valley into a reservoir received national coverage shortly after the San Francisco Earthquake of 1906. Hetch Hetchy pitted San Francisco and extractive conservationists such as Gifford Pinchot against aesthetic conservationists such as John Muir, Robert Underwood Johnson, J. Horace McFarland, and Frederick Law Olmstead, Jr. in a long-term battle.[24] Ultimately, the proponents of development prevailed when President Woodrow Wilson granted the valley to San Francisco in late 1913. Yet, even in defeat, aesthetic conservationists had reason to celebrate. Hetch Hetchy had consolidated a social movement and it would symbolize the costs of simple obedience to the ethic of progress for decades to come. As Nash (1982:181) observes:

> Previously most Americans had not felt compelled to rationalize the conquest of wild country...For three centuries they had chosen civilization [over unspoiled nature] without any hesitation. By 1913 they were no longer sure.

Dissatisfied with inconsistent management of national parks, aesthetic conservationists lobbied the legislative and executive branches of government for a federal park service during the first decade of the century. A park service was strongly opposed by Pinchot, who preferred to keep potential park lands under the control of the USFS.

In 1913, aesthetic conservationists persuaded President William Howard Taft to recommend a park agency to Congress. Finally, in 1916, legislation was passed creating the National Park Service within the Department of Interior. Thus, the two sides of conservation--extractive conservation and aesthetic conservation--were institutionalized in the federal government in the USFS and NPS.

Modern America

Following World War I, federal attention to natural resources was limited and ineffective under the administrations of Warren G. Harding, Calvin Coolidge, and Herbert Hoover.[25] Meanwhile, the field of wildlife conservation experienced substantial growth. The National Association of

Audubon Societies (which had been formed in 1905 with George Bird
Grinnell as director), was joined by the American Game Protective Society
(AGPS) in 1911, and the Izaak Walton League in 1922. In the 1920s and
1930s, the managerial professionals in the Audubon association and the AGPS
quarreled with their constituencies over organization goals and ties to gun and
ammunition manufacturers.26

When Franklin Delano Roosevelt assumed the presidency in 1933,
conservation policies based on Republican individualism and decentralization
were replaced with the New Deal. In the face of the Great Depression,
Roosevelt had the conviction that comprehensive attention to the conservation
of natural resources would result in long-term economic security. In the
1930s, he coordinated a dynamic federal conservation policy (Riesch 1968).
Roosevelt's commitment to natural resources is reflected in the 1933 creation
of the Civilian Conservation Corps (CCC) and the Tennessee Valley Authority
(TVA). The CCC assigned two million unemployed men in several thousand
camps to address problems of forestry, soil erosion, and flood control. The
TVA demonstrated that grass roots regional planning could resolve issues of
conservation and development while providing for the social and economic
welfare of the nation.

Throughout the 1930s, the theme of extractive conservation waned
while aesthetic conservation waxed. Interestingly, important stimuli for a
reconsideration of traditional attitudes towards nature emanated from
management bureaucracies. Most notably, Robert Marshall and Aldo
Leopold, both of whom had experience as foresters, were effective in this
regard. Leopold, who founded the field of wildlife management and pioneered
wilderness preservation, was experienced in outdoor recreation and strongly
objected to what he considered to be myopic commodity-production
perspectives on forest, fisheries, agriculture, and wildlife management.27 As
an alternative, he promoted a holistic and ecological "land ethic":

> ...quit thinking about decent land-use as solely an economic
> problem. Examine each question in terms of what is
> ethically and esthetically right, as well as what is
> economically expedient. A thing is right when it tends to
> preserve the integrity, stability, and beauty of the biotic
> community. It is wrong when it tends otherwise. (Leopold
> 1966 [1949]:262)

Marshall was especially concerned about the disappearance of
wilderness. He worked tirelessly to develop USFS "U" regulations
establishing wilderness recreation as a dominant use in parts of National

Forests.28 In 1935, Marshall and Leopold helped to found the Wilderness Society.

After World War II, internecine struggle within the conservation movement resumed. Although the post-war decade marked the maturation of what President Dwight D. Eisenhower termed the "military-industrial complex," private organizations and public servants made strides in advancing the theme of aesthetic conservation and its variant, outdoor recreation. In 1952, Resources for the Future (RFF) was established with a Ford Foundation grant to advance education in the field of natural resource development and conservation. RFF's first president and chairman was Horace M. Albright, who years earlier succeeded Stephen T. Mather to be second director of the National Park Service. In 1958, Eisenhower created the Outdoor Recreation Resources Review Commission to prepare an inventory of the nation's recreational resources and provide wildlife refuge, park, and forest policy recommendations.

The most significant conservation story of the 1950s, however, was the virtual replay of Hetch Hetchy on the Utah border in the northwest corner of Colorado, this time with a reversed outcome. In the first years of the decade, the Bureau of Reclamation within the Department of Interior unveiled a plan for an Echo Park dam at the junction of the Green and Yampa rivers in Dinosaur National Monument. Aesthetic preservationists, outraged that the dam would flood part of a national monument, resisted in dramatic fashion. Led by David Brower of the Sierra Club and Howard C. Zahniser of the Wilderness Society, the consolidated forces of preservation prevailed in the end, and the dam plan was discredited.

In the 1960s, quality of life and outdoor recreation continued to be topics of widespread interest. The Wilderness Act of 1964 established the National Trails System, and 1968 legislation created the National Wild and Scenic Rivers System and the National Wilderness Preservation System. In between, President Lyndon B. Johnson convened the White House Conference on Natural Beauty in 1965. This conference resembled that of Theodore Roosevelt in having the Executive Office as the sponsor. The important difference was that aesthetic conservation, rather than Gifford Pinchot's extractive conservation, was the preeminent theme.

In 1962, Rachel Carson, who had worked as an aquatic biologist and an editor-in-chief for the U.S. Fish and Wildlife Service, published the enormously provocative *Silent Spring*, documenting the injurious effects of pesticides on ecosystems. This work had an impact reminiscent of George Perkins Marsh's *Man and Nature* and was a harbinger of the environmental movement and the messages of Barry Commoner, Paul Ehrlich, Ralph Nader, and Victor Yannacone (cf., Fox 1981). To a large degree, conservation issues as phrased in traditional extractive-aesthetic terms (and as debated by

traditionally white Anglo-Saxon protestant [WASP] publics) were
overshadowed in the late 1960s and 1970s by the even more complex and
generally frightening problems of pollution, population, nuclear war, and
energy.[29]

Legislation in the 1970s transformed management objectives and
procedures in natural resource management systems. The National
Environmental Policy Act (NEPA) of 1969 asserts that it is national policy to
protect and enhance the environment. The Act requires the preparation of
environmental impact statements prior to major federal actions significantly
affecting the human environment. The passage of NEPA revolutionized the
ways citizens could participate in, and challenge, administrative decisions of
federal agencies pursuant to a great body of law treating air, water, noise,
oceans, energy, historic preservation, land use, natural areas, parks, recreation,
wildlife, solid waste, toxic substances, transportation, and resource
conservation (cf., Sive 1976). The passage of legislation such as the Marine
Mammal Protection Act of 1972 (which introduced the concept of optimum
sustainable population), the Endangered Species Act of 1973, and the
Magnuson Fishery Conservation and Management Act of 1976 (which
introduced the concept of optimum yield) confirmed that the objective of
maximum physical production was no longer justifiable on an *a priori* basis.[30]

In response to the energy crisis of the Carter administration,
strategies for the federal disposal of public lands and resources were
resurrected during the presidency of Ronald Reagan. Most controversially, the
Department of Interior under the leadership of James Watt espoused not only
extractive conservation, but "privatization" of oil, gas, coal and other
resources. For this, for accelerated federal oil, gas, and mineral leasing in
designated wilderness areas, for support of the Sagebrush Rebellion (in which
miners and stock raisers in the West sought to transfer BLM and USFS lands
to state and private ownership [cf., Shanks 1984]), and for a proclivity for
glibness, Watt is regarded by aesthetic conservationists as more notorious than
the Secretary of Interior of the Progressive Era, Richard A. Ballinger.

Today, all three social elements of natural resource management
systems are mature. Profit-seeking industries have consistently benefited from
technological innovations. Management bureaucracies have benefited from
advances in the applied natural resource services. Diverse publics have
benefited from legislation legitimating their stakes and participation in the
resource policy arena. All elements have benefited from computer data
analysis and a general rise of citizen awareness of natural resource
management issues. This has made for leveling of the balance of power
among the three.

Perhaps the most interesting new sociological feature of natural resource management systems is that the historically strong correlation of extractive conservation with bureaucracies and aesthetic conservation with publics is breaking down. Parties are becoming more sophisticated about the rules of the policy process, opposition, and science. Individuals increasingly design career paths which crisscross the elements of resource systems. This could well mean that management efforts to discover the correct attitude of humankind to the environment and natural resources will lead less often to ideological stalemates and more frequently to educated compromises. Should this transpire, the full array of applied natural resource sciences will be challenged to assist in the policy definition of natural resource conservation.

COMPARATIVE STUDY OF NATURAL RESOURCE MANAGEMENT SYSTEMS

Authority over natural resources has always been fragmented in the government. Although there have been numerous plans for federal reorganization (many of these realized), the idea of a comprehensive Department of Natural Resources has never found wide acceptance. Similarly, universities have rarely endorsed the consolidation of natural resource disciplines.[31] The unfortunate result is that the natural science, social science, and humanistic literatures of natural resources are poorly coordinated.

Interest in natural resource management systems by social scientists is a rather recent phenomenon.[32] The classics begin with Selznick's (1949) *TVA and Grass Roots: A Study of Formal Organization*; Maass's (1951) *Muddy Waters: The Army Engineers and the Nation's Rivers;* Hays's (1959) *Conservation and the Gospel of Efficiency: The Progressive Conservation Movement 1890-1920*; Kaufman's (1960) *The Forest Ranger: A Study in Administrative Behavior*; and Foss's (1960) *Politics and Grass*, which concentrates on the Bureau of Land Management.

Except for Hays, these authors each examine a single resource management bureaucracy. Although valued as important contributions to the study of formal organizations, neither academics nor practitioners viewed them as precursors to a new social science concerned with natural resource management. One reason may have been that few applied roles existed for social scientists in the management of natural resources and public lands.

Between 1960 and 1980, social scientists continued to focus on single agencies or systems. Influential works include Cooley's (1963) *Politics and Conservation: The Decline and Fall of the Alaskan Salmon*; Darling et al.'s (1967) *Man and Nature in the National Parks*; Clawson's (1971) *The Bureau of Land Management*; and Richardson's (1973) *Dams, Parks, and Politics*.

The passage of the National Environmental Policy Act (NEPA) in 1969 motivated social scientists to look to the design and implementation of environmental policy. Studies by Andrews (1976) and Liroff (1976) exemplify the shift from structural to policy analyses of resource systems. Concurrently, the growth of environmental and natural resource law stimulated legal scholarship (cf., Sax 1970, Anderson 1973).

A decade after NEPA and the first Earthday (22 April 1970), two important studies by social scientists appeared. These were Mazmanian and Nienaber's (1979) *Can Organizations Change? Environmental Protection, Citizen Participation, and the Corps of Engineers*; and Fairfax's revised and updated edition of Dana's landmark (1956) *Forest and Range Policy: Its Development in the United States* (Dana and Fairfax 1980).

In recent years, social scientists have extended the insights found in the classic works to produce comparative studies of natural resource management systems. One of the first in this genre is Culhane's (1981) *Public Lands Politics: Interest Group Influence on the Forest Service and the Bureau of Land Management*. Similarly, Twight (1983) reports on conflict between the USFS and the National Park Service (NPS), Taylor (1984) examines adaptations of the USFS and the U.S. Army Corps of Engineers (COE) to NEPA, and Nienaber (1983) and Clarke and McCool (1985) compare the USFS, the BLM, the NPS, the COE, the Soil Conservation Service, the U.S. Fish and Wildlife Service, and the Bureau of Reclamation. Gale (1985), Fricke (1985), and Miller and Gale (1986) compared the USFS with the National Marine Fisheries Service.[33]

Legal mandates spur this comparative emphasis by requiring the incorporation of social science in natural resource policy decisions. Resource management, however, has yet to become a widely distributed social science specialty (cf., Burton *et al.* 1986). Development of an integrated social science of natural resource management systems has also been hampered by the fact that scientists, policymakers, industries, and publics familiar with one resource system habitually stress the unique qualities of that system's resources and management regime. This parochial emphasis discourages comparative analyses of natural resource management systems.

A comparative orientation, however, has two benefits. First, it causes social scientists studying a specific natural resource system to track the work of social science colleagues examining other systems. Thus, resource social scientists who have diversified to study those natural sciences (e.g., forestry, fisheries biology, ornithology, zoology, hydrology) most influential in specific resource systems, will profit as well from following social science developments in different natural resource systems.[34] Such a perspective is necessary to avoid theoretical, methodological, and applied duplications in natural resource social science.

Second, modern legal, economic, political, and social events force the attention of social scientists to conflicts which connect natural resource systems. Increasingly elaborate natural resource systems are internally characterized by competing profit-seeking industries, such as commercial and recreational extractive industries, and service industries; competing publics, such as sportsmen, environmental, preservationist constituencies; and competing sciences. All parties engaged in resource management are increasingly sophisticated in recognizing scientific, bureaucratic, political, and moral options in resource management. This compels social science researchers to be alert to policy developments in multiple natural resource management systems.

A RESEARCH AGENDA FOR NATURAL RESOURCE MANAGEMENT SYSTEMS

Any agenda for integrating social science into natural resource management systems must acknowledge common researchable topics across systems. In the remainder of this section, we briefly identify research issues that we see to be especially persistent and pervasive. A triadic schema shows these problems pertain to the dominant resource management decision--*allocation*; the basic mechanism for making resource policy--*representative government*; and the fundamental dynamic in natural resource management systems--*social change*.

Allocation

Careful inspection of conservation history reveals that resource management objectives derive not from the natural sciences, but from the values of society. For example, calculations of maximum sustainable yields, rebuilding rates, and the selection of which particular resources merit management all reflect implicit assumptions about preferred distribution effects of resource policies.

Research opportunities in this area for social scientists lie in the construction of equitable formulas of resource allocation, and in the measurement of the sociological, demographic, and other implications of such prescriptions.[35]

Representative Government

Scrutiny of resource legislation of the last quarter century confirms that resource management is social policy. This, coupled with spectacular post-World War II advances in extractive technologies, means that people and industries shape natural resource management systems by the rules of a zero-sum game. The resulting resource decisions are extra-scientific, influenced by philosophical and political arguments, as well as by applied science. This

arrangement cannot be remedied. Moreover, many believe that the resource
policy process is correctly a product of representative government.

Social scientists thus have the opportunity to monitor natural resource
policy processes through the phases of design, implementation, and
enforcement. Topics for research include familiar ones: the degree of
openness in the the policy arena, the possibility of agency or scientific capture
by industry (or public) interests, and the evaluation of agency performance.

Social Change

Natural resource management systems respond to social change
under three conditions: when any of the three human elements of systems
(industries, agencies, and publics) change, when the relationship between
system elements is restructured, and when the relationship between systems is
restructured. In the first two cases, social change can emanate from the
industry, public, or bureaucratic element. Thus, industries can expand,
diversify, decline, and clash. The rise of recreational and service industries
and the survival problems of harvesting industries (for example, in forest and
marine fisheries systems) illustrate how industrial balances of power shift.
Social change in the public element can be based on political, economic, or
ideological discontent. The environmental movement (including associated
submovements concerned with pollution, nuclear waste, wilderness and
wildlife protection), political movements, and consumer rights activities all
have the potential to influence natural resource management. Finally, the
bureaucratic element of natural resource systems can be restructured, as has
occurred by federal reorganizations of government.[36]

The third case, involving relations between systems, promises to be
the most troublesome in natural resource management. Problems here are of
two types. First, resource agencies are plagued by serious and longstanding
differences that create obstacles to cooperation. This is illustrated by
jurisdictional and philosophical clashes between the USFS and the NPS
throughout most of the century. Second, the ecological boundaries of
resources often fit poorly with the jurisdictions of existing agencies.
Management of ecological systems have received special designation is
especially complex, as is seen in instances where Wild and Scenic Rivers
cross agency boundaries.

Despite the lack of cooperation among agencies, no large-scale
federal effort to create a Department of Natural Resources appears imminent.
Social scientists can bridge the gap by helping to improve communication
across natural resource systems. Better communication would bring agencies
closer together. For example, the USFS could learn from the NMFS about
public participation in open policy-making arenas; the BLM could learn from
the USFS about multiple-use management; and those working in the National

Wildlife Refuge System could learn from the NPS about visitor and tourism management.

DISCUSSION

In this article we have argued that it is both appropriate and timely for social scientists working in natural resource management systems to share results and methods, and to collaborate in the design of future research. In particular, we have called for comparative studies of decisions, policy processes, and social change. The rationale for this comparative perspective is found in the facts that conservation concerns have not represented the peripheral and temporary ideas of a few, but instead have been widely distributed across society and American history. If the natural resource management systems of today do not exactly have a common origin, their roots are clearly intertwined.

We are optimistic about the prospects for applied research in natural resource management, but we make one final observation on the status of the allied social science disciplines in this field. Natural resource management has always depended first on the natural sciences. The grass-roots environmental legislation of the 1960s and 1970s and the burgeoning recreational use of resources have provided the impetus for social scientists to contribute to resource policy. Unfortunately, many agency administrators (and natural scientists) still believe that social sciences have little to offer to policy deliberations.

Social scientists, then, must establish their own niche in natural resource management systems. In our estimation, and as we feel the following articles demonstrate, social scientists are prepared for this challenge. The bringing of social science to bear on natural resource policy is achievable. Practitioners have only to formulate socially responsible research questions and attack these with the scientific method.

ACKNOWLEDGMENTS

The authors express their gratitude to David L. Fluharty, Curtis E. Johnson, and Robert L. Stokes for valuable comments on drafts of this article.

NOTES

1. Throughout this article, we employ *extractive conservation* to abbreviate a "wise-use" regulatory ethic emphasizing a sustainable production orientation to natural resource management. The term thus encompasses the harvesting of renewable resources such as forests and fisheries, as well as the extraction of nonrenewable resources such as minerals (cp., Barnett and Morse 1963). In contradistinction, *aesthetic conservation* connotes an ethic stressing preservation of resources, but permitting human access for transcendental and recreational purposes.

2. This is, of course, a semantic simplification of the notion that integrated ecosystems, rather than single resources, are the objects of management.

3. Useful appendices describing the chronology of public land and natural resource legislation and regulation are found in Clawson and Held (1957), Matthiessen (1959), Steen (1977), Dana and Fairfax (1980), and Zaslowsky and the Wilderness Society (1986). Also, see Sive (1976).

4. This phase was repeated between 1960 and 1980 with the acquisition of tidelands, outer continental shelf areas, fisheries, and Alaskan lands (Clawson 1983).

5. Culhane (1981) generally agrees with Clawson's partitions, but describes the present phase as *Extensive Preservation* beginning in 1964.

6. Less than 5 percent of the nearly 500 personalities identified as leaders of conservation in American history by Stroud (1985) are women. Fox (1981:341-345), however, correctly points out that the important roles women have played in conservation have been systematically understudied.

7. As one biblical injunction for the subjugation of nature, Nash (1968:3) cites Genesis 1:28. Here the first couple is instructed to:

> ...be fruitful, and multiply, and replenish the earth, and subdue it: and have dominion over the fish of the sea, and over the fowl of the air, and over every living thing that moveth upon the earth.

8. Nash's well-received treatment of changing American attitudes toward nature is complemented by Huth's (1957) equally fine work.

9. The Commission evolved into the Bureau of Fisheries in 1903 and then into the NMFS with the creation of the National Oceanic and Atmospheric Administration in 1970. The U.S. Fish and Wildlife Service created in 1940 is also traced to the 1895 creation of the Bureau of Biological Survey in the Department of Agriculture. Before this, the bureau was the Division of Biological Survey (1891), first established in 1886 as a Division of Economic Ornithology and Mammalogy.

10. In revising the historiography of conservation, Reiger (1986) notes that historical figures committed to the code of the sportsman have been variously labeled by historians as nature lovers, experts, scientists, naturalists, preservationists, nature writers, ornithologists, artists, and politicians, among others.

11. In 1854 bark stripped from one of the California Big Trees which measured 315 feet in height and 61 feet in circumference was exhibited in London. Although the showing was unsuccessful (Londoners refused to believe in such a tree), it provoked American anger at the entrepreneurs and inspired the first of a number of testimonials in the 1850s to the beauty of the California trees (Huth 1957:143).

12. Gifford Pinchot helped to found the Society of American Foresters in 1900.

13. Under the law, the State of California acted as trustee for the federal government. In 1906, Yosemite Valley and neighboring lands reverted to federal control and were merged to form Yosemite National Park.

14. Unlike Yosemite, Yellowstone was situated in a territory. As a consequence, it could not be given in trusteeship to a state. As Huth (1957:153) reports, "the way to segregate the vast area 'as a public or pleasuring ground for the benefit and enjoyment of people'...was to establish it as a park under immediate federal administration."

15. That these included Grand Canyon National Park (1908) is tribute to the popular writings of Major John Wesley Powell which appeared in 1874-1875 describing his pioneering navigation of the Colorado River circa 1870 (Huth 1957:159-161).

16. Earlier Audubon Societies had been established for the propagation of game species. Grinnell's society was discontinued in 1889, but

by then it had served as a model for sportsman-naturalist William Brewster's Massachusetts Audubon Society (1896).

17. Grinnell received delayed satisfaction in the 1900 passage of the Lacey Act prohibiting the commercial hunting and interstate transport of wildlife and wildlife products taken in violation of state law. Grinnell's 1894 *Forest and Stream* editorial calling for sportsmen to adopt as a plank that "the sale of game should be forbidden at all seasons" is reprinted in Reiger (1986:70-72).

18. Hornaday (1931) vividly describes the decline of game species and the early need for bag limits and open season reductions as hedges against the excesses of "game-hogs."

19. Two influential leaders of the Boone and Crockett Club in this era were Theodore Roosevelt and Gifford Pinchot.

20. The Appalachian Mountain Club, established in 1872, was a forerunner of associations devoted to nature education and maintenance of trailways.

21. For the details of Pinchot's resignation, see Richardson (1962: 65-85).

22. For comment on Pinchot's famous management objective "the greatest good for the greatest number in the long run," see McConnell (1960).

23. For an introduction to the diffusion of wilderness and park management to other industrialized nations, see Nash (1978).

24. Empathizing with both sides, Roosevelt was ambivalent about the San Francisco solution for Hetch Hetchy (Nash 1982:162-164).

25. Swain (1968) argues that Hoover, who found it difficult to reconcile conservation and ideological objectives, did allow agencies to lay the foundation for the conservation achievements of the Franklin Delano Roosevelt administration.

26. Fox (1981:148-182) describes the activities of "radical amateurs" including William T. Hornaday, W. H. Dilg, Willard Van Name, William E. Dutcher, and Rosalie Edge (the first highly visible female conservationist) in reforming these organizations.

27. Leopold (1966:284-295) describes the components of outdoor recreation in terms of trophies, feeling of isolation, fresh air and change of scene, perception, and husbandry.

28. It was Leopold who was mainly responsible for the first wilderness designation in the National Forest system, the Gila Wilderness Area.

29. Fox (1981:315) reports that the combined annual growth rate in five major conservation groups (Izaak Walton League, National Audubon Society, National Wildlife Federation, Sierra Club, Wilderness Society) ranged between 12.2 and 18 percent for the years 1966-1970; for the next 5 years the growth rate diminished to range between 6.1 percent and 8.5 percent.

30. Similar law covering National Forests is found in the Multiple Use and Sustained Yield Act of 1960. In the 1970s, policy guidelines and procedures of the USFS and BLM were stipulated in the Forest and Rangeland Renewable Resource Planning Act (1974), the National Forest Management Act (1976), and Federal Land Policy and Management Act (1976).

31. Currently, 23 educational institutions in the U.S. offer a doctorate as their highest degree in the field of natural resource management. Eighteen institutions offer a master's as their highest degree in this field. For the combined categories of forestry, natural resource management, agricultural and forest technologies, range management, water resources, and fish, game, and wildlife management, 39 institutions list a doctorate (and 33 institutions offer a master's) as their highest degree. In the field of environmental studies, 24 institutions offer a doctorate (and 37 institutions offer a master's) as their highest degree. (GRE/CGS, 1985).

32. The following influential works bring other perspectives to bear on natural resource management systems: *natural science and nature*--Emerson (1833-1893), Parkman (1849), Thoreau (1906), Marsh (1864), Muir (1888), Leopold (1949), Carson (1961, 1962); *social histories*--Huth (1957), Matthiessen (1959), Burton and Kates (1960), Brower (1961, 1964), Richardson (1962), Udall (1963), Nash (1968, 1982), Hofstadter and Lipset (1968), Graham (1971), McPhee (1971), Wenk (1972), Trefethen (1975), Runte (1979), Fox (1981), Shanks (1984), Chase (1986), Reiger (1986), Zaslowsky and the Wilderness Society (1986); *management texts*--Brockman (1959), Stoddart, Smith and Box (1975), Hendee, Stankey, and Lucas (1978), Lackey and Nielsen (1980), Royce (1984), Sharpe, Hendee, and Sharpe (1986); *agency histories/(auto)biographies*--Hornaday (1931), Albright and

Taylor (1947), Pinchot (1947), Clawson (1951, 1971, 1983), Frome (1962, 1971), Fitch and Shanklin (1970), Swain (1970), Warne (1973), Robinson (1975), Steen (1977), Everhart (1983), Foresta (1984), Reed and Drabelle (1984), Stroud (1985).

33. Other recent volumes by social scientists, which do not emphasize comparisons of natural resource systems include Hoole, Friedheim, and Hennessey (1981); Maiolo and Orbach (1982); Young (1982); Devall and Sessions (1985); Kamieniecki, O'Brien, and Clarke (1986); Manning (1986), and Silva (1986).

34. The social science with the longest tenure and greatest representation in natural resource management systems is economics. As a consequence, practitioners of the other social sciences frequently diversify in this direction (cf., Barnett and Morse 1963, Miles et al. 1986).

35. One of the most basic of allocation decisions concerns access to resources. The first director of the National Park Service, Stephen T. Mather (also a Sierra Club member and an enormously successful businessman), was one of the earliest to realize the great appeal of the natural environment to people. His philosophy that parks should be made accessible to people (and automobiles) has, of course, long been challenged by preservationists, most recently by Edward Abbey (1968) and Garrett Hardin. In the management of contemporary marine fisheries, limited entry (cf., Rettig and Ginter 1978; Wilson 1982) is a highly celebrated (by resource economists) and hotly contested tool for regulating fishing effort.

36. Sometimes stimuli for reorganization come from the judicial branch of government. The Boldt Decision (cf., Broches and Miller 1985) illustrates how an activist judiciary has restructured social policy concerning salmon resources in the Pacific Northwest. In the 1980s, two bureaucratic developments of interest are the creation of entirely new federal entities with natural resource responsibilities (e.g., the Northwest Power Planning Council, the Klamath Fishery Management Council), and the Reagan Administration's tendency to weigh executive experience more than resource (and scientific) experience in searches for top-level administrators of natural resource agencies (cf., Miller and Gale 1986).

REFERENCES

Abbey, E. 1968. *Desert Solitaire*. New York: Ballantine Books.

Albright, H.M. and F.J. Taylor. 1947. *"Oh Ranger!" A Book About the National Parks*. New York: Dodd, Mead.

Anderson, F. 1973. *NEPA in the Courts*. Baltimore: The Johns Hopkins Press.

Andrews, R.N.L. 1976. *Environmental Policy and Administrative Change*. Lexington, MA: D.C. Heath.

Barnett, H.J. and C. Morse. 1963. *Scarcity and Growth: The Economics of Natural Resource Availability*. Baltimore: The Johns Hopkins Press (Resources for the Future).

Broches, C.F. and M.L. Miller. 1985. "Public Law Litigation and Marine Affairs: The Boldt Decision." *Coastal Zone Management Journal* 13:99-130.

Brockman, C.F. 1959. *Recreational Use of Wild Lands*. New York: McGraw-Hill Book Company, Inc.

Brower, D. (ed.). 1961. *Wilderness: America's Living Heritage*. San Francisco: Sierra Club.

_____ 1964. *Wildlands in Our Civilization*. San Francisco: Sierra Club.

Burton, I., and R.W. Kates (eds.). 1960. *Readings in Resource Management and Conservation*. Chicago: The University of Chicago Press.

Burton, M.L., G.M. Shoepfle, and M.L. Miller. 1986. "Natural Resource Anthropology." *Human Organization* 45:261-269.

Carson, R. 1961 [1951]. *The Sea Around Us*. New York: New American Library.

_____ 1962. *Silent Spring*. New York: Fawcett Crest.

Chase, A. 1986. *Playing God in Yellowstone: The Destruction of America's First National Park.* Boston: The Atlantic Monthly Press.

Clarke, J.N. and D. McCool. 1985. *Staking Out the Terrain: Power Differentials Among Natural Resource Management Agencies.* Albany: State University of New York Press.

Clawson, M. 1951. *Uncle Sam's Acres.* New York: Dodd and Mead.

_____ 1971. *The Bureau of Land Management.* New York: Praeger Publishers.

_____ 1983. *The Federal Lands Revisited.* Washington, D.C.: Resources for the Future.

Clawson, M. and B. Held. 1957. *The Federal Lands: Their Use and Management.* Baltimore: The Johns Hopkins Press.

Cooley, R.A. 1963. *Politics and Conservation: The Decline and Fall of the Alaskan Salmon.* New York: Harper and Row.

Cronon, W. 1983. *Changes in the Land: Indians, Colonists, and the Ecology of New England.* New York: Hill and Wang (Farrar, Strauss, and Giroux).

Culhane, P.J. 1981. *Public Lands Politics: Interest Group Influence on the Forest Service and the Bureau of Land Management.* Baltimore: The Johns Hopkins University Press (Resources for the Future).

Dana, S.T. and S.K. Fairfax. 1980. *Forest and Range Policy: Its Development in the United States.* New York: McGraw-Hill Book Company, Inc. (second edition).

Darling, F.F. and N.D. Eichhorn. 1967. *Man and Nature in the National Parks.* Washington, D.C.: The Conservation Foundation.

Devall, B. and G. Sessions. 1985. *Deep Ecology: Living as if Nature Mattered.* Layton, UT: Gibbs M. Smith, Inc.

Emerson, R. W. 1833-1893. *Emerson's Complete Works.* Boston: Houghton Mifflin (Riverside edition, 12 volumes).

Everhart, W.C. 1983. *The National Park Service*. Boulder: Westview Press.

Fitch, E.M. and J.E. Shanklin. 1970. *The Bureau of Outdoor Recreation*. New York: Praeger Publications.

Foresta, R.A. 1984. *America's National Parks and Their Keepers*. Baltimore: The Johns Hopkins University Press.

Foss, P. 1960. *Politics and Grass*. Seattle: University of Washington Press.

Fox, S. 1981. *John Muir and His Legacy: The American Conservation Movement*. Boston: Little, Brown and Company.

Fricke, P. 1985. "Use of Sociological Data in the Allocation of Common Property Resources." *Marine Policy* 9: 39-52.

Frome, M. 1962. *Whose Woods These Are: The Story of the National Forests*. Garden City, NY: Doubleday and Company.

_____ 1971. *The Forest Service*. New York: Praeger Publications.

Gale, R.P. 1985. "Federal Management of Forests and Marine Fisheries." *Natural Resources Journal* 25: 275-316.

Gale, R.P. and M.L. Miller. 1985. "Professional and Public Natural Resource Management Arenas: Forests and Marine Fisheries." *Environment and Behavior* 17:651-678.

Graduate Record Examinations Board and the Council of Graduate Schools in the U.S. (GRE/CGS). 1985. *Directory of Graduate Programs: 1986 and 1987*. Princeton: Educational Testing Service.

Graham, F., Jr. 1971. *Man's Dominion: The Story of Conservation in America*. New York: M. Evans and Company.

Hays, S.P. 1975 [1959]. *Conservation and The Gospel of Efficiency: The Progressive Conservation Movement 1890-1920*. New York: Atheneum.

Hendee, J.C., G.H. Stankey, and R.C. Lucas. 1978. *Wilderness Management*. Washington, D.C.: U.S. Forest Service, Department of Agriculture, Chapter 3: 43-59.

Hofstadter, R. and S.M. Lipset (eds.). 1968. *Turner and the Sociology of the Frontier*. New York: Basic Books, Inc.

Hoole, F.W., R.L. Friedheim, and T.M. Hennessey (eds.). 1981. *Making Ocean Policy: The Politics of Government Organization and Management*. Boulder: Westview Press.

Hornaday, W.T. 1931. *Thirty Years War for Wild Life: Gains and Losses in the Thankless Task*. New York: Charles Scribner's Sons.

Huth, H. 1957. *Nature and the American: Three Centuries of Changing Attitudes*. Berkeley: University of California Press (Bison Book edition).

Kamieniecki, S., R. O'Brien, and M. Clarke (eds.). 1986. *Controversies in Environmental Policy*. Albany: State University of New York Press.

Kaufman, H. 1960. *The Forest Ranger: A Study in Administrative Behavior*. Baltimore: The Johns Hopkins University Press.

Lackey, R.T. and L.A. Nielsen (eds.). 1980. *Fisheries Management*. New York: John Wiley and Sons.

Leopold, A. 1966 [1949]. *A Sand County Almanac*. New York: Ballantine Books.

Liroff, R. 1976. *National Policy for the Environment: NEPA and Its Aftermath*. Bloomington: Indiana University Press.

Maiolo, J.R. and M.K. Orbach (eds.). 1982. *Modernization and Marine Fisheries Policy*. Ann Arbor: Ann Arbor Science.

Manning, R.E. 1986. *Studies in Outdoor Recreation: Search and Research for Satisfaction*. Corvallis: Oregon State University Press.

Marsh, G.P. 1965 [1864]. *Man and Nature*. Cambridge: The Belknap Press of Harvard University Press.

Maass, A. 1951. *Muddy Waters: The Army Engineers and the Nation's Rivers*. Cambridge: Harvard University Press.

Matthiessen, P. 1959. *Wildlife in America*. New York: Viking Press.

Mazmanian, D., and J. Nienaber. 1979. *Can Organizations Change? Environmental Protection, Citizen Participation, and the Corps of Engineers.* Washington, D.C.: Brookings Institution.

McConnell, G. 1960 [1954]. "The Conservation Movement--Past and Present." In I. Burton and R.W. Kates (eds.), *Readings in Resource Management and Conservation.* Chicago: The University of Chicago Press. 189-201.

McPhee, J. 1971. *Encounters with the Archdruid.* New York: Farrar, Strauss and Giroux.

Miles, E.L., R. Pealy and R.L. Stokes (eds.). 1986. *Natural Resources Economics and Policy Applications: Essays in Honor of James A. Crutchfield.* Seattle: Institute for Marine Studies, the Graduate School of Public Affairs, and the Institute for Public Policy and Management of the University of Washington.

Miller, M.L. and R.P. Gale. 1986. "Professional Styles of Federal Forest and Marine Fisheries Resource Managers." *North American Journal of Fisheries Management* 6:141-148.

Muir, J. (ed.). 1888. *Picturesque California and the Region West of the Rocky Mountains, from Alaska to Mexico.* San Francisco: (2 volumes).

Nash, R. (ed.). 1968. *The American Environment: Readings in the History of Conservation.* Reading, MA: Addison-Wesley Publishing Company.

Nash, R. 1978. "International Concepts of Wilderness Preservation." In J.C. Hendee, G.H. Stankey, and R.C. Lucas (eds.), *Wilderness Management.* Washington, D.C.: U.S. Forest Service, Department of Agriculture. Chapter 3: 43-59.

_____ 1982 [1967]. *Wilderness and the American Mind.* New Haven: Yale University Press (third edition).

Nienaber, J. 1983. "Two Faces of Scarcity: Bureaucratic Creativity and Constraints." In S. Welch and R. Miewald (eds.), *Scarce Natural Resources: The Challenge to Public Policy Making.* Beverly Hills: Sage Publications. 151-177.

Parkman, F. 1910 [1849]. *The Oregon Trail*. (Otis B. Sperlin, ed.) New York: Longmans, Green.

Pinchot, G. 1947. *Breaking New Ground*. Seattle: University of Washington Press.

Reed, N.P. and D. Drabelle. 1984. *The United States Fish and Wildlife Service*. Boulder: Westview Press.

Reiger, J.F. 1986. *American Sportsmen and the Origins of Conservation*. Norman: University of Oklahoma Press (revised edition).

Rettig, R. B. and J.J.C. Ginter (eds.). 1978. *Limited Entry As a Fishery Management Tool*. Seattle: University of Washington Press.

Richardson, E.R. 1962. *The Politics of Conservation: Crusades and Controversies 1897-1913*. Berkeley: University of California Press.

_____ 1973. *Dams, Parks, and Politics*. Lexington: University of Kentucky Press.

Riesch, A.L. 1968 [1952]. "Conservation Under Franklin Delano Roosevelt." In R. Nash (ed.), *The American Environment: Readings in the History of Conservation*. 147-151.

Robinson, G.O. 1975. *The Forest Service: A Study in Public Land Management*. Baltimore: The Johns Hopkins University Press.

Royce, W.F. 1984. *Introduction to the Practice of Fishery Science*. New York: Academic Press, Inc.

Runte, A. 1979. *National Parks: The American Experience*. Lincoln: University of Nebraska Press.

Sax, J. 1970. *Defending the Environment*. New York: Alfred A. Knopf.

Selznick, P. 1966 [1949]. *TVA and the Grass Roots: A Study in the Sociology of Formal Organization*. New York: Harper Torchbooks.

Shanks, B. 1984. *This Land is Your Land: The Struggle to Save America's Public Lands*. San Francisco: Sierra Club Books.

Sharpe, G.W., C.W. Hendee, and W.E. Sharpe. 1986. *Introduction to Forestry*. New York: McGraw-Hill Book Company, Inc. (fifth edition).

Silva, M. (ed.). 1986. *Ocean Resources and U.S. Intergovernmental Relations in the 1980s*. Boulder: Westview Press.

Sive, M.R. 1976. *Environmental Legislation: A Sourcebook*. New York: Praeger Publishers.

Steen, H.K. 1977 [1976]. *The U.S. Forest Service: A History*. Seattle: University of Washington Press (second printing, with corrections).

Stroud, R.H. (ed.). 1985. *National Leaders of American Conservation*. Washington: Smithsonian Institution Press (sponsored by the National Resources Council of America).

Stoddart, L.A., A.D. Smith, T.W. Box. 1975. *Range Management*. New York: McGraw-Hill Book Co., Inc.

Swain, D.C. 1968 [1966]. "Conservation Accomplishments, 1921-1933." In R. Nash (ed.), *The American Environment: Readings in the History of Conservation*. Reading, MA: Addison-Wesley Publishing Company. 139-147.

_____ 1970. *Wilderness Defender: Horace M. Albright and Conservation*. Chicago: University of Chicago Press.

Taylor, S. 1984. *Making Bureaucracies Think: The Environmental Impact Statement Strategy of Administrative Reform*. Stanford: Stanford University Press.

Thoreau, H.D. 1906. *The Writings of Henry David Thoreau*. Boston: Houghton Mifflin (20 volumes; Volumes (VII-XX) are Thoreau's *Journal* [Bradford Torrey, ed.]).

Trefethen, J.B. 1975. *An American Crusade for Wildlife*. New York: Winchester Press and the Boone and Crockett Club.

Twight, B.W. 1983. *Organizational Values and Political Power: The Forest Service Versus the Olympic National Park*. University Park: The Pennsylvania State University Press.

32   Miller/Gale/Brown

Udall, S.L. 1963. *The Quiet Crisis*. New York: Holt, Rinehart and Winston.

Warne, W.E. 1973. *The Bureau of Reclamation*. New York: Praeger Publications.

Wenk, E., Jr. 1972. *The Politics of the Ocean*. Seattle: University of Washington Press.

Wilson, J.A. 1982. "The Economical Management of Multispecies Fisheries." *Land Economics* 58:417-434.

Young, O.R. 1982. *Resource Regimes: Natural Resources and Social Institutions*. Berkeley: University of California Press.

Zaslowsky, D. and The Wilderness Society. 1986. *These American Lands*. New York: Henry Holt and Company.

II

ROLES OF SCIENCE

INTRODUCTION TO PART II

Marc L. Miller
Richard P. Gale
Perry J. Brown

Social science in natural resource management systems can be discussed in terms of mandate and status. Three cross-referenced mandates have generated normative variations on the role of applied social science. A legal mandate is found in natural resource legislation. An institutional mandate is found in the standard operating procedures and rules of management bureaucracies. Finally, a social mandate is found in the will of industry and public constituencies. These three mandates are solid testimony that social science belongs in the natural resource management arena.

The status of social science in natural resource management systems is influenced by such factors as the distribution and recruitment of sociological expertise, philosophies of management, agency budgets, and cross-scientific competition, not to mention the severity of social problems attributed to the use of resources.

Employing examples from a mix of natural resource systems, six articles in this section treat the normative and sociological dimensions of applied social science. To introduce these works, we make the following few observations.

The Interactive Process of Applied Research: A Partnership Between Scientists and Park and Resource Managers.

A professional riddle which faces all scientists in natural resource management systems centers on how research might be designed so that it is simultaneously socially meaningful and intellectually rewarding. Sometimes this riddle causes scientists to engage in seemingly interminable, and ultimately unprofitable, debate over whether abstract research is preferable to applied research, or vice versa.

In this article, Donald R. Field and Darryll R. Johnson take a different tack. In their view, the success of a research project fundamentally depends upon a shared understanding of its purpose by researchers and sponsors. While it is uncontroversial that information should flow in both directions between scientists and managers, the Field and Johnson injunction is that communication must occur at all of the four stages of science--research design, data collection, analysis, and write-up.

Natural Resource Sociology: Forests and Marine Fisheries.

Social scientists who work in natural resource management systems consistently find that management bureaucracies strongly endorse the scientific ethic and the concept of a pluralistic applied scientific community. This means that for social science to be productive, its practitioners must learn to work both with managers and with scientists with different specialities.

In this article, Marc L. Miller and Richard P. Gale examine the niches of social science in forest and marine fisheries systems, particularly insofar as these are influenced by the pervasive themes of professional specialization and executivism. In providing direction to future researchers, these authors stress the importance of promoting sociology as a science, of appreciating the subtle differences between research grants and contracts, and of taking the initiative to disseminate results to multiple audiences.

The Practice and Promise of Social Science in the U.S. Forest Service.

Renowned for its *esprit de corps* and decentralized authority, the U.S. Forest Service, more than any other natural resource bureaucracy, has been identified with scientific management. Moreover, the adaptive behavior of the agency in response to changing social conditions over the last quarter century has been consistently professional. Today, the extraordinary *Forest Service Handbook* codifies procedures and standards for every conceivable type of applied social science. Lambert N. Wenner shows that this prepares the USFS to communicate with diverse industry groups, "silent publics," and other constituencies; to engage in long-range planning and consensus-building exercises; to conduct complex social impact assessments; and even to recommend mitigation.

Unfortunately, this good news is balanced with the bad news that few in the service have expertise in the social sciences. Lambert fully describes this situation and then is specific in suggesting how the state of the social sciences can be raised to a higher and more socially responsible level.

Integrating Social Science into Wildlife Management.

Ironically, the argument that the social sciences belong in natural resource management systems seems to have greater appeal the further one moves from the management arena. To illustrate, Daniel J. Decker, Tommy L. Brown, and George F. Mattfeld report a tendency of wildlife managers to endlessly seek additional biological and ecological data, while misunderstanding scientific paradigms for the study of human behavior. The Decker *et al.* conclusion is that any breakdown of this resistance will require the integration of social science into wildlife management curricula. The authors also reiterate our injunction that social scientists of different kinds and in different systems arrange for their professional activities to intersect, and put more energy into the transfer of research results across resource system boundaries.

The Sociology of Science in Natural Resource Management Systems: Observations on Forests and Marine Fisheries in the Pacific Northwest.

Science has contributed much to the understanding of natural resource problems. However, the practice of science is inevitably influenced by the often conflicting social elements of natural resource management systems. Thus, profit-seeking industries, agencies, and organized publics battle over whose science is correct and whose research agenda should be used to resolve resource controversies.

This article by Richard P. Gale and Marc L. Miller describes the basic structure of natural resource science with examples from the federal forest and marine fisheries regimes. In these systems, few opportunities exist for a pure science divorced from resource conflicts. Thus, most science in these systems, whether the focus is production or impacts, is advocacy science. Gale and Miller argue that natural resource research which is attuned to the needs of all constituencies, but which is debated by the rules of science, best informs resource policy.

Social Impact Assessment in New Zealand Resource Management.

Natural resource management is not, of course, a strictly American experiment. Numerous nations have now designated elements of government to oversee the use of resources and the protection of the environment. In many of these systems, concern for human problems stemming from resource policies has resulted in formal requirements for the scientific study of social change. In the manner of the Santa Barbara oil spill (1969), a controversial proposal to utilize Lake Manapouri to generate electricity in the late 1960s sparked widespread grass roots support in New Zealand for a revised policy of resource conservation. Subsequently, the Labor Government (1972-1975) instituted a new agency, the Commission for the Environment, to incorporate social science in the auditing of Environmental Impact Reports.

In this article, C. Nick Taylor and C. Hobson Bryan point out that social impact assessment in New Zealand and the United States have similar origins. These authors note that the effectiveness (indeed, existence) of the Commission has been greatly shaped by changes in federal administrations. Against the backdrop of a new conservative "free market" economic policy, Taylor and Bryan consider the future of social impact assessment programs in light of a new Ministry for the Environment, and an agenda for new state corporations.

2

THE INTERACTIVE PROCESS OF APPLIED RESEARCH: A PARTNERSHIP BETWEEN SCIENTISTS AND PARK AND RESOURCE MANAGERS

Donald R. Field
Department of Resource Recreation Management
Oregon State University

Darryll R. Johnson
Cooperative Park Studies Unit
College of Forest Resources
University of Washington

Regardless of the discipline involved, the person conducting the inquiry, or the setting in which the inquiry occurs, the principles of science are universal. It is appropriate, however, to distinguish between applied and basic research. This distinction is not made with regard to the activity of science, but with regard to the social origin of the inquiry and the goals for which the results of the research are commissioned (Johnson and Field 1981, Hobbs 1969, Rossi *et al.* 1978). A brief comparison between basic and applied research illustrates this point.

Basic research has as its primary goal the creation of knowledge to advance disciplinary theory and understanding; applied research has as its primary goal the creation of knowledge for problem solving. In short, applied research is mission-oriented. The impetus for basic research is intellectual curiosity, a gap in knowledge, or the personal interests of the scientist, whereas the impetus for applied research is a policy issue, a management or client problem, or program evaluation (Rossi *et al*. 1978, Johnson and Field 1981, Freeman *et al*. 1983, Lazarsfeld *et al*. 1975).

The general orientation of scientific inquiry within public land management agencies, state parks, and forest preserves is applied, and it is usually expected that researchers will embrace a practical or problem-solving orientation. For those scientists (government and university) under contract to such clients, an applied orientation, and the fulfillment of its requisite responsibilities, are essential.

At the heart of applied science is the formation of a partnership between management (client) and scientist. That partnership rests upon interaction and communication throughout the research endeavor--from establishing a research agenda to the presentation of the results of research (Figure 1). The purpose of this article is to explore an interactive process that underlies applied science activity and that is essential to the integration of research results into a decision-making process. Such a process includes the following steps: (1) establishing a research agenda, (2) defining the research question, (3) conducting research, and (4) reporting the results of research. The discussion is presented in the context of a public natural resource management agency, but has applicability to any more general administrative audience where science is used in the decision-making process.

ESTABLISHING A RESEARCH AGENDA

The first step in applied science is the joint interaction of the client and the scientist in the definition of a program of research. The ultimate responsibility, however, for defining a research agenda lies with the management of the agency commissioning the research. It may appear inconsistent to suggest initially that research agendas are a product of interaction between scientist and management and then to argue that the responsibility for an agenda rests with management. The important word here is "ultimate." In practice, of course, research projects undertaken are a result of a negotiation process, availability of funds, scientific expertise to conduct the research, and so on. Managers will benefit from scientific input on an agenda and should modify priorities accordingly.

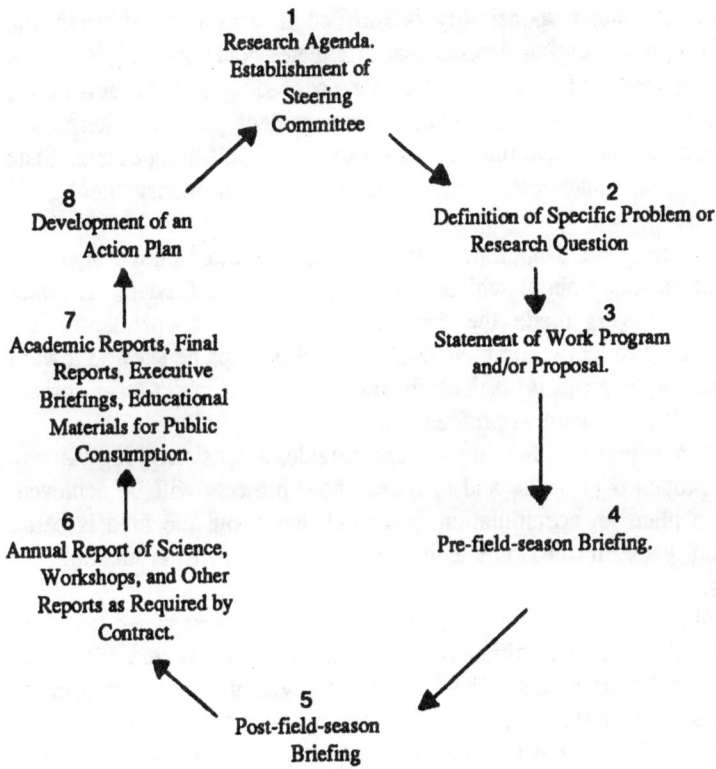

Figure 1 Steps in the communication of science to park and resource
managers

This ultimate responsibility is fulfilled in a number of ways, but primarily through a planning process that articulates goals and objectives for the area being managed. For example, for each administrative unit of the National Park Service there is a general management plan, an interpretive plan, a resource-management plan, and a visitor-use plan, among others. State and local park units have comparable documents defining management goals and objectives.

With the limited appropriations available to most public agencies, choices must be made about which research projects are funded. If either scientists or managers made the decision on projects independently, the priority list would reflect incomplete analysis, and perhaps be skewed toward long-term research projects (scientific preference), or short-term, crisis-oriented projects (management preference).

The management planning process provides a consistent, logical way to evaluate proposed projects, and to assess how projects will be achieved. Because of a plan, an accumulation of knowledge about the area is being recorded and gaps in the knowledge available for decision making are documented.

Similarly, management planning provides a basis on which decision-makers and scientists can initiate research, monitor social and biological change, and resolve problems. These documents with their research agendas can be modified as research projects are accomplished and information is infused into a park/resource management program. A constant updating of research needs will necessitate regular interaction between scientists and managers as to what a new agenda should be.

The interactive process also provides a forum for discussion about the role of science in park management and resource management. Through interaction between management and scientists, both should develop an understanding of the limitations of science in solving management problems and the constraints management must face in incorporating science into the decision-making process.

THE RESEARCH QUESTION

The interaction of management and scientists does not end with a plan. Both must be involved in establishing the specific research question to be investigated. A partnership in this stage of the applied research process is essential for several reasons. Many management issues cannot be answered by scientific inquiry, and only through communication and, perhaps, education of the manager by the scientist can it be determined if scientific inquiry is appropriate.

There are examples of land-management agencies where research has been commissioned for the wrong reasons and the results of scientific inquiry rejected for the wrong reasons. Evaluation research studies of public policies such as the establishment of carrying capacities or use limits for wildlands and designated wilderness areas are classic examples. Management often implements a policy (especially if there is a public outcry or legal action over the decision). Seldom has research been conducted on such areas before the implementation of the policy. For this reason, baseline data on human-use patterns by which change or effect can be measured are frequently not available. Debates often ensue over the research findings depending upon which side of the policy a group is supporting. Acceptance or rejection of the research may depend on who speaks the loudest, or has the most power, and may not be based on the merits of the research itself.

At times the failure of manager and scientist to communicate has led the scientist to undertake expensive and relatively long-term research, when a literature review and a state-of-the-art assessment by a scientist would do. At other times, management may request research that cannot provide the desired solutions. Scientists and managers have a responsibility to each other to articulate clearly the reasons for requesting research and whether or not research is appropriate, and, if it is, to state clearly the research question and the results expected based upon the way the research question is posed.

CONDUCTING THE RESEARCH

There are several problems inherent in the contribution of research to the solution of management issues that should be addressed and understood by manager and scientist alike. Three issues in particular should be addressed in the early stages of the research project: (1) the timing and pacing of the research itself, (2) the research design, and (3) variable selection.

First, the timing and pacing of the research must match the client's problem-solving time schedule. Information is many times requested requiring a long-term design to obtain (two, three, or five years) when a project must be completed within one year. Second, the time frame in which a decision must be made, and the funds available, guide the selection of the research design. Social scientists, for example, may prefer sophisticated sampling designs and survey research, when such may not be practical or required. Participation observation, time budget studies, and unobtrusive measures are alternatives to survey research and may be sufficient to provide the kind of information and accuracy desired. Often, scientists must modify the research design in the field in response to existing conditions.

Finally, the selection of variables to study is sometimes dictated by whether or not management teams can prescribe action to mediate a problem. Attitude and value research serves to illustrate this point. Through planning and design, regulations, permit systems, campground design, parking lot configuration, and admission fees, for example, managers can modify the behavior of individuals; they have little or no ability to change attitudes or values. If a management goal is to measure behavioral response to a set of conditions, then assessing only the attitudes and values of a recreation clientele may be insufficient to measure such a response.

Communication between scientists and management during the research process keeps both informed of the progress being made. A mistake often made by scientists is assuming that once a contract is awarded, communication responsibilities about the research become less important. Pre-field-season briefings and briefings during the data collection phase keep management informed of progress and modifications in research plans. The critical period of uncertainty for management is at the end of a field season and before the first interim report. Communication at this stage of the process enhances credibility of, support for, and confidence in the project. A close-out interview at this time, reviewing work accomplished and establishing the next step in the research program, reinforces the management/scientist partnership.

REPORTING THE RESULTS OF SCIENCE

The way the results of research are reported has been changing during the past 10 years. Traditional publication responsibilities to the academic community remain, but the need to disseminate scientific information to special-interest groups and the general public has increased. Scientists are being asked to serve in a "technology transfer" role, explaining what their research means, identifying alternatives for management action suggested by their research, and helping to design management programs based upon research results. Machlis and Field (1974) and Machlis and McDonough (1978) have, for example, described theories of human behavior and then used these theories to develop and propose specific environmental education programs for children.

Reporting the results of science has taken on a new meaning, thanks to the increased diversity of the audiences for those results, all requiring different means of presentation. For example, research addressing a political question, research used within the public involvement process, and research used in the preparation of an environmental statement or social impact assessment will all require alternative formats for the presentation of scientific

RESEARCH AREA	CLIENT					PUBLIC			ACADEMIC COMMUNITY		
	Management Plan	Training Program	Annual Rpts. of Science & CPSU Rpts.	Executive Summaries	Alternative and Action Plans	Audio Visual	Pamphlets and Brochures	Park Science	Dissertations	Masters Theses	Journal Articles
FIRE	Resource Management Plan		Prescribed Fire in Crater Lake / Fire Research needs in NPS Areas of Ore. and Wash. / Annual Rpts. 1977-79		Fire Restoration at Sun Creek, Mgmt. Recommendations / Fire Monitoring Techniques (CRLP)	Slide Program	Fire in Pac. NW Natl. Parks	Vol. 1, No. 1 / Vol. 2, No. 1	Forest & Avifaunal Structure in W. Montane Oly. Mts.	Interp. Natural Role of Fire / Forest Res. at Sun Creek	Fire Effects on Pac. NW Forests / First Year Ecolog. Effects of Hoh Fire / Large Lightning Fires in Oly. Mts.
ELK	Resource Management Plan	Aerial Censusing Training	Elk Ecology & Mgmt. at Mt. Rainier / Annual Rpts. 1977-79	Annually at Elk Mgmt Comm. Mtgs. (at Park)	Elk Monitoring Techniques - Population & Habitat	Talks before local interest groups		Vol. 1, No. 3	History, Ecology & Mgmt of Introduced Wapiti Population in Mt. Rainier		Multiple-Agency Mgmt. of a Common Resource
SOCIAL SCIENCE RESEARCH FOR INTERPRETATION	Interp. Management Plan / Strategy for Social Sci. Res.	Resources Mgmt. / Basic Interp.	Children's Interp. / Interp. for Handicapped / Annual Rpts. 1977-78	Whitman Mission Data: Interp. Activity Inventory	Design Monitoring Program / Visitor Observation for Interp.		Splash! (game) / Coloring Books / Design for Bulletins / Clams of Garrison Bay	Vol. 1, No. 1 / Vol. 2, No. 1 / Vol. 2, No. 2		Retirees in Parks / Preparation and Career Dev. of Interp. Personnel / Interpretive Activity Inventory	Cruiseship Travelers: Onboard Interp. / Applying Soc. Res. to Interp. in NW / Getting Connected: An Approach to Child's Interp.
SOCIAL SCIENCE RESEARCH ON BACKCOUNTRY MANAGEMENT	Backcountry Management Plan / Strategy for Social Sci. Res.		Hikers on the Chilkoot Trail / Annual Rpts. 1977-79	Executive Summary Rec's for McKinley	Design Monitoring Program			Vol. 1, No. 2	Study of Crowding and Social Gatherings in Alaska Natl. Parks	Visitor Use Data in the Dev. of Interp. Services	Study of Backpacker's Preferences / Backcountry Use at Mt. McKinley / Crowding at Katmai NP / Interp. and Backcountry Mgmt.

Figure 2 Reporting results of applied science

information. Likewise, if scientists are expected to testify in courts of law or represent agencies at public hearings, the manner of presentation will also vary.

While scientific journal articles, dissertations, and masters' theses maintain the scientific credibility of the researcher, management often requires separate reports prescribing how the research answered the questions posed and the alternative actions that management can consider to solve a problem (Foote 1975). Executive summaries and action documents noting implications and alternatives are essential for management action plans.

Often research lends itself to popular reports or brochures for dissemination to the public. Slide/tape programs can be prepared to communicate the results of the research. Scientists should think in terms of a multifaceted science publication/reports program for management, the public, and the scientific community. Alternative formats for the display of scientific results are depicted in Figure 2. Managers working with their staffs can use the categories depicted as a checklist in negotiating with scientists about the potential of their work for presentation.

The wider the distribution of scientific results, the wider the audience which gains an appreciation for the role of science in park management. Numerous interpretive naturalists and communication experts within and outside of recreation agencies are more often than not willing to help the scientist in translating science into a popular publication or program.

CONCLUDING REMARKS

The integration of research into resource management decision making more often depends upon the way in which the research is undertaken and communicated to park management than on the subject area under study. This article has explored an interactive process involving scientist and manager that underlies an applied science perspective and that is essential for the application of science to problem solving. This process facilitates the formation of a partnership between manager (client) and scientist in which both are involved in decisions about what research is to be undertaken, how and in what order research issues will be addressed, and in what time frame research will be accomplished.

Regardless of the organizational structure supporting scientific inquiry, the interactive process between manager and scientist is fundamental. The science programs within the National Park Service and many state departments of fish and game, for example, are divisions within the "line" management system. In many state and local park units, scientific inquiry is a function with a division such as interpretation or visitor services, or a science activity may not even receive a separate designation. In both the U.S. Forest Service and the U.S. Fish and Wildlife Service, scientific activity is located within a separate administrative arm. Nevertheless scientists and managers alike acknowledge the importance of working together to ensure that high-quality research findings support management decisions.

Such a partnership has been underdeveloped in the past because the reward structure has not acknowledged the responsibilities for interaction between manager and scientist. Few managers have among their performance standards a requirement that they use science in decision making. Similarly, few scientists have in their job descriptions the successful communication or application of scientific information within a problem-solving management framework. This fact is particularly apparent in the cases of university scientists who undertake contract research for recreation agencies.

This partnership will also face numerous challenges in the future. Perhaps the most important area for discussion involves the question of what research will be required in the next 20 years to preserve the social and biological integrity of the nation's parks and to plan for the orderly extraction of renewable resources from the nation's forest system. Managers and scientists should seriously consider the formation of a think tank, a strategic planning task force, to chart a course of action that will provide necessary information for the management of park environments in conjunction with resource-management activities around parks.

During the remaining two decades of this century, competing demands for scarce resources will accelerate. Managers and scientists must both be concerned with integrated resource management. They must consider events taking place within and outside parks, such as commercial development, hydroelectric power development, forestry products, fisheries management, mining, agriculture, visitor use and tourism, regional urbanization, and rural population growth. There must be increasing awareness that parks are not islands, but rather integral components of a larger natural and social system, subject to a myriad of external or internal forces, and should be managed accordingly.

Some have argued that park ecosystems are becoming distinct biological islands. This concept has merit for assessing the ecological change taking place within a park, species and habitat relationships, and so on; but it must be understood that such distinctiveness arises because of ecological interdependency within the region in which the park is located (Machlis, Field, and Campbell 1981). To consider such issues, however, will require an expanded scientific effort beyond park boundaries to provide the necessary information for decision makers. A communication effort with a network of scientists and land managers at the federal, state, and local levels, which has yet to be firmly established, must be forged. A new partnership will be required to examine and resolve the complex issues appearing on the horizon.

ACKNOWLEDGMENTS

This article is reprinted from the Journal of Park and Recreation Administration 1983:18-27 (adapted from Johnson and Field 1981) with the permission of the American Academy for Park and Recreation Administration.

REFERENCES

Foote, N.H. 1975. "Putting Sociologists to Work." In D.H. Demerath, III, O. Larsen, and K.F. Schuessler (eds.), *Social Policy and Sociology*, New York: Academic Press.

Freeman, H., R.R. Dynes, P.H. Rossi, and W.F. Whyte, (eds.). 1983. *Applied Sociology*. San Francisco: Jossey-Bass.

Hobbs, D. 1969. "A Comment on Applied Sociological Research." *Rural Sociology* (June):224-45.

Johnson, D.R., and D.R. Field. 1981. "Applied and Basic Social Research: A Difference in Social Context." *Leisure Sciences* 4:269-79.

Lazarsfeld, P.F., and J.G. Reitz. 1975. *An Introduction to Applied Sociology*. New York: Elsevier.

Machlis, G., and D.R. Field. 1974. "Interpreting Parks For Kids--Making It Real." *Trends* II (Spring):19-25.

Machlis, G., and M. McDonough. 1978. *Children's Interpretation: A Discovery Book For Interpreters*. Cooperative Park Studies Unit, College of Forest Resources, University of Washington.

Machlis, G., D.R. Field, and F. Campbell. 1981. "The Human Ecology of Parks." *Leisure Sciences* 4:195-212.

Rossi, P.H., J.D. Wright and S.R. Wright. 1978. "The Theory and Practice of Applied Social Research." *Evaluation Quarterly* 2:171-91.

3

NATURAL RESOURCE SOCIOLOGY: FORESTS AND MARINE FISHERIES

Marc L. Miller
Institute for Marine Studies
College of Ocean and Fishery Sciences
University of Washington

Richard P. Gale
Department of Sociology
University of Oregon

> *"I was slow to observe the development of what, in the terms of our formulae, is becoming something like a third culture."*
>
> (C.P. Snow on the status of sociology and affiliated fields 1964:70)

Environmental legislation in the 1970s recruited the social sciences to the field of natural resource management. This development was spurred not so much by a social science lobby as by lawmakers and general publics awakened through popular writings (e.g., Carson 1962, Udall 1963, Ehrlich 1968, Commoner 1971) to the costs and uncertainties of technological progress (cf., Miller, Gale, and Brown This Volume). Before federal initiatives were undertaken to develop or otherwise transform natural resources, society wanted to know the human, as well as the environmental, consequences. The idea was that an array of social sciences could be applied to natural resource management topics to complement the physical and natural sciences.

In the early 1970s, sociology was not entirely prepared to fill applied niches in natural resource management systems. To be sure, sociologists had treated social disorganization, criminal behavior, poverty, ethnicity, urbanization, and education for most of the century.[1] But they had only just begun to study public bureaucracies, and very few of these were embedded in natural resource management systems. While sociologists did have a variety of theories to test, they did not have a research agenda attuned to the practical problems of resource policy. Equally seriously, little sociological baseline or time-series data existed other than census materials.

Over the last 15 years, sociologists working outward from academe, but also working as independent practitioners, have gradually brought their expertise to the natural resource policy arena. Sociologists increasingly provide contractual services to profit-seeking industries and various publics, but they are most frequently employed by resource management bureaucracies. In the latter role, sociologists aspire to a status comparable to tenured natural resource professionals who specialize in other sciences.[2]

Of all the federal agencies which manage natural resources, the U.S. Forest Service (USFS) has the longest experience with the use and employment of sociologists. The National Marine Fisheries Service (NMFS) stands at the opposite extreme with the least experience with sociologists. Drawing examples from the USFS and NMFS, this article considers the contemporary place of sociology in natural resource systems. A first section introduces the setting for applied sociology in two natural resource systems. A second section notes the significance of the social facts of professional *specialization* and *executivism* for natural resource sociology. A final section suggests how applied sociologists might enhance their contribution to natural resource management.

CONTEMPORARY NICHE

As practiced in natural resource management systems, sociology is a descendent of applied community sociology of another era. However, natural resource sociology occurs today in a special sociological, institutional, and intellectual context.

Sociologically, natural resource sociology is conducted within the same *natural resource management systems* which the discipline defines as objects of study. These systems are composed of natural resources, profit-seeking industries, diverse publics, and management bureaucracies (cf., Gale and Miller 1985, Miller and Gale 1986).[3] Throughout this century, the three social elements of natural resource management systems have debated the merits of *extractive* and *aesthetic* conservation philosophies of resource management (Miller, Gale, and Brown This Volume).

The history of natural resource management at the federal, regional, and state levels shows that the social elements of individual systems have bonded as a by-product of the policy process. Today, for example, managers, industries, and publics in both the forest and marine fisheries systems are highly conversant about such topics as federalism, laissez-faire philosophy, conservation, and the policy process.[4]

This sophistication has fostered communication about natural resource conflicts, but it has also helped all parties to evaluate the performances of a spectrum of natural resource professionals, including legal specialists, public relations experts, and scientists. For natural resource sociologists, this means that applied sociology will be scrutinized by a complex community of extractive and aesthetic conservationists, industry and social movement representatives, judiciaries, scholars, scientists, and journalists, among other analysts.

Institutionally, much contemporary natural resource sociology is a direct result of innovative law. The National Environmental Policy Act of 1969 was an organic stimulus to the field of social impact assessment. In 1976, the Magnuson Fishery Conservation and Management Act and the National Forest Management Act mandated formal attention to social and economic consequences of resource policy (cf., Orbach 1977, Dana and Fairfax 1980, Fairfax and Burton 1983).

Critically, the opening for sociology in natural resource management systems provided by this legislation had virtually no basis in any solid record of sociological achievements in resource management. In the forest case, the opportunity arose in response to the environmental movement's concern over the extra-exploitative tendencies of extractive resource industries. In fisheries, the sociological participation resulted from dissatisfaction with policies which ostensibly were made strictly on biological grounds, but which clearly were motivated as well by social and economic considerations (Miller and Gale 1986). The genesis of sociology in forests and fisheries management is that sociology was not so much invited by enlightened managers as it was Congressionally ordained.

Intellectually, natural resource sociology is assessed by the rules of science. The scientific doctrine has been a major force in the management of forests and fisheries for the entire history of the USFS and the NMFS. The impact of this understanding is that phenomenological, hermeneutic, humanistic and other forms of non-scientific sociology have had no application in resource management systems.

Sociologists who have been involved with forest and fisheries management bureaucracies over the last decade quickly discovered that research was to be judged by the paradigms of scientific communities. As relative newcomers to applied natural resource science, sociologists are expected (in particular by foresters and fishery biologists) to demonstrate a commitment to objectivity and a familiarity with the basic measurement concepts of reliability and validity. Sociologists, and other natural resource scientists, are discredited when they behave as advocates or policy makers.

CHANGES IN NATURAL RESOURCE SOCIOLOGY

Like other collective human endeavors, natural resource sociology is subject to change. In the cases of sociology supported by the U.S. Forest Service and the National Marine Fisheries Service, two pressures, or themes are noteworthy.

The first theme, professional *specialization*, has been pervasive in American life. As Becker *et al.* (1961:5) observe:

> Our social and technical order requires more and more services which depend upon esoteric knowledge and skills; so esoteric, in fact, that each of us--no matter how skilled and full of knowledge in his own specialty--must accept them on trust. When some people apply such knowledge and skill in performing services for other men, for organizations, or for society at large, and when these services are accepted on trust...they are practicing a profession. Of professions so-defined, we have more than ever before and will have more in the future as scientific knowledge is increasingly applied and as social organization becomes more complex.

In the formal organizations which house natural resource sociologists, specialization shapes role behavior.

The second theme, *executivism*, surfaces in the professional style of natural resource line managers (Miller and Gale 1986). It is the executive privilege of managers to create new expectations about the role of applied sociology. Insofar as sociologists operate in a staff relation to managers, this process leads to changes in role behavior of sociologists as well.

Specialization

In forest and marine fisheries resource systems, the lead management agencies are the USFS and the NMFS. These complex bureaucracies are highly stratified and specialized. Their behavior is that of rationalized organizations.

Specialization is traditional in the application of the sciences to real-world problems. At the beginning of this century, for example, fisheries science was strictly a biological activity. Since then two trends have been evident in the field. First, fisheries science has increasingly come to rely on quantitative and modelling expertise. This is illustrated in the rise of population dynamics. Second, fisheries science has expanded from a biological base to embrace other expertise, notably that of the oceanographic and social sciences (cf., Royce 1984).

The Magnuson Fishery Conservation and Management Act (MFCMA) of 1976 signalled a Kuhnian revolution in applied fisheries science. In recognition of the social policy aspects of fishery management, the Act freed fisheries managers from obligations to defend policy solely on biological grounds. In essence, managers were encouraged to behave less as *specialists*, and more as *politicians* (Miller and Gale 1986).[5]

Sociologists operating in the fisheries management system should not misunderstand the MFCMA. The message of the Act to scientists is different from its signal to managers. Sociologists are in the system to face the challenge of interdisciplinary research, not to make policy. In this role, sociologists are expected to master a quantitative and technical vocabulary.

Major differences in policy process distinguish marine fisheries and forest management (Gale and Miller 1985). In the fisheries system of the NMFS, policy unfolds in a public management arena in which the time horizon is short, and the information base is experimental and relatively nonstandardized. If the fisheries system's support of specialization continues, its public management arena will likely come to resemble the professional management arena of the USFS' forest system, with its long time horizon and technical, standardized information base.

The applied sciences in forestry are facing a post-specialization adjustment. Here, more than in fisheries, research agendas are well established and experts are accustomed to team research, judicial review, and the political re-alignments of industries and publics. Indeed, many of the technical methods utilized in forestry have been borrowed and used effectively by the timber industry and environmental constituencies. This democratization of science is shown, for example, in the familiarity of the Sierra Club with silviculture and sectorial input-output economics.

Sociology in the forest system is an established specialty. USFS sociologists have engaged in recreation research since the mid-1950s. This history of participation makes for a different opportunity structure than that of sociologists in fisheries.

Although sociology in forestry is relatively secure, it is not well integrated with other science. This has meant that research in the USFS is more multidisciplinary than interdisciplinary in character. Sociologists who would remedy this situation might look to the fishery format for team research. Under the MFCMA, fishery plan development teams include social

and natural scientists.   Ideally, this arrangement generates bio-economic
models of fisheries.

Executivism

A second theme in natural resource management systems stems from
the emergence of the line manager qua *executive*.[6] Executive managers are
committed first to bureaucracies, rather than to constituencies, applied
sciences, or resources. In forestry, where it is still very much the rule that
managers rise from within the USFS, few have backgrounds which include
administrative experience with private or public bureaucracies outside of the
forest system. In contrast, executive line managers are beginning to appear in
the marine fisheries system. In recent times, executives with legal experience
have functioned at the Deputy Assistant Administrator and Assistant
Administrator levels in the NMFS, as well as at the Administrator level in the
National Oceanic and Atmospheric Administration (Miller and Gale 1986).
Because executives are trained in fields other than natural resource
management, and because they are sometimes politically implanted in
resource management positions, executives are not easily or universally
accepted inside resource bureaucracies.

Professionally socialized to corporate and public administration
models of organizations, executive managers bring entirely new perspectives
to natural resource problems. Application of the corporate model poses a
threat of anomie for sociologists because executives have little experience
working with social scientists to develop policy.[7] In the corporate world,
where sociological expertise is diffused in public relations, marketing, and
personnel departments, sociologists encounter much the same problem they
did in fisheries management prior to the MFCMA. They are stigmatized as a
pre-professional and human resource. Resource managers familiar with the
corporate model would expect to employ lawyers, not social scientists, to
inform policy decisions.

Executives versed in the public administration model of organizations
can influence natural resource sociology in a different way. These resource
managers would expect sociologists to do policy analysis.

This vision is certain to create ambivalence in sociologists because
policy analysis is not academically identical to sociology.   Sociology is
generally understood to be an empirical science. Policy analysis has been
defined as marshalling information to support decisions. It is commonly
spiced with normative economics. As such, policy analysis is part science and
part craft (cf., Williams 1982).

Natural resource sociology stands along a continuum between basic
sociology and policy analysis (cp., Field and Johnson This Volume, Moore
and Brickler This Volume, Decker *et al*. This Volume). To be of service to

the executive manager using the public administration model, sociologists would have to consider the merits of an intellectual diversification. Indeed, proficiency at policy analysis could become requisite for survival for sociologists whose career aspirations are to work for resource agencies.

DISCUSSION

This article has examined existing and potential niches for sociology in forest and fishery resource management systems. For the benefits of natural resource sociology to materialize, sociologists will have to re-examine their professional practice in light of the persistence of specialization and the spectre of executivism. Needed is the spirit for strengthening natural resource sociology to be responsive to shifting social, political, and economic realities, while remaining intellectually rewarding. To this end, we conclude with several recommendations.

First, sociologists must emphasize a commitment to the scientific ethic. In modern natural resource management systems, where scientific pluralism is the rule instead of the exception, professionals must speak the language of science. By this, we do not suggest that sociologists become natural scientists, or that they should accept any subordination of sociological research. Instead, we mean that social scientists should prepare to defend their research with scientific logic.

Second, sociologists must realize that increasingly the foundation of applied sociology is the contract, rather than the research grant. Although both require specifications of problem, theory, and procedure, contracts differ from grants in that pragmatic results are expected in the short term. Sociologists should take obligations in contracts very seriously. While it is important to be precise about what is promised in a research proposal, it is more important to deliver what is promised in a timely manner. Moreover, it is guaranteed that many in the system will be informally assessing the worth of natural resource sociology.

Third, sociologists must design research questions which are grounded in policy decisions. Natural resource managers in the forest and fishery systems are much less certain how to allocate resources among users than how to preserve species. Sociologists need a research agenda attuned to the zero-sum nature of allocation decisions, as well as to the efficiency-equality tradeoffs in social policy (cf., Okun 1975). On demand, sociologists must answer the question of how their work fits, or does not fit, with that of other social scientists.[8] But, they must also be able to explain how their work complements that of natural scientists (cf., Gale and Miller This Volume).

Finally, sociologists must experiment with qualitatively different research products. To be more effective as scientists in the policy arena, sociologists must learn to be creative in the presentation of technical results, testimony, and formal reports. Becker (1964) has commented on the multiple benefits which accrue from attention to the professional responsibility to disseminate findings to those who sponsor research.

During the presidency of Ronald Reagan, natural resource sociology has suffered with other science from a withering of the federal research budget. This has resulted in hiring ceilings and cut-backs in agency programs. At the same time, support for contracts linking agencies with sociologists in universities and the private sector has diminished. While it is reassuring that environmental law remains in place, the administrative climate for natural resource sociology is not destined to be more receptive in the near term.

Nevertheless, we are optimistic about the future of sociology in natural resource management systems. In the essay containing the quotation which begins this article, Lord Snow apologizes for an English upbringing which conditioned him to be suspicious of all but the "hard" intellectual disciplines. With Lord Snow, we are confident that sociologists, as representative of the third culture, will play an important role bridging the gulf between traditional scientists and literary intellectuals.[9]

Sociology is ready to increase its productivity in natural resource management systems. For this to transpire, practitioners must not only empathize equally with those in profit-seeking industries, public interest groups, and management bureaucracies, but they must also perform as scientists.

ACKNOWLEDGMENTS

The authors are indebted to Perry J. Brown, David L. Fluharty, Arnold G. Holden, and Robert G. Lee for constructive comments on drafts of this article.

NOTES

1. In this article, we use the term "sociologist" generically to refer to several categories of social scientists (esp., sociologists, political scientists,

and cultural anthropologists) with the important exclusion of economists. Our arguments apply in a somewhat looser way to persons with other professional identities (e.g., foresters, rangers, managers) but who nonetheless have responsibility for the study of social systems. For the meaning of "sociologist" in the U.S. Forest Service, see Wenner (This Volume). See also Burton *et al.* 1986.

2. By definition, the work of professionals (and necessarily that of scientists) is characterized by freedom from interference. As Braude (1975:105) comments:

> The professional is an autonomous person, in principle responsible to none save his peers. To the degree that a worker is constrained in the performance of his work by the controls and demands of others, that individual is less a professional.

3. The ethnic, small-community, and other cultural groups commonly studied by ethnographers fall into the industry and/or public categories. The few subsistence groups which remain can be treated as "industrial" user groups (sometimes with special treaty privileges, as, for example, in the Pacific Northwest management of anadromous species) or as special publics.

4. Of course, management bureaucracies, industries, and publics require time to communicate their very different perspectives on resource management. For an illustration of how mutual understandings, if not policy agreement, have been fostered in fisheries, compare Miller and Van Maanen (1978) and Miller and Van Maanen (1983).

5. These idealized types, and two others, are defined in the following way:

> The *forstmeister* (and variants such as *fishmaster*, *mineralmaster*) has a professional style characterized by an intuitive understanding of natural resources; the resource management system is controlled as a family. The *specialist* has a style rooted in professional education; the resource management system is controlled with an intellectual paradigm. The *politician* has a negotiating style most attuned to extra-scientific problem solving that involves conflicting constituencies; the resource management system is controlled by the minimization of conflict. The *executive*

has a non-resource-specific style of facilitating cooperation, whatever the bureaucracy; the resource management system is controlled as an organization. (Miller and Gale 1986:143)

6. See note 5.

7. Sociologists have, of course, been useful to corporate executives in studying the means (cp., ends) of organizational behavior.

8. It is intolerable for sociologists, political scientists, and cultural anthropologists to fail at interdisciplinary communication. At the very least, sociologists and anthropologists should dispel the myth that ethnography and survey research are incompatible.

9. In clarification, Lord Snow (1964:60-61) adds:

I did not mean that literary intellectuals act as the main decision makers of the western world. I meant that literary intellectuals represent, vocalize, and to some extent shape and predict the mood of the non-scientific culture: they do not make the decisions, but their moods seep into the minds of those who do.

REFERENCES

Becker, H.S. 1964. "Problems in the Publication of Field Studies." In A.J. Vidich, J. Bensman, and M.R. Stein (eds.), *Reflections on Community Studies*. New York: Harper and Row. 415-425.

Becker, H.S., B. Geer, E.C. Hughes, and A.L. Strauss. 1961. *Boys in White: Student Culture in Medical School.* New Brunswick: Transaction Books.

Braude, L. 1975. *Work and Workers: A Sociological Analysis.* New York: Praeger Publishers.

Burton, M.L., G.M. Schoepfle, and M.L. Miller. 1986. "Natural Resource Anthropology." *Human Organization* 45:261-269.

Carson, R. 1962. *Silent Spring.* New York: Fawcett Crest.

Commoner, B. 1971. *The Closing Circle.* New York: Alfred A. Knopf.

Dana, S.T. and S.F. Fairfax. 1980. *Forest and Range Policy: Its Development in the United States.* New York: McGraw-Hill.

Ehrlich, P.R. 1968. *The Population Bomb.* New York: Ballantine (Sierra Club).

Fairfax, S.F. and L. Burton. 1983. "A Decade of NEPA: Milestone or Millstone?" *Fisheries* 8:5-9.

Gale, R.P. and M.L. Miller. 1985. "Professional and Public Natural Resource Management Arenas: Forests and Marine Fisheries." *Environment and Behavior* 17:651-678.

Miller, M.L. and R.P. Gale. 1986. "Professional Styles of Federal Forest and Marine Fisheries Resource Managers." *North American Journal of Fisheries Management* 6:141-148.

Miller, M.L. and J. Van Maanen. 1978. "'Boats Don't Fish, People Do': Ethnographic Notes on the Federal Management of Fisheries in Gloucester." *Human Organization* 38:377-385.

_____ 1983. "The Emerging Organization of Fisheries in the United States." *Coastal Zone Management Journal* 10:369-386.

Okun, A.M. 1975. *Equality and Efficiency*. Washington: The Brookings Institution.

Orbach, M.K. (ed.). 1977. *Report of the National Workshop on the Concept of Optimum Yield in Fisheries Management*. Washington: U.S. Department of Commerce (NOAA, NMFS).

Royce, W.F. 1984. *Introduction to the Practice of Fishery Science*. New York: Academic Press, Inc.

Snow, C.P. 1964. *The Two Cultures and A Second Look: An Expanded Version of the Two Cultures and the Scientific Revolution*. Forage Village, MA: Murray Printing Company (London: Cambridge University Press).

Udall, S.L. 1963. *The Quiet Crisis*. New York: Holt, Rinehart and Winston.

Williams, W. (ed.). 1982. *Studying Implementation*. Chatham, NJ: Chatham House Publishers.

4

THE PRACTICE AND PROMISE OF SOCIAL SCIENCE IN THE U.S. FOREST SERVICE

Lambert N. Wenner
Office of Environmental Coordination
U. S. Forest Service

The U.S. Forest Service (USFS) manages 191 million acres of land in 45 states and the West Indies. It exercises forestry and conservation leadership in about one-third of the nation's land area. Because the agency is decentralized, many important management decisions are made in the 9 regions, 1 area, 156 national forests, and 9 research stations.

The USFS is committed by law and tradition to multiple-use management of national forest resources. Strong programs exist for managing wilderness areas, timber, wildlife, recreation, minerals, range, fisheries, soil, and air and water quality, and for cooperation with state and private forestry. Both environmental protection and consumer needs are considered in developing and adapting these programs. A variety of support services such as research, fire and pest control, engineering, personnel, public information, and social economic analysis help resource professionals achieve agency goals.

In 1985, the USFS hosted 225 million forest recreation visitor-days, provided forage for 8.8 million animal-months, constructed 721 miles of trail, constructed or improved 8 thousand miles of road, and sold 10.8 billion board feet of timber. In addition, the agency processed 28.5 thousand minerals cases, reforested 370 thousand acres, improved 355 thousand acres of wildlife habitat, purchased or exchanged 166 thousand acres of land, and protected 800 million of acres of land from fires (USFS 1985).

Under federal law, the "best" plans and decisions are those which consider all relevant social, economic, biological, and physical factors. This article examines present and potential applications of social science in national forest management. The first section explains the need for current, accurate social information in planning and implementing natural resource programs. The next section describes the organization and extent of social science activity in the USFS. A third section identifies barriers to the expanded use of social science expertise within the agency. The final section shows how social science knowledge and expertise can be used to achieve agency goals and summarizes recent efforts to make better use of this potential.

SOCIAL INFORMATION NEEDS

A major barrier to effective resource management is an incomplete understanding of the relationship between agency activities and public expectations and needs. Projects are sometimes initiated with insufficient information about how publics will be affected. Resource managers need answers to such questions as the following:

1. Who has an interest in USFS activities and who is most affected by changes?
   How do they view agency programs and how do they react?
   What is happening or will happen to them? Why?
   Are external costs and benefits equitably distributed?
   Can unwanted social and economic impacts be avoided or mitigated?

2. What social, economic, and technological trends affect the agency's mission and performance?
   What kind of a future would the agency prefer?
   Can and should the agency influence changes? Two examples are changes in its mission or changes in the way national forests are used.
   How can the USFS best identify and meet public needs?

3. What are the characteristics of the agency and its work force?
   How do these affect performance?
   Do they affect interaction with publics?

Some of this information seems self-evident. Some is readily volunteered by publics. But much of it is best obtained and validated using social science methods. The use of social science methodology helps to ensure that the information collected is current, valid, and relevant, and that the analysis is credible. Properly applied, social science helps to evaluate findings, for example, by estimating how people are affected and how important the effects are.

Rationale for Social Science Analysis

In the USFS, people often use the term *social analysis* as an umbrella concept for all of the following activities:

1. Collecting social and economic information relating to USFS programs, projects, and policies

2. Organizing, analyzing, and evaluating social data

3. Estimating the social and economic consequences of agency actions

However, this article focuses on *social science analysis*, with emphasis on social impact analysis. Science implies higher standards: the use of established social science methods to collect and interpret information relevant to national forest management.

National forest resources are owned by and managed for the American people. Resource decisions are shaped by Congress, administrative policies, tradition, and the values and needs of a variety of publics, including commercial forest users, forest products consumers (all of us), recreationists, state and local governments, and local residents affected by USFS programs. Each public has somewhat different expectations for forest management. The chief concern of some publics is to protect their interests as commercial or recreational forest users. Other publics, which include people who seldom visit a national forest, are concerned about maintaining environmental quality, preserving wildernesses and endangered species, and ensuring future supplies of forest products.

There are also "silent" publics with no publicly expressed expectations for national forests. Often their membership greatly exceeds the more vocal groups and some of them are directly affected by USFS activities. Agency credibility with these and other publics is enhanced by evidence that systematic social impact analysis of proposed actions is done to obtain a balanced view of potential impacts and to identify mitigation opportunities. Social science provides tested procedures for identifying a wide range of affected publics and for estimating the types and importance of potential impacts on each.

The National Environmental Policy Act of 1969 (NEPA) requires the integrated use of the natural and social sciences in federal agency planning and decision making that may have an impact on the human environment (P.L. 91-190, Section 102 (2) (A)). The National Forest Management Act of 1976 (NFMA) reaffirms this obligation (P.L. 94-580, Section 6(g)(1)). Both laws also require public involvement in agency planning and decision making.

PRACTICE OF SOCIAL SCIENCE

The USFS now has formal procedures for both public participation and social impact analysis. It also has conducted or contracted for social science research in selected problem areas, such as nonmarket resource values, issue identification and consensus building techniques, national trends affecting the agency, social impacts of minerals and energy development, recreation research, and urban forestry.

Public Participation

The most institutionalized and widely used USFS procedure for collecting and evaluating social data is the public participation program of the Public Affairs Office (PAO), which dates back to the early 1960s. PAO has a professional and technical staff of about 20 in Washington, staffs of 3 to 13 in each regional office, and part- or full-time public information officers in each national forest.

The PAO keeps the public apprised of agency activities, prepares educational materials for public use, and monitors public and media responses to announced projects and programs. This office plans and administers the public involvement activities required by NEPA (U.S. Government 1978) and the NFMA (USFS 1982).

Public participation takes various forms. Public comment frequently is requested when the agency proposes new projects, policy changes, or program modifications. These comments are analyzed and considered before making a final agency decision on the proposal. Unsolicited public comments such as media reports, letters to the editor, oral opinions, and correspondence are also taken into account. Some Forest Service units routinely collect and analyze these.

Public participation is sometimes structured with specific goals in mind. Examples of this participation are town meetings to discuss proposals, informal "open house" gatherings to explain the agency's programs and respond to questions, information exchanges among competing interest groups seeking a mutually acceptable solution, and the convening of advisory councils to discuss problems such as grazing allotments.

Social science methods are sometimes used in collecting and analyzing public responses to agency proposals. Content analysis increases the objectivity of recorded responses and the validity of findings. One content analysis procedure called "codinvolve" (USFS 1981) uses a computer to code, display, record, store, and retrieve large-volume public responses. Codinvolve can display the number, categories, and content of such data to facilitate summaries and evaluation.

Social Impact Analysis

Social impact analysis (SIA) is a procedure for estimating the social and economic effects of proposed actions and their alternatives (Finsterbusch et al. 1983, Leistritz and Ekstrom 1986). The *Forest Service Manual* mandates the use of SIA when the potential social effects of agency policies or actions are important to the decision (USFS 1985c).

Experience demonstrates that the great majority of people likely to be affected by an agency proposal do not provide input to resource managers. Many of these people feel they lack the time, information, communications skills, or other resources (money, power, etc.) to respond effectively. In other cases, they are unaware of the proposed action or its potential direct, indirect, and cumulative effects.

Hence, much public input is from organized, vested and special interest groups with a specific stake in the action. Some of the responses are not carefully researched, are biased, and fail to consider the needs of other groups. Responses from other agencies usually are well informed, but tend to be limited to technical or procedural judgments about the management of particular physical and biological resources. Thus, whether by design or default, silent publics leave it to the agency to be aware of their needs and to take necessary actions. If the USFS does not respond to their needs, silent publics may eventually mobilize and be heard through organized protests, lawsuits, and appeals. This has happened on grazing, mineral development, timber harvesting, pest management, and water rights issues.

The *Forest Service Handbook* 1909.17 (USFS 1985a, chapter 30) sets forth social impact analysis procedures. Social impact analysis is an integral part of environmental analysis and must meet Council on Environmental Quality (CEQ) and USFS analysis standards. Both natural and social science knowledge must be utilized in preparing environmental impact statements and preparers must be from appropriate disciplines (USG CEQ 1978 40 CFR 1501.2 (a) and 1502.6).

The *Forest Service Handbook* recommends using social science expertise to accomplish the following objectives:

1. To obtain a balanced view of the preferences and needs of individuals, communities, and special-interest publics potentially affected by agency activities

2. To learn the details of major agency proposals that may have an impact on the human environment

3. To make careful estimates of the economic and social effects of proposed actions including direct, indirect, and cumulative effects of each alternative for the foreseeable future

4. To suggest ways to avoid or mitigate adverse effects and to enhance public benefits

5. To monitor ongoing activities to ensure that program objectives are met and that mitigation is effective

Coordination of SIA

The Forest Service has a loosely organized network of employees (Table 1) who guide, conduct, and evaluate social impact analysis at the national, regional, and forest levels.

The social impact analysis network in the Forest Service is guided by the Office of Environmental Coordination in Washington. This office monitors agency activities to ensure compliance with NEPA and its supporting regulations. The sociologist in this office has several complementary roles:

1. Developing and coordinating training in social impact analysis, including in-service training seminars, inter-agency sessions at professional conferences, a library of useful sources, and annotated bibliographies of these sources

2. Participating in national-level agency and inter-agency activities with social analysis components

3. Monitoring National Environmental Policy Act compliance.

Each region and area has a regional social science coordinator to guide and monitor social science analysis at that level. One regional coordinator is a sociologist (Ph.D) but most other coordinators are from fields such as forestry, economics, and public administration. All but one have primary responsibilities in other specialities.

Several sociologists and social scientists[1] are employed at the forest and zone (multiforest) levels. Some regions have social science coordinators for each forest. All national forests have social impact analysis responsibilities, but most such analysis is done by agency employees in other specialities (Table 1) or by outside contractors, some of whom are also drawn from other specialities. For this reason persons doing social impact analysis are called "social science analysts," rather than social scientists.

Table 1   Professions that perform social impact analysis in the forest service. A survey of six Forest Service Regions and the Northeastern Area provided the following data on the backgrounds of people doing social analysis in 1983-1984.

Job Title	Percent	Academic Degrees	Percent
Forest planner	20	Forestry	13
Economist	18	Forest management	7
Public affairs officer	8	Natural resource economics	7
Forester	6	Economics	7
Community planner	5	Sociology	5
Sociologist	5	Business & bus. adm.	5
Operations research	4	Political science	5
Program analyst	4	Agricultural economics	4
Social scientist	3	Social science	3
Archaeologist	2	Public administration	3
Ethnologist	1	Regional and city planning	3
16 other titles	24	Geography	2
	100	Social anthropology	2
N=94		Landscape Architecture	2
		35 other degrees	32
			100
		N=129	

Role of Social Science Analyst
        Social science analysts compile and interpret social and economic information relating to agency programs, policies, and projects. Often a member of an interdisciplinary environmental analysis team is assigned to identify relevant public and agency concerns about an agency proposal, to develop agency alternatives, to project and compare the probable social effects of each alternative, and to suggest possible mitigation procedures. Along with other specialists, social science analysts monitor ongoing programs and projects to ensure compliance with laws, regulations, planned impact mitigation, and negotiated agreements.
        The analyst focuses mainly on the social, economic, and cultural impacts of agency activities on people outside the agency. This work includes an analysis of socioeconomic effects, such as changes in per capita income, employment, secondary business activity, population shifts, and the fiscal situation of state and local governments. In practice, the economic impacts of agency activities are analyzed more frequently and extensively than other social and cultural effects. The agency has many more economists than sociologists; thus, quantified economic data are more readily available.
        Social and economic impact analysis differs from economic efficiency analysis, which estimates the monetary costs and benefits of an activity for its sponsors. The most economically efficient alternative for an agency or its permittees (for example, commercial producers of timber, recreation opportunities, minerals, or hydropower) may produce unacceptable external social and economic impacts.
        Agency social analysts usually work with existing information gathered from a variety of secondary sources, such as U.S. Census data, county data, and comments on public response forms. Although some agency social analysts are professionally qualified to do field work to develop additional data, limitations of time and budget often discourage it. Some proposals for social science analysis and research are contracted to university departments or private consultants who must meet specifications and standards set by the Forest Service. When available, agency social scientists help to prepare these proposals and review the contractor's work, just as engineers or wildlife biologists review the work of contractors in their areas of expertise.

Other Applications of Social Science
        Social science research is not mandated by the Forest and Rangeland Research Act of 1978 (P.L. 95-307). However, Sections 3(a) and 6(d) suggest the need for such research and also authorize it.
        USFS Research Stations employ about a dozen sociologists and social scientists, whose primary assignments are forest recreation, urban forestry, and state and private forest utilization. Forest recreation research

provides agency managers with the information and technology needed to meet the growing public demand for a wide spectrum of both developed and dispersed outdoor recreation. Urban forestry research seeks ways to use vegetation to enhance the social, economic, and natural environments of urban areas. Both types of research include studies of the preferences and use patterns of their respective publics. For example, research social scientists are examining the social distribution of recreation opportunities and the possible consequences of policy changes, such as increased fees and reduced options.

Research social scientists monitor selected social and economic trends relevant to natural resource management. They also analyze the social consequences of alternative scenarios for natural resource management, such as those found in both the periodic assessment of forest and range land needs and the resources program developed under the Resources Planning Act (RPA).

Agency economists have developed and are refining a system of input-output models for planning (IMPLAN). These models estimate employment, income, and population impacts of different alternatives for forest land management plans and for large-scale projects.

Applying Social Theory and Research

Social theory and research methodology are used by the small core of social scientists in the agency. For reasons mentioned below, applications are sometimes very pragmatic and may be more intuitive than formal. For example, social theory helps to explain the structure and behavior of the Forest Service organization and its local community and larger political contexts. Ecological theories help to explain the existing population distribution and patterns of resource use. Theories of socioeconomic change guide the prediction of population shifts resulting from agency program changes.

USFS social scientists look to external sources for social science knowledge and analytical techniques needed to investigate forest-dependent communities and to estimate the potential social effects of various program alternatives. Case studies of communities where similar actions have occurred provide clues to research methods, possible impacts, and appropriate mitigation measures.

CONSTRAINTS TO WIDER APPLICATION

Perhaps more than ever before, USFS managers and their professional staffs are open to new ideas and approaches, including the broader use of the social sciences in resource management, especially in impact and trend analysis. Important social changes are occurring and many publics show an increased interest in the policies, techniques, and effects of public resource management. However, the application of social science knowledge and skills is limited by inadequate staffing, the traditional natural resource orientation of the agency, and several other factors discussed below.

Inadequate Staffing

The agency has relatively few social scientists[2] and most outside of research have primary assignments in other specialities. They are also unevenly distributed; the majority of regional and forest social scientists are in California, Oregon and Montana.

Social scientists tend to be clustered at the lower levels of the administrative-professional staff (GS-9 to 12). In contrast to the situation in resource areas such as timber, wildlife, or minerals, no staff units encourage, guide, and coordinate social science work in the National Forest System.

About ten sociologists, social scientists, and anthropologists in the agency currently coordinate or do social impact analysis as part of their assigned duties.[3] Another ten employees with these job titles have full-time assignments in other specialities such as land management planning or public affairs. About ten more do research in recreation, urban forestry, and forest utilization. A few others have been promoted into other specialities with different job titles. The estimated 30 social scientists in the agency make up about one-fourth of one percent of the total professional-administrative work force. Table 2 compares the number of social scientists with specialists in several other professional fields within the USFS.

The network of agency social scientists is too small and too unevenly distributed to meet all of the agency's needs. Its members lack the authority, autonomy, time, and budget to become an innovative force in the agency--as engineers, landscape architects, wildlife biologists, and archeologists have done previously. Few opportunities exist for original field work, contacts with others in the same discipline, or on-the-job training in social science procedures. Five of the nine national forest regions currently have neither sociologists nor social scientists (except economists).

Unrecognized Potentials

Most agency managers and professionals are trained in the natural sciences and readily see the need for data from the physical and biological sciences in their work. But some fail to see the parallel need for social science data to help understand the social context within which the agency functions. Many have had little or no course work in the social sciences. At least a few believe the natural sciences are "exact" while social sciences are "soft" (neither is either), when, in truth, the essence of science is the rigor of the method and the validity of the results--not the type of data studied.

Table 2   Total forest service professional-administrative staff in selected job titles, October 1985 *(Compiled by Rick Wetherill from USFS personnel files)*

Sociology	3	Forestry	5282
Anthropology, General	2	Engineering, Civil	1068
Social Science	20	Engineering, General	46
		Range Conservation	441
		Soil Science	255
Biology, General	195	Hydrology	205
Wildlife Biology	489		
Entomology	140		
		Landscape Architecture	212
Fishery Biology	122		
		Archaeology	140
Geology	157	Public Affairs	161
Chemistry	53	Economics	72
Plant Pathology	92		

Most agency professionals live and communicate in a universe of natural resource specialists and seldom encounter social scientists or have detailed knowledge of their work. Some use sociological sources or approaches in their work, but do not associate them with the field.

Tentative Guidance
Detailed, approved, national direction for social impact analysis procedures was not available until 1985. Before that a variety of national, regional, and forest-level procedures was evolving, providing a fund of good ideas, regional variations in procedures, and some confusion. People were

uncertain about when and how to do social impact analysis. In addition, training was not available in most locations.

Some agency personnel think that public involvement and consensus-building procedures are all that NEPA requires. In fact, social impact analysis is also necessary to estimate the social effects of a proposed action and its alternatives, to identify feasible mitigation, and to determine if desired results are achieved.

Uncertain Responsibility

Sometimes social impacts are not carefully estimated and addressed because USFS personnel assume that other agencies and state and local governments have the major responsibility for mitigating social effects, and that the Forest Service has no authority to deal with off-site effects. The agency has a responsibility under the NEPA (P.L. 91-190, Sec. 102(2)) to identify the potential social effects of its programs, to share this information with public officials and interested or affected citizens, and to cooperate with other governments and agencies to avoid or minimize adverse effects.

Restrictions on Field Work

Short time schedules, budget limitations, and social survey restrictions enforced by the federal Office of Management and Budget sometimes discourage field work to fill social (and resource) information gaps. However, field work is possible in most situations that require it--if the skills and opportunity are available. Outside contractors or persons on detail from other units may be used when the need for social science expertise is recognized but locally unavailable.

Complexity of Social Environment

Major agency proposals sometimes have local, regional, and national effects. A wide range of people may experience direct or indirect effects. Identifying potentially affected people; focusing the analysis on the most important issues; estimating the location, magnitude, and duration of effects; and recommending feasible mitigation for unwanted effects can be demanding, even for agency social scientists.

Wish to Avoid Controversy

Some employees are reluctant to inform potentially affected publics promptly and fully about proposed agency actions, either because the social impacts are not yet clear or because of concern that early communication may initiate unproductive controversy. Such delays may instead reduce the value of public contributions; force the public to get its initial information through rumor, speculation, and messages from special interests; intensify controversy;

and decrease agency credibility. This underscores the need to begin SIA early in the environmental analysis process and to share findings with others.

Low Priority

Some managers believe that the analysis and mitigation of social impacts is not as urgent or binding a requirement as the analysis and protection of cultural resources, endangered species, or soil, air, and water, because the latter are protected by additional legislation with more specific provisions than NEPA. Faced with limited budgets and staffing, they devote most of their effort to analyzing effects on resources protected by legal mandates.

A few managers have employed or contracted social scientists, but found their products unsatisfactory for one or more of these reasons:

1. Too voluminous to read and use efficiently

2. Not clearly applicable to the decision

3. Written in obscure prose and/or social science jargon

4. Naive, reflecting insufficient understanding of management options and constraints

5. Seemingly biased toward certain interest groups

Traditional Resource Orientation

For most of its 90-year history the National Forest System has been administered by resource professionals trained in the natural sciences. Some resource managers are convinced that they have the necessary expertise and authority, and are doing what is best. Even though some members of the public may disagree with their decisions, they believe that most people support them. The self-image of many agency professionals is one of competent, responsible people doing a good job of resource stewardship.

Declining Budgets and Ceilings

USFS budgets and staffing declined sharply from 1980 to 1985. The number of full-time equivalent employees decreased about 21 percent (USFS 1985) and further reductions are expected during 1986-1988. To avoid laying off employees, many vacated positions are now left unfilled. Although the total number of professional employees remained fairly constant during 1980-1985, few new positions were created and most vacated social science positions were not filled.

PROMISE OF SOCIAL SCIENCE

Forest Service managers and staffs must function within limits established by law and administrative policy. However, they usually have sufficient flexibility to consider a range of alternatives and to build an optimal program within these limits. The quality of their program depends on the adequacy of their social and resource information.

The USFS and other natural resource agencies could reap many benefits from a broader and more professional application of social science knowledge and methods, including social impact analysis. The challenge is to build a more effective program in a time of agency retrenchment.

With more effective social impact analysis, the agency would more fully comply with NEPA and NFMA requirements. This, in turn, should better serve the public, reduce the volume of administrative appeals and costly litigation of agency decisions, increase agency credibility, and strengthen public support for resource programs and projects.

Agency managers are increasingly aware that organizational factors contribute to successes and failures. Peters and Waterman (1983) stress the importance of qualities such as a preference for action, autonomy, respect for the individual employee, and being close to the customer. Social science analysis and feedback can be used to critique and improve agency performance in each of these areas.

Potential Uses of Social Science

The following examples drawn from the author's own experience within the agency illustrate the range of potential applications of social science expertise to resource management. Some of the listed activities are already well institutionalized by certain forests and/or staff units. Others suggest new opportunities. The following is a list of appropriate tasks for social scientists in resource management:

1. Identify currently or potentially affected human populations and estimate the social and economic impacts of agency activities, such as recreation projects, land exchanges, mineral projects, pest management programs, and forest planning. In environmental documents, clearly present the types, duration, and the intensity of potentially important social impacts of resource management alternatives. These must be considered by the decision-maker in combination with natural resource impacts and economic efficiency. Inform potentially affected communities about proposed actions, the expected effects of each, and options for dealing with unwanted effects. For major actions, help to evaluate the capacity of affected communities to adapt to growth or decline and associated changes.

2. Determine existing and emerging public and agency needs using objective indicators, such as demographic trends, technological changes, consumption levels, attitude surveys, forest use patterns, and case studies of similar situations. Include the special needs of minorities, the handicapped, women, and the elderly, and ways to meet these needs. Discover and clarify the opportunities for redirection of USFS programs to meet verified public needs. This can be done at the local, regional, and national levels.

3. Anticipate public concerns *before* they result in organized opposition. Help to develop appropriate social, economic, and fiscal mitigation *before* actions are implemented. Monitor program implementation and provide feedback from each category of interested and affected people, including previously unrecognized publics.

4. Improve agency guidance in social science analysis. Help to train personnel to be more sensitive to social factors and economic concerns, and to use these insights in planning and decision making.
Coordinate social science analysis to avoid duplication of effort and to share available knowledge. Develop and publish relevant statistical data and case studies of ongoing activities and lessons learned, so that other units in the agency and affected publics will make fewer mistakes in designing and carrying out effective programs.

5. Analyze and share information about broad or persistent social changes that affect environmental protection, forest products and uses, and agency functions. This can be done at the regional and national levels for cost efficiency. Examples of change are numerous:

Decline of traditional occupations	Changes in consumption patterns
Urban-rural population shifts	Electronic revolution
Interregional migration patterns	New lifestyles and recreation
Increase in rural retirees	Preferences affecting forests
Changes in rural institutions	Environmental movements
Level of unemployment	Civil rights responsibilities

6. Monitor international trends. We are increasingly involved in a world market economy, share environmental impacts, and are asked to provide expertise to developing nations. Innovations should be compatible with cultural needs and expectations both in developing countries and our own society.

7. Use social theory to explain relationships, identify missing data, and predict consequences.

8. Help other federal and state agencies and private sector developers to be aware of the importance of social and local economic factors in program design and implementation.

9. Develop effective interdisciplinary training texts. Compile and integrate under one cover the technological, social, economic, and resource implications of each major field activity, such as the recreation program, energy development, hard-rock mining, timber harvest, ski area development, land management planning, and livestock grazing.

10. Assist in the preparation of contract proposals for social science services. This will help to ensure that products received are responsive to USFS needs, methodologically sound, meet time schedules, and make sense to prospective users in other fields.

Increasing the Effectiveness of Existing Staff
A small cadre of professional social scientists[4] could make important additional contributions in many of these areas, provided they were well qualified through training and experience, reasonably creative, and self-motivated. Several options exist for increasing the effectiveness of USFS social science analysis activities with existing staff:

1. Expanding the training program for upgrading the knowledge and skills of social science analysts, especially those with limited formal training or field experience in social analysis.

2. Contracting qualified social scientists to assist in the environmental analysis of programs or projects with potentially significant social effects. This is now agency policy when Forest Service staff cannot provide needed expertise (USFS 1985c, sec. 1973.03).

3. Utilizing agency social scientists as efficiently as possible by creating zone (multiforest) assignments, using regional social scientists as consultants and reviewers, and identifying appropriately trained, socially sensitive economists, archeologists, geographers, or others who are able to assist. Encouraging regional social science coordinators to devote more time to social impact analysis, providing information and feedback. This should be a specific element in their performance standards.

4. Establishing liaisons with university social science institutes that would be willing to work with Forest Service units, supplying information and doing applied research.   Coordinating with university departments of sociology or natural resources to establish stipends for Ph.D candidates doing research valuable to the agency.   Establishing campus-based graduate programs (a semester or year in duration) for intensive training in social science, including social impact analysis procedures.

Strengthening Social Impact Analysis Skills
Currently, several efforts are underway to improve the quality of applied social science in the agency.   In 1984 each region and area formally appointed social science coordinators to guide and monitor social impact analysis and related activities including conducting training sessions, reviewing documents, and visiting forests.
During 1983-1985 the Washington office developed a social impact analysis training program, which was tested and evaluated at pilot sessions held in Washington and Sacramento. Detailed lesson plans and supplementary handout materials have been completed and distributed to the Regions.
In 1985 the *Economic and Social Analysis Handbook* was published, providing the first official detailed instructions for doing social impact analysis as an integral part of environmental analysis. The Washington office also maintains an up-to-date social science reference library for field and inter-agency use. A published annotated bibliography lists available sources.
The Forest Service, in cooperation with the Rural Sociologicial Society, organized Inter-agency Social Science Symposia as presessions to the 1983, 1984, 1985, and 1987 annual meetings of the Society. These symposia provide an opportunity for agency and university social scientists to meet and share mutual interests.   Proceedings are published and distributed to participants.

CONCLUSIONS

The scope and depth of USFS social science analysis, including social impact analysis, is still limited. Several factors, including inadequate staffing, insufficient training, and agency inertia, have hindered the development of this program. However, the agency is taking steps to increase the effectiveness of social impact analysis.   The USFS can and should continue to increase the effective use of social science in natural resource management.   Social science expertise is needed to identify human populations who are affected by agency programs, to determine the impacts of agency activities, and to develop feasible mitigation for unwanted effects. It can also provide information and methods to help meet a wide range of management needs, such as improved public relations, trend monitoring, forest-user data, civil rights compliance, contracting, and training.

The several options for increasing the use of social science in the agency include increased staffing of experienced resource sociologists, closer coordination with universities, training in social sensitivity and impact analysis procedures, and more effective utilization of existing agency social scientists.

NOTES

1. In the Forest Service "social scientist" is a job description for a person who works with social data. Qualifications vary by position but generally include a bachelor's degree, credit hours in specified social science fields, and relevant experience for higher-level positions. Sociologist positions have similar minimum standards and may also be filled at the bachelor's level. This is considered equivalent to the entry requirements for foresters, biologists, or engineers. A graduate degree in social science is a competitive advantage at the entry level for social science positions and essential for "research social scientist" positions in the agency's research program.

2. The emphasis here is on social scientists in fields that study the social and cultural patterns and trends of contemporary people. Most economists in the agency are involved mainly in economic efficiency analysis; they are not included in these computations.

3. Estimates in this section are based on official personnel statistics supplemented by discussions with other agency social scientists.

4. The cadre could include a regional social scientist, one or more forest or zone (multiforest) social scientists in each region, and two in the Washington office, for a total of 20 professionals nationwide with social science as their primary responsibility. Several more can be utilized effectively in problem-oriented research (as is now being done).

REFERENCES

Finsterbusch, K., L. Llewellyn, and C. Wolf. 1983. *Social Impact Assessment Methods*. Beverly Hills: Sage Publications.

Leistritz, F., L. Ekstrom and B.L. Ekstrom. 1986. *Social Impact Assessment and Management: An Annotated Bibliography*. New York: Garland.

Peters, T.J. and R.H. Waterman, Jr. 1983. *In Search of Excellence*. New York: Harper and Row.

U.S. Forest Service (USFS, Department of Agriculture). 1981. *Forest Service Handbook 1609.13, Public Participation*. Washington, DC: USFS.

_____ 1982. *National Forest Land Resource Management Planning Regulations*. 36 DFR part 219. Washington, DC: USFS.

_____ 1985. *Report of the Forest Service 1985*. Washington, DC: USFS.

_____ 1985a. *Forest Service Handbook 1909.17, Economic and Social Analysis*. Washington, DC: USFS. Chapter 30.

_____ 1985c. *Forest Service Manual 1970, Economic and Social Analysis*. Washington, DC: USFS.

U.S. Government, Executive Office of the President, Council on Environmental Quality. 1978. *Regulations for Implementing the Procedural Provisions of the National Environmental Policy Act*. 40 CFR Parts 1500-1508.

5

INTEGRATING SOCIAL SCIENCE INTO WILDLIFE MANAGEMENT: BARRIERS AND LIMITATIONS

Daniel J. Decker
Department of Natural Resources
Cornell University

Tommy L. Brown
Department of Natural Resources
Cornell University

George F. Mattfeld
New York State Department of Environmental Conservation

The need to integrate social science perspectives into wildlife management has never been greater. The complexity of management issues has increased and public involvement in wildlife management is at an all time high. Every wildlife management program has one or more constituencies. Sometimes they share common views of how wildlife should be managed, sometimes their views are polarized, but their interest in management approaches and outcomes is keen. The complexity of wildlife management has increased partially because management programs have attempted to serve broader publics than they did two decades ago. This trend has resulted from agency reaction in some instances, proaction in others. The dynamic interplay of the human and biophysical dimensions of wildlife management creates the imperative to integrate social science perspectives within the management process. Langenau (1987) predicts that the need for integrating social science into wildlife management will continue to grow. If management hopes to be successful in achieving societal goals using wildlife resources, responsiveness and adaptiveness to these needs are essential.

Recent examples of diverse and intense public interest in wildlife management are numerous. Sometimes such interest results in conflict between an agency and a constituency or between constituencies. For example, the Department of Interior's decision in 1982 to permit deer hunting on Loxahatchee National Wildlife Refuge in Florida was opposed by many people, as the Department learned after making the decision. The hunt was subsequently cancelled (Audubon Society 1985). Deer hunters, local residents, anti-hunters, and people opposed to hunting particularly in state parks became embroiled in a controversy over the need to reduce deer overpopulations in Harriman State Park, New York, north of New York City. A high degree of interaction between the state wildlife and parks agencies resulted in a special weekday-only hunt to reduce populations, despite an unsuccessful court suit from anti-hunting groups (Cobb 1982). Kellert (1986) noted the high degree of public interest and controversy in Minnesota as an eastern timber wolf recovery plan was introduced first in 1978, and again in 1980, by the state wildlife agency. Livestock producers, trappers, and hunters favored the plan, but environmentalists blocked the plan via litigation. A survey of various publics sponsored by the U.S. Fish and Wildlife Service revealed areas of public information needs regarding the issues and areas of possible agreement.

As these examples demonstrate, successful wildlife management requires the adoption of a dynamic, comprehensive model that integrates social science into the management process. Krueger et al. (In Press) recently proposed such a model for resource management. In their conceptualization of the process, social science information is an equal partner with biophysical information in the establishment of management objectives, identification of problems, selection of management actions, and evaluation of achievement. Their process model is conceptually set within a "management environment" that has cultural, economic, and political, as well as ecological arenas as major elements. Thus, a broad range of societal values is explicitly recognized as the basis of resource management. Such an approach to integrate social science into wildlife management is necessary for effectively maximizing resource benefits (including nonmarket ecological benefits) to society, but has seldom been accomplished.

Use of social science information in wildlife management has been improving. Mattfeld et al. (1984) traced the general development of human dimensions inquiry in the wildlife field using the categories of surrogate biology, basic audience profiles, administrative justification of programs, user satisfactions and management preferences, and integrated human dimensions inquiry. Evidence of this development has been apparent in papers presented at the 49th North American Wildlife and Natural Resources Conference (Sabol 1984) and at a recent symposium on the economic and social values of the wildlife resource (Decker and Goff 1987).

Despite the examples of social science applications in wildlife management that can be found, the integration of social science and ecological information to achieve wildlife management usually occurs unsystematically and at a superficial level. Berryman (1987) recognized this and challenged the wildlife profession to improve upon it. Significant barriers and limitations to the integration of social science into wildlife management exist; it is the purpose of this article to identify some of the major hindrances. The suggestions offered for overcoming these are not guaranteed, but problem identification is a necessary first step toward problem solution. This paper is directed at that first step.

IMPEDIMENTS TO INTEGRATION

Three general and pervasive impediments greatly limit the extent to which social science has been and will become a part of wildlife management. First, a tradition exists in wildlife management that biological considerations are the primary determinants of management decisions. This bias makes little sense, even if the effort is limited to conservative utilization of extant resource supplies, because management is conducted by humans and primarily for humans. Second, a communications gap of considerable breadth exists between many wildlife managers with traditional biological backgrounds and those "mavericks" who are dealing in the social science aspects of management. Furthermore, within the social sciences, communications gaps exist (e.g., between economists and other social scientists). Third, the image of social science among wildlife managers needs improvement. Each of the impediments is discussed below.

Biological Bias

Wildlife management agencies are staffed at all levels with individuals educated in biology, a specialized area of applied ecology, or some other natural science discipline. Typically, they have emerged from curricula that concentrated on the biotic and abiotic elements of the system to be "managed," but provided little preparation for the human aspects of management. Coursework begins with basic natural sciences then moves to specific courses on techniques for bio-physical data collection and for manipulation of the biological and physical elements of natural systems to obtain a particular response (e.g., habitat manipulation to increase deer populations). These curricula seldom deal with understanding human values and desires, with evaluating how well management met those desires, or with decision making in human-dominated ecosystems.

The biological bias has been perpetuated by the coursework requirements for entry-level positions in state and federal agencies that are responsible for wildlife management. Similarly, course completion requirements for certification by the Wildlife Society reflect the biological bias. Because most administrators in state and federal agencies (except political appointments, such as commissioners of state agencies) arrive at their positions by advancement through the ranks where they began by meeting the basic biological coursework requirements mentioned above, agencies tend to perpetuate the biological bias. Underlying and more important than the focus of training is the narrowness of perspective and the "biology or ecology first" philosophy that is transmitted, and later reinforced by peers of similar descent. This philosophical barrier is a much greater hindrance than deficiencies in particular skills.

An article in the *Wildlife Society Bulletin* by Fraser (1985) effectively pointed out the fallacy of the current norm in wildlife management. Dubbing it the Great Assumption, he depicted the wildlife management establishment as being of the mind that regardless of the problem, it is assumed that the solution is to collect as much biological data as possible about the problem and that somehow solutions will emerge. He indicated that the profession is largely preoccupied with techniques, particularly those used to collect field data and regulate resource use. He argued for a more systematic approach to wildlife management, using his experience in swine production as a metaphor for an approach that might be followed in wildlife management. Nevertheless, Fraser exhibited the "biological bias" in the omission of any reference to the role of social science in a management system. Similarly, no mention was made of the process that sets management objectives and evaluates their achievement. Overlooked was the fact that objectives are human, not biological constructs, and require social science approaches to define them in the complex resource-management arena that currently exists.

Adoption of a management model that explicitly depicts the breadth of factors affecting wildlife management and identifies the concomitant range of expertise required to address such factors is inhibited by the "biological bias." The inertia that must be overcome in the typical wildlife management agency before the adoption of a comprehensive model of management can be realized is significant.

The people who are most influential in introducing and encouraging change, the policy-level wildlife administrators, have generally come from the biological community. They are steeped in the tradition of seeking biological solutions. This situation is similar to that found in forestry and marine fishery resource management agencies (Miller and Gale 1986). Even those enlightened wildlife administrators who recognize the need for a broader approach are often limited by their lack of background in social science concepts. That understanding is a prerequisite to their commitment to change. They need more than an intuitive notion of necessity before they are willing to support an approach similar to that espoused by Krueger *et al.* (In Press).

Academia also has maintained a narrow view of wildlife management, for the most part. The biological bias runs rampant in many traditional natural resource departments in colleges and universities. Few academics teaching wildlife management have any education in the workings of organizations. To exacerbate this situation, few academics teaching management have real-world management experience, particularly in the contemporary environment of wildlife management. Professors are isolated from the multitude of "people pressures" that impinge on management in practice. They are hired because of their biological or ecological interest and expertise, particularly as it is demonstrated through research. Their teaching typically and quite naturally reflects these interests. The importance of integrating social sciences into a management paradigm too often goes unrecognized. The old biological concepts and habitat or population management techniques are still over-emphasized. The biological bias is perpetuated. Would-be wildlife managers who emerge from this educational setting are ill-prepared to deal with the complexities of management in the social environment that awaits them.

Communications Gap

Another significant barrier to integrating social science into wildlife management is miscommunication. As in any discipline, social science has its unique terminology. Understanding this terminology is a key to effective communication, but social scientists often use the terminology with wildlife professionals who may not understand it, resulting in miscommunication. Although wildlife managers and administrators use a biological jargon of their own, they often criticize social scientists for similar behavior. Somehow, terms like biological carrying capacity, ecotone, edge effect, limiting factors, and MSY are acceptable. But, role model, social referent, innovation adoption, belief-attitude-behavioral intention systems, and motivation are considered jargon. Certainly the social science disciplines have a great deal of specialized terminology that an individual with a traditional wildlife management background may not readily understand. This must be recognized by social scientists and dealt with effectively, particularly by teaching others the meaning of special terms used in communicating with them.

Any serious attempt by social scientists and managers to integrate social science into wildlife management must pay close attention to communication. When messages are encoded, assumptions about the receiver warrant careful examination. How much social science "terminology" do agency administrators know? How much do they need to know? How can frustration with social science information be reduced, understanding be facilitated, and utilization in management be improved? As these questions indicate, the adoption of social science into the mainstream of wildlife management carries significant educational and communications challenges. These are challenges that social scientists, by the nature of their profession, should take the lead in addressing.

This is no small task for social scientists, however, when even they do not all speak the same language. Of special concern is the communications gap that seems to have developed between economists and other social scientists. This gap has been generally tacit, and is therefore difficult to document, but economists, other social scientists, and wildlife managers sense its presence. The communications gap between economists and other social scientists may be based on their different assumptions about the basis for human behavior and their different methodologies for examining such behavior. Economists view most human behavior in terms of rational choices that maximize utility. Other social scientists generally take the view that internal motivational orientations or external social influences (including culture) influence human behavior.

The field of economics uses not only highly theoretical conceptual constructs, but also highly quantitative methods. The general field has become specialized to the degree that resource economists typically work quite separately from other social scientists. Resource economists are concerned not only with valuing market and nonmarket goods, but also with decision making more generally. Thus, these economists have a great deal to offer the wildlife administrator, particularly when wildlife management decisions become entangled in political processes that rely on economic arguments.

In addition to needs for economic information, administrators need an understanding of the causes or antecedents of wildlife valuing behavior. Psychologists, sociologists, and other social scientists have the expertise to develop this understanding. Psychologists can help explain why individuals value wildlife as they do and what their motivations are for certain behaviors vis-a-vis wildlife. Sociologists can help develop understanding of the role of wildlife interests in stimulating group action and the implications of such action for wildlife conservation. Cultural anthropologists can help decision-makers understand the importance of wildlife-related recreation and symbolism in maintaining traditional rural cultures. Thus, all of the social sciences can make valuable contributions to wildlife management decision making, and no one social science discipline by itself is sufficient. Consequently, communication among disciplines is vital.

One way of narrowing the communications gap between economists and other social scientists is to provide forums for them to interact more frequently. The Economic and Social Values of the Wildlife Resource Symposium held in Syracuse, New York, in 1986, is an example of a forum that was useful in this regard. However, simply bringing representatives of these disciplines together is not enough. Thorough integration of economics and other social sciences in individual sessions is needed if we are to expect growth across these disciplines. In an agency setting, economists and other social scientists could be required to work together. Joint research and planning tasks could be assigned, or joint solutions to management problems could be expected.

Image

The third barrier to the integration of social science in wildlife management, a poor image of social science among wildlife managers, has at least two dimensions. The first is a lack of recognition of training and qualifications necessary for social science research, embodied in comments such as "anyone can do survey research." The second is a disbelief that social science produces valid and trustworthy data.

The "anyone can do it" attitude is troublesome because people who are not prepared to conduct valid and reliable social science research nevertheless "do surveys." Scientific sampling procedures, rigorous instrument development, and careful implementation are often ignored. Regardless, decisions are made and results are published. Experience with these "results" leads to the second dimension, the belief that social science research findings are not trustworthy. When social science research is developed, implemented, and analyzed by qualified social researchers, it is trustworthy. Potential users of social science information need to recognize the difference. Help in differentiation should be part of the educational communication challenge discussed above.

Social scientists participating in wildlife management will have to take a more active role in eliminating the unreliable reports that appear in the wildlife management literature, and mislabeled social science. Peer-reviewed journals in the wildlife field seem to be maintaining high quality. However, some conference and symposia proceedings contain unacceptable papers based on social science "research" conducted by unqualified people who have the "anyone can do it" attitude. These bogus pieces should be called to task. It is not a pleasant undertaking, but our mutual professional integrity is at stake. When such data are used to make poor decisions, with false confidence, it is the broader credibility of social science that is diminished as well as the effectiveness of wildlife management. Social scientists working in the arena of wildlife management also have the obligation to measure their qualifications, techniques, and theories in the full social science forum, not simply against the applied social scientists acting in partnership with ecologists to provide better wildlife management. Inappropriate or inadequate biological research to support wildlife management would not go unnoticed or unquestioned; poor social science research should be examined just as closely.

BOTTOM LINE

Probably the best way to expedite the integration of social science into wildlife management is the steady accumulation of success stories. Documentation is needed to show how social science was used in wildlife management decisions and how these applications resulted in better programs (e.g., higher rates of objective achievement and greater human benefit). It is the lack of such successes that is pointed to by skeptics as a reason for not supporting the integration of social science in wildlife management.

The three barriers discussed earlier make this goal difficult to achieve. The image problem, the communications gap, and the biological bias all work against the acquisition of support for social science research initially, and then decrease the probability of the data from good research being used effectively. Nevertheless, successes have occurred, as evidenced by the numerous examples reported in the session, Using Socioeconomics in Resource Management at the 49th North American Wildlife and Natural Resources Conference in 1984 (Sabol 1984). And some people in the highest administrative circles of wildlife management are calling for greater application of social science information (e.g., Berryman 1987, Doig 1987). Furthermore, it is becoming increasingly common (e.g., Krueger et al. In Press) for the traditional paradigm of resource management to be criticized and for more comprehensive alternatives, which include the sociological dimension, to be advocated. These developments are causes for at least cautious optimism.

FUTURE

Some positive movement is occurring in the direction of improving the outlook for social science in wildlife management. The establishment of the Human Dimensions in Wildlife Study Group as a formal professional organization of social scientists, wildlife and other natural resource managers, and educators, should go a long way in narrowing the communications gap and improving the image of social science for resource management. Symposia such as the First National Symposium on Social Science in Resource Management held in 1986 are attracting the attention and attendance of resource managers who want to learn more about the social science dimensions of resource management. Gradually, course offerings for aspiring resource managers are broadening to include social science aspects of resource management; at least four universities now offer specific courses on human dimensions in wildlife management. The "standard" literature of wildlife managers now includes more social science topics. For example, *The Wildlife Society Bulletin* has an associate editor assigned specifically to work with human dimensions papers.

As we approach the end of this decade, the importance of integrating social science into resource management will increase. Soon, the imperative for such integration will become obvious to even the most traditional resource agencies. Those that move in this direction early and sincerely will be in the best position to operate successfully in the management environment that surrounds them. Others will falter, then adopt social science perspectives, for change in this direction seems inevitable.

Professionals who are interested in accelerating the adoption process must work steadfastly toward bridging the communications gap and improving the image of social science among the wildlife management establishment. The transition period may not go as rapidly as social scientists would like, but if they continue to work toward alleviating the barriers that currently exist, the next generation of wildlife management may be the balanced, comprehensive, responsive-adaptive process required to meet the challenges of wildlife conservation that lie ahead.

REFERENCES

Audubon Society. 1985. *Audubon Wildlife Report 1985*. R.L.D. Silvestro (ed.). New York: The National Audubon Society.

Berryman, J.H. 1987. "Socioeconomic Values of the Wildlife Resource: Are We Really Serious?" In D.J. Decker and G. R. Goff (eds.), *Valuing Wildlife: Economic and Social Perspectives*. Boulder: Westview Press. 5-11.

92   Decker/Brown/Mattfeld

Cobb, T.L. 1982. "Deer Management Unit-53." *The Conservationist* 37(2): 12-17.

Decker, D.J., and G.R. Goff (eds.). 1987. *Valuing Wildlife: Economic and Social Perspectives.* Boulder: Westview Press. 424pp.

Doig, H.E. 1987. "Applying Wildlife Values Information in Management Planning and Policy Making." In D.J. Decker and G. R. Goff (eds.), *Valuing Wildlife: Economic and Social Perspectives.* Boulder: Westview Press. 305-308.

Fraser, D. 1985. "Piggery Perspectives on Wildlife Management and Research." *Wildlife Society Bulletin* 13: 183-187.

Kellert, S.L. 1986. "The Public and the Timber Wolf in Minnesota." *Transactions of the 51st North American Wildlife and Natural Resources Conference.* 193-200.

Krueger, C.C., D.J. Decker, and T.A. Gavin. In Press. "A Concept of Natural Resource Management: An Application to Unicorns." *Transactions of the 42nd Northeast Fish and Wildlife Conference* (27-30 April 1986, Hershey, Pennsylvania).

Langenau, E.E., Jr. 1987. "Anticipating Wildlife Values of Tomorrow." In D. J. Decker and G. R. Goff (eds.), *Valuing Wildlife: Economic and Social Perspectives.* Boulder: Westview Press. 309-317.

Mattfeld, G.F., D.J. Decker, T.L. Brown, S.L. Free, and P.R. Sauer 1984. "Developing Human Dimensions in New York's Wildlife Research Program." *Transactions of the 49th North American Wildlife and Natural Resources Conference.* 54-65.

Miller, M.L., and R.P. Gale. 1986. "Professional Styles of Federal Forest and Marine Fisheries Resource Managers." *North American Journal of Fisheries Management* 6: 141-148.

Sabol, K. (ed.). 1984. *Transactions of the 49th North American Wildlife and Natural Resources Conference.*

6

THE SOCIOLOGY OF SCIENCE IN NATURAL RESOURCE MANAGEMENT SYSTEMS: OBSERVATIONS ON FORESTS AND MARINE FISHERIES IN THE PACIFIC NORTHWEST

Richard P. Gale
Department of Sociology
University of Oregon

Marc L. Miller
Institute for Marine Studies
College of Ocean and Fishery Sciences
University of Washington

Natural resource management systems (NRMSs) are composed of four elements. Three are social: profit-seeking resource industries, organized and unorganized publics, and management bureaucracies (Gale and Miller 1985, Miller, Gale, and Brown This Volume). The fourth element is the resource itself.[1]

The NRMS concept stresses the basic notion that natural resources are socially defined, and are therefore products of society. Each of the three social elements is likely to operate with differing social definitions of resources. To the timber industry, a 400-year old Douglas fir with a rotting center is best chipped up for wood pulp; to an environmentalist the same tree may exemplify the need to preserve old growth stands of timber. On a fundamental level, then, natural resource conflicts are based on competing social definitions of natural resources and different notions about the future of those resources.

These competing definitions clearly affect natural resource science. How science operates in NRMSs is a topic which can be addressed within the general framework of the sociology of knowledge or sociology of science. This sociological perspective, seen in the classic works of Merton (1973) and Kuhn (1962) and in the more recent work of observers such as DiMento (1981), suggests that science is significantly shaped by differing conceptions of scientific inquiry, as well as by social and economic forces. The multiple elements of NRMSs at times employ inconsistent definitions of science in the interpretation of natural resource conflicts. This can lead to changes in resource science.

Three observations are central to understanding the role of science in NRMSs.[2] A first observation is that science underlies the informational and inventory bases of natural resources. However, the high costs and technical difficulties of studying resources such as fish populations, sea bed minerals, and habitat requirements result in incomplete and debatable resource knowledge.

The second observation concerns kinds of natural resource science. Schnaiberg (1980) notes that while most science under the research and development umbrella is oriented toward improving production efficiency and profitability, another (typically less developed) side of science focuses on the impacts of production on social and environmental conditions. Schnaiberg refers to these two kinds of science as *production* science and *impact* science. This production-impact distinction clearly applies to the natural resource and environmental sciences. Whereas production forest science develops new fertilization processes, impact forest science worries about residual soil impacts and contamination of forest streams. Whereas production fishery science produces "improved" fish, impact fishery science worries about mixing these fish with wild and hatchery-produced stocks. Thus, integral to the highly politicized setting of resource conflicts is the struggle between practitioners of production and impact natural resource science.

A third observation is that science often becomes part of a natural resource constituency's arsenal of tools with which to influence resource policy. Many natural resource conflicts can only be fully understood with an examination of the competing perspectives of resource science relevant to the issues. Science is an especially crucial factor whenever social elements of NRMSs fight over resource allocation and access.

These three observations--that resource inventories are scientifically derived, that resource science treats both production and impacts, and that science can be used as an interest group tool--serve as background to this discussion. Two additional points focus our analysis. First, since science is unlikely to operate uniformly across NRMSs, a comparative resource approach is necessary to build cross-resource generalizations and theory (Gale 1985; Miller, Gale, and Brown This Volume). Second, management bureaucracies, profit-seeking industries, and diverse publics have different views of how science should operate. Profit-seeking industries emphasize production science, as in, for example, the development of genetically enhanced trees. At the same time, some publics emphasize impact science as in the study of impacts of forest monoculture on soil fertility.

This article focuses on two NRMSs in the Pacific Northwest--forests and marine fisheries. In the following sections, we describe three central features of natural resource science: relations between agency, academic, and private research scientists; links between scientists and resource constituencies; and differential paths of controversy-generated research.[3]

AGENCY, ACADEMY, AND PRIVATE SECTOR NATURAL RESOURCE SCIENCE

Agency Science

The lead federal agencies in forest and marine fisheries management systems--the U.S. Forest Service (USFS) and National Marine Fisheries Service (NMFS)--each have a research arm. The USFS Forest and Range Experiment Station research system is composed of eight experiment stations. Research in these stations is organized by "project." The scope of projects, however, can be broader. For example, the project titled "Integrating Dispersed Recreation and Other Forest Uses" at the Pacific Northwest Forest and Range Experiment Station has, over the years, addressed topics including wilderness recreation, perceptions of recreational experience, the incorporation of recreation alternatives into resource management, and campground vandalism. Its current work extends research to recreation in Alaska.

This organizational structure has both positive and negative implications for the practice of science in the forest NRMS. On the positive side, the multi-topic project provides some job security to research personnel while encouraging scientific diversification. Long-term research fits nicely into this framework, although levels of funding vary annually. The project structure provides an umbrella under which different, but related, topics can be studied. The Alaskan recreational research study mentioned above also includes analysis of subsistence use of National Forests in Alaska.

Less positively, project science has little flexibility to adjust to new topics which do not neatly fit within established agendas. Many forest policy issues crosscut existing projects and consequently receive little direct funding. Sometimes, however, ongoing projects contribute to the resolution of these complex issues. For example, several Pacific Northwest regional laboratories have directed funds and effort toward development of a USFS recreational planning system, although the system was not a mission of any specific project. A second less positive feature stems from the tendencey of personnel to narrowly identify academic disciplines with a particular project or type of project. Throughout the USFS Experiment Station system, sociology is perceived as nearly synonymous with recreation research. This has made it difficult for sociologists interested in broader policy issues to establish professional niches.[4]

In the marine fisheries system, the NMFS has four Fisheries Centers such as the Northwest and Alaska Fisheries Center in Seattle. Agency science within the marine fisheries system occurs in a relatively unique public arena-- the Regional Fishery Management Council system established by the Magnuson Fishery Conservation and Management Act of 1976 (Miller and Van Maanen 1983). Each of eight Councils has a legislatively mandated Scientific and Statistical Committee (SSC) to provide evaluations of Council actions. While SSC scientists are asked to make rapid judgements (Paredes 1985), and Councils lack uniformity in their role and influence (Miller 1986), the SSCs at least provide a stage for multi disciplinary input from agency and academic scientists. This setting for the practice of science is found in only a few other NRMSs. The Cooperative Park Studies Units of the National Park Service and the Scientific and Statistical Advisory Committee to the Northwest Regional Power Planning Council occasionally engage in similar scientific activities. The impact estimation tasks of SSCs, would, in the forest system, be carried out in the quite different setting of a Forest Service Planning Team or Regional Office staff unit.

Since basic and applied science functions are often separated, one would not expect resource management units to directly undertake basic scientific research. However, one example is found in the forest system in the Pacific Northwest. Embroiled in protracted conflict over soil stability on the Mapleton District of the Siuslaw National Forest in Oregon, the USFS established a special research unit at the Pacific Northwest Forest Science Laboratory on the Oregon State University campus. Here, district staff members work with resource scientists to study the soil impacts of logging and road construction. This arrangement is, however, temporary, and related to the specific conflict.

Academic Science

In the academy, forest and fisheries science are firmly based in natural resource schools and colleges at major universities. In the Pacific Northwest, as elsewhere, both sciences are located at land and sea grant institutions. Scientists thus benefit from federal research funds provided by the USFS Experiment Stations, Sea Grant, Agricultural Experiment Stations, and NMFS research centers. This situation provides researchers with access to funds earmarked for applied natural resource science.

Natural resource scientists in the academy are also supported by general science agencies such as the National Science Foundation (NSF). Predictably, topics investigated bear more on discovering basic ecological relations than solving practical resource management problems. Forest scientists at the University of Washington, for example, have received NSF support to study soil development in the Arctic, and to examine vegetative and soil changes associated with the eruption of Mt. St. Helens.

Forest and fisheries academic science generally share three important sociological characteristics. First, it is problematic where in the academy social scientists interested in natural resources are found. For example, social scientists in the Institute for Marine Studies at the University of Washington vary in their formal and informal affiliations with traditional academic departments. Some administrators at the University of Oregon view research on natural resource policy as the exclusive province of the School of Law, despite the fact that many social science faculty in the liberal arts college are also interested in natural resource policy.

Second, the larger campus community (particularly the liberal arts unit) is prone to view both forest and fisheries science as having a strongly applied emphasis. This can lead to lost opportunities for coordination. For example, the basic research emphasis of the University of Washington's Institute for Environmental Studies is seen by some as incompatible with the more applied research programs in the College of Ocean and Fishery Sciences and the College of Forest Resources.

Finally, forest and fisheries academics have different reputations with environmentalist interests. Although management of either resource can attract environmentalist fire, it is forest science which is most typically seen by environmentalists as captured by development or resource exploitive interests.

Private Sector Science

Private sector natural resource science in the Pacific Northwest is conducted by corporate research units, consulting firms, and interest groups. Large land-owning timber companies, such as the Weyerhaeuser Company, operate research laboratories and also contract with university scientists.

Because these firms are vertically integrated and resource-owning, corporate research on natural resources covers activities ranging from the development of genetically superior trees to fertilization, harvest, processing, new product development, and marketing. Corporate research in fisheries occurs on a smaller scale. Large multi-product food conglomerates, such as the Ralston Purina Company, do have research laboratories, but the segmented nature of the industry, and the absence of very large vertically integrated corporations combine with the common property characteristics of fish to produce corporate research less integrated than research in the forest system. In short, there is no marine fisheries equivalent of Weyerhaeuser or the Georgia-Pacific Corporation.[5]

Consulting firms range from part-time operations to large, national firms such as the Battelle Memorial Institute of Columbus, Ohio. These large firms show a much greater interest in oil, natural gas, and toxic wastes than in forests and marine fisheries.

Small consulting firms do operate in NRMSs for both forests and fisheries, particularly the latter. In the forest system, some small research and consulting firms such as Mason, Bruce and Girard in Portland, serve private forest industry clients, provide expertise in the major resource profession (forestry and forest economics), and assist agencies and corporations in natural resource conflicts. The experience the forest system has had as the locus of production vs. impact struggles has resulted in the emergence of small impact research firms. For example Cascade Holistic Economic Consultants engage in issue-oriented research, often under contract to interest groups and state agencies. It also publishes *Forest Watch*, a monthly newsletter which focuses on Pacific Northwest forestry. The forest system also includes sociological, anthropological, and archeological research, typically in the form of project-specific assessments. This research is provided by an array of small, often university-based, firms under contract to forest agencies.

Small private firms are found in both production and impact marine fisheries science. However, there are few marine fisheries counterparts to Mason, Bruce, and Girard. Instead, the complexity of marine fisheries issues and the existence of what we elsewhere term a *public arena* policy-making system (Gale and Miller 1985) have created an unusual applied research and consulting market. Examples of firms operating in this market are the Seattle-based Natural Resource Consultants, in which prominent fisheries scientists such as James A. Crutchfield and Dayton L. Alverson are active, and the California-based Meyer Associates. These firms provide both consulting and applied research. Small, local firms also undertake funded research. Recently, discussions on increasing recreational harvest of coho salmon were spurred when the Oregon Department of Fish and Wildlife hired a private consultant based in Yachats, Oregon, to survey fishermen.

Research in forests and marine fisheries is also sponsored by interest groups. These include industry-related organizations such as the the Electric Power Research Institute which has funded research on acid rain by scientists on the faculty of the College of Forest Resources, University of Washington.

A different type of interest group has been involved in forest policy research. Supporting resource privatization and reduced regulation, the Montana-based Center for Political Economy and Natural Resources has aggressively researched alternative management systems for land-based resources. The center has yet to turn its attention to marine resources.

Finally, environmental organizations such as Greenpeace and the Sierra Club Foundation provide limited research support for forest and marine fisheries science. The Wilderness Society has its own research division. More typically, however, such groups advocate government funding of research likely to uncover support for their positions.

SCIENTISTS AND THEIR RESOURCE CONSTITUENCIES

This section briefly describes relations between resource scientists and four constituencies--resource managers, resource-dependent industries, resource-dependent communities, and the environmental movement.

Resource Managers

Central to the quality of relations between managers and scientists is what we elsewhere (Miller and Gale 1985) term resource management style. We have argued that four styles--those of *forstmeister*, disciplinary *specialist*, *politician*, and *executive*--can occur within NRMSs. Each management style has different implications for natural resource science. Traditional forstmeister management is probably least receptive to applied science. Strong administrators, relying on their personal manner and longstanding involvement in NRMSs lack tolerance for research contributions, especially those from social scientists. To illustrate, a manager who fits the regional "fishmaster" model explained that economic analysis usually told him what he already knew, and that he preferred to run his large organization with the informal help of six persons whom he always consulted for disciplinary-based advice. (No social scientists were among the six.)

Managers with a disciplinary specialty such as forestry or fisheries biology favor resource science, perhaps in part because it has been relatively uncritical of management. As Dana and Fairfax (1980:227) note with respect to USFS investigations into clearcutting:

They [USFS managers] failed to recognize that land management decisions were frequently matters of value or preference rather than technique and that being a forester does not necessarily qualify one to decide what are appropriate goals for public land management.

The politician strives to mediate conflict between constituencies. Managers who adopt the politician style commonly support scientists' contributions to resource controversies, especially when adversaries accept scientific findings. In contrast, what we term the executive, the manager whose forte is managing bureaucracies rather than resources, is apt to confuse the role of the research scientist, which is to create new knowledge, with that of the policy analyst, which is to study the effect of new knowledge and new policies upon an organization and its constituencies (cf., Miller and Gale This Volume). Relations between all styles of resource managers and scientists are strained when managers' timeframes do not fit those of the scientist, and when research on pressing management problems competes for funding with more basic research.

Resource-Dependent Industries

Both forest and marine fisheries NRMSs are characterized by linkages between resource-dependent industries and scientists. These links can be manifest in direct corporate research as described above. In other cases, these ties occur through industry advisors such as the West Coast Fisheries Development Foundation, which reviews research proposals for the Oregon Sea Grant Program.

Relationships between scientists and industry are generally more positive in fisheries than in forestry, although strong links exist between forestry academic scientists and segments of the forest products industry. This is due, in part, to the fact that fisheries scientists share the ocean environment with people economically dependent on the resource. Then too, commercial fishing boats are sometimes chartered for research purposes, and scientists depend a great deal on catch data provided by fishermen. Countering this closeness and cooperation is the fact that fishermen are quick to challenge the relatively new scientific base of marine fisheries when fish quotas are allocated to competing domestic fleets.

Resource-Dependent Communities

The practice of science confers mixed stakes upon many communities dependent upon forest and marine resources. The balance, however, often appears to weigh against local community interests. Accordingly, communities may resist scientific conclusions which question longstanding resource harvest practices. Technological innovation often requires higher capital outlays and displacement of traditional harvest techniques. The result is often lost jobs. In California, for example, development of a system to raise abalone completely on shore (Fishermen's News 1986) affected a highly visible and specialized harvesting occupation--abalone diving. Science may also contribute to increased size and geographical mobility for resource industries, making it more difficult to maintain local economies. Finally, science which generates major controversies may ultimately reduce community access to resources. Communities near controversial areas of the Siuslaw National Forest in Oregon have protested a court injunction prohibiting certain timber sales until USFS analyses of soil stability are complete. These communities argue that an environmental court victory has reduced the availability of timber for local mills.

Environmental Movement

The maturation of the environmental movement has brought increasingly complex relations between the movement, countermovement, and natural resource agencies (Gale 1986). Traditionally, the movement has viewed agency science with suspicion. A major tactic has been to use Environmental Impact Statements (EISs) as devices to force agency analysis and disclosure of potentially adverse consequences of policy. While few would argue that preparing EISs represents the best of science, legal requirements for EISs have caused agencies to fund research in areas that might otherwise have been ignored.

The environmental countermovement also employs science to support its goals. For example, proponents of at-sea incineration of toxic wastes have pushed for authority to test the concept scientifically, arguing that the Environmental Protection Agency justifiably granted a permit for experimental tests of incinerator ship technology. Opponents in the environmental movement argue that the full impacts of the tests are unknown, and that the private firm under contract for the testing is using the tests as a way to establish a market for its waste disposal services (Stutz 1986). In the forest system, environmental countermovement interests such as sawmill operators carefully monitor outcome of scientific research on the amount of forest area needed to protect spotted owls. Not surprisingly, the environmental countermovement resists all research which would delay resource development.

In general, then, movement-scientist relations are conditioned by how science informs particular controversies. In some controversies, adversaries may push for judicial and legislative resolution of science-based resource conflicts. In other situations, adversaries may argue instead for additional research. The usual environmentalist assumption is that full scientific analyses of environmental impacts will produce results in support of the environmental objectives. Conversely, the environmental countermovement often views impact-evaluation science as unnecessarily impeding economic and technological progress. Caught in the middle, of course, are agency scientists, whose work is often distrusted by both movement and countermovement interests.

PATHS OF CONTROVERSY-GENERATED RESEARCH

Both of the NRMSs under examination here are frequently marked by management controversies in which science plays a complex role. Within the forest system, conflicts involving such timber harvest practices as clearcutting and the use of pesticides and herbicides have embroiled the USFS and the Bureau of Land Management in major disputes. Fisheries have struggled with issues such as the impacts of dam construction, the decline of king crab, mixing of wild and hatchery stocks, and fish-mammal interactions.

The role of science in resource controversies is influenced by three variables: (1) the ideology of management, (2) the scientific legitimacy of controversies, and (3) the role of the market in resolving resource conflicts.

Management Ideology

Ideology, or general philosophy, influences management decisions to channel issues into the scientific arena. This professional ideology becomes an agency ideology when one or two allied natural resource professions dominate an agency. In forestry, the basic ideology leans toward *extractive conservation* and resource development rather than *aesthetic conservation* and resource preservation (cf., Miller, Gale, and Brown This Volume). The model for forestry is agriculture, with intensively managed tree farms as an ideal. In fishery sciences, the basic ideology favors resource preservation rather than resource development. For many, the model is a restored wild fish run. One could argue that forestry encourages production science, while fisheries foster impact science.

Scientific Legitimacy

Forest and fisheries systems exhibit important differences in the timing and difficulty with which resource controversies move into the natural resource science system. In forestry, controversy frequently begins with public criticism of forest management. The need for research on issues highly critical of management is slow to gain either legitimacy within the USFS or research support. Issues such as clearcutting, slash disposal, and the use of herbicides and pesticides long stood in the public spotlight before receiving substantial attention from agency scientists.

Our observations suggest that for some fishery issues, the path to scientific legitimacy is somewhat shorter and more direct than it is for forest issues. In general, controversial fisheries management topics are seen as opportunities for fisheries science. For example, funding of research on the decline of the king crab and the feasibility of limited entry programs in other fisheries in recent years has been welcomed, since conservation-oriented managers long feared consequences of heavy harvests. The following quote from a fisheries scientist reflects this caution:

> Under conditions of high uncertainty about yields, new assessment and management techniques must be developed ...Here, utmost attention must be paid to the avoidance of a disasterous collapse of the fishery, given the realisation that there will be little forewarning. (Francis 1980:99)

Of course, issues receive differential priority depending on their regional saliency and economic importance. In the Pacific Northwest and Alaska, funding for research on salmon is much higher than for marine mammals.

Role of the Market

In some instances, it is the market, rather than science, that first finds a solution to a resource problem. Changing technologies and associated costs can result in strong incentives for new products and uses for natural resources. Although the USFS was slow to fund Pacific Northwest studies of slash disposal, emergence of a market for chips and the development of portable chippers which could be used at logging sites "solved" a portion of the problem of logging residues. Similarly, wood fiber markets improved to the point that polluting "wigwam" burners were phased out. In fisheries, surimi and other innovative seafood products show promise to minimize problems of "trash" fish caught along with higher value species.

DISCUSSION

Just as natural resource ecosystems are exceedingly complex, so is the sociology of the sciences which study those ecosystems. Pure science, in an ideal sense, exists nowhere in the system. Instead, science typically emerges in the context of resource conflict. As a result, then, most science within NRMSs--whether it is of the production or impact kind--is inevitably

advocacy science. Because natural resource science does not exist apart from
the three social elements of NRMSs--management bureaucracies, organized
and unorganized publics, and profit-seeking resource industries--good science
will display an openness to all three elements. In our opinion, natural resource
controversies are most likely to be judiciously resolved when adversaries
support open scientific inquiry. Fortunately, the forest and marine fisheries
systems in the Pacific Northwest display secure, accessible, and increasingly
interdisciplinary natural resource science.

NOTES

1. This definition implies a different system for each resource, such
as forests, marine fisheries, and seabed minerals. Conceptually, however,
multiple natural resource management systems could be defined for a single
ecosystem or management unit. Forest ecosystems, such as National Forests,
include multiple resources, such as trees, fish, mountains, minerals, and
geothermal sites. For each, there could be a separate natural resource
management system.

2. While it is possible to distinguish between "science" and
"research," these terms are used interchangeably here. In NRMSs, research
activities produce the scientific knowledge that underpins resource
management. NRMSs are typically organized so that scientific disputes lead
directly to changes in research agendas.

3. Our observations reflect intermittent ethnographic work by the
authors within forestry and fishery systems. Gale's observation of the U.S.
Forest Service spans 15 years. Miller has observed the fishery management
system for 10 years, and serves on the Scientific and Statistical Committee of
the Pacific Fishery Management Council. In addition, the paper is informed by
a two-year period in which Gale held visiting appointments in the College of
Forest Resources (1983-84) and Institute for Marine Studies (1984-85) at the
University of Washington.

4. The difficulty of fitting traditional social science disciplines into
"policy analysis" also occurs for sociologists in agency staff positions (Miller
and Gale This Volume). One research unit that does address broader
organizational issues is the U.S. Forest Service Management Sciences Staff, a
small group of social scientists who carry out applied organizational research

for the agency. A topic currently under study by that group, administrative appeals, does not fit neatly into existing Experiment Station projects.

     5. Recent involvement of the Weyerhaeuser Company in aquaculture is thus an interesting exception, although the company hopes to sell its operation to the state of Oregon. A key issue in the experimental ocean ranching project was the degree to which a specific, highly mobile resource (salmon) can be privatized within a multi-resource common property natural environment or ecosystem.

REFERENCES

Dana, S.T. and S.K. Fairfax. 1980. *Forest and Range Policy*. New York: McGraw-Hill.

DiMento, J.F. 1981. "Making Usable Information on Environmental Stressors: Opportunities for the Research and Policy Communities." *Journal of Social Issues* 37:172-204.

Fishermen's News. 1986. "Abalone Commercially Farmed Entirely on Shore." 42(3):19.

Francis, R.C. 1980. "Fisheries Science Now and in the Future: A Personal View." *New Zealand Journal of Marine and Freshwater Research* 14:95-100.

Gale, R.P. 1985. "Federal Management of Forests and Marine Fisheries: A Comparative Analysis of Renewable Resource Management." *Natural Resources Journal* 25:275-315.

_____ 1986. "Social Movements and the State: the Environmental Movement, Countermovement, and the Transformation of Natural Resource Agencies." *Sociological Perspectives* 29:202-40.

Gale, R.P. and M.L. Miller. 1985. "Professional and Public Natural Resource Management Arenas: Forests and Marine Fisheries." *Environment and Behavior* 17:651-78.

Kuhn, T. 1962. *The Structure of Scientific Revolutions*. Chicago: University of Chicago Press.

Merton, R. 1973. *The Sociology of Science: Theoretical and Empirical Investigations*. Chicago: University of Chicago Press.

Miller, M.L. 1986. "Regional Fishery Management Councils and the Display of Scientific Authority." Presented at the Annual Meeting, American Society for Public Administration, Anaheim, California.

Miller, M.L. and R.P. Gale. 1985. "Professional Styles of Federal Forest and Marine Fisheries Resource Managers." *North American Journal of Fisheries Management* 6:141-8.

Miller, M.L. and J. Van Maanen. 1983. "The Emerging Organization of Fisheries in the United States." *Coastal Zone Management Journal* 10:369-86.

Paredes, J.A. 1985. "'Any comments on the Sociology section, Tony?': Committee Work as Applied Anthropology in Fisheries Management." *Human Organization* 44:177-82.

Schnaiberg, A. 1980. *The Environment: From Surplus to Scarcity.* New York: Oxford University Press.

Stutz, B. 1986. "Protests Mount as EPA Pushes Ahead with At-sea-burning Plans." *National Fisherman* 66(12):14-15,64.

7

SOCIAL IMPACT ASSESSMENT IN NEW ZEALAND RESOURCE MANAGEMENT

C. Nick Taylor
Center for Resource Management
University of Canterbury and Lincoln College

C. Hobson Bryan
Department of Sociology
University of Alabama

New Zealand is experiencing rapid economic and environmental change. As a South Pacific island nation located midway between the Equator and the South Pole, the country is approximately 1,000 miles long, with no point further than 90 miles from the sea. Mostly urban dwellers comprise its three million population. Resource use, however, is primarily agricultural. The loss of New Zealand's "favoured trade" status with its major trading partner, Great Britain (after Britain joined the European Common Market), and lessening world demand for agricultural products have caused major upheavals in the country. Moreover, New Zealand must face the same energy shortages and associated economic problems as the rest of the world.

In response, New Zealand has attempted to diversify its export base and promote more energy self-sufficiency. This turn toward industrialization and resource exploitation (e.g., hydro-electric generation, metals processing, manufacturing, construction of energy plants and mining) provoked controversy in a country in which quality of life, as measured by traditional social and economic indicators, has been among the highest in the world. Inflation and overseas debt in the last 10 years have taken their toll, and resource conflicts have been escalating. These conflicts include dams for hydro-electric development versus rivers for recreation; preservation of valleys for agricultural purposes and irrigation diversion versus maintenance of water flows for fishing and boating; and preservation of native forests for aesthetic and ecological reasons versus the planting of non-native trees for faster timber production or additional clearing of bush for sheep production.

This article addresses the role of social impact assessment (SIA) in New Zealand's resource management. A first section provides an overview of environmental administration and the basis for original SIA work. A Second section examines recent changes in the institutional basis for environmental administration and links these changes to current SIA. A third section discusses the role SIA might play in future New Zealand resource management through understanding of conflicts common to the field. Finally, some productive areas of work are presented based on the New Zealand experiences.

ENVIRONMENTAL ADMINISTRATION IN NEW ZEALAND

The original system of formal environmental administration in New Zealand was established in the early 1970s, in the climate set by a strong environmental and conservation movement. In fact, similarities exist between New Zealand and the United States with regard to environmental events, subsequent legislation, and the development of SIA (Bryan and Taylor 1984). Of relevance here is that impetus for New Zealand's 1973 Environmental Protection and Enhancement Procedures was public outrage resembling that following the 1969 Santa Barbara oil spill in the United States. In the case of New Zealand, the controversy resulted from a proposal to raise Lake Manapouri to facilitate electricity generation to use for aluminum smelting. This incident struck a note of widespread discord in the country, which led to a major public campaign against the proposed project. Increased awareness of environmental issues led also to a new formal "green" party to fight the 1972 general election (Gilbert 1986). Official recognition of environmental issues was stimulated further by the 1972 Stockholm Conference on the Environment and the 1970 implementation of the National Environmental Policy Act (NEPA) in the United States. The new Labour government of 1972-1975, conscious of the political importance of environmental concerns among the public, established a new government agency, the Commission for the Environment, under a Minister for the Environment. The Commission staff grew from 3 to 56 from 1972 to 1985 (Gilbert 1986:89). It is located separately from other decision-making and resource managment agencies, and some of its most important work has been conducted through such channels as inter-departmental committees and informal liaison. The new advisory agency had no legislative backing, but was provided with a basis for operation under the Environmental Protection and Enhancement Procedures (EPEP) introduced in 1973. These require government agencies to prepare environmental assessments of proposals, including Environmental Impact Reports (EIRs) for large developments. The Commission formally audits these reports, a process which includes public submissions, and otherwise advises the government on the environmental implications of planned developments. Although the procedures did not spell out a requirement for SIA work, they did provide an early impetus for formal SIA work (Gilbert 1986). In addition, a number of legislative provisions also require government agencies to consider social issues and effects. These include legislation for town and country planning, public works, local government and mining (Conland 1985:16). The Ministries of Works and Development, and Energy have therefore become particularly important in conducting and promoting SIA work in development planning.

Since the inception of the EPEP there has been a considerable development of social assessment methods as part of environmental assessment, resource planning, and project/policy evaluation and monitoring. Early EIRs and audits made little or no mention of social impacts. One exception, a major social-monitoring research project initiated in the mid-1970s, provided a mass of data about the Huntly thermal power project on the Waikako River (Fookes 1981). This research gained substantial government funding and some international recognition. Nonetheless, as McPherson (1985) points out, it was seen by many planners, developers and others involved in the practical side of impact assessment and mitigation as largely an academic exercise. Later funding and institutional support for SIA were therefore hindered by skepticism from both government officials and community groups. But, lessons learned led towards a process for SIA that merged data collection, early identification of social issues, and mitigation action at a community level. This was prerequisite for the "rapid growth" phase of SIA that followed.

The EPEP have been modified since 1973, with considerable limits placed on the scope of assessment and public involvement, as described in detail by Morgan (1983). The changes to the procedures were initiated with the emergence of the 1975-1984 National Government. (The Commission acts at the pleasure of Government, for there is no legal mandate as there is for the U.S. Environmental Protection Agency.) The most important changes came with the National Government's agenda of major industrial developments, under a "think big" economic growth strategy. Several projects were promoted based on exploitation of oil and gas, coal, and hydro electricity. A "fast-track" piece of legislation, called the National Development Act (NDA) was introduced in 1979 and amended in 1981. The aim of this act was to streamline environmental and planning procedures and to thwart opposition to development priorities of the National Government.

As the round of major energy projects unfolded under think-big, their very real social impacts became clear and were an important focus for social impact assessment initiatives. Impacts in such areas as housing and social services were documented in monitoring research. In addition, this research facilitated comparisons between New Zealand projects and overseas energy projects, particularly those in North America (Taylor and Sharp 1983). Suggestions for future planning covered such topics as improved workforce planning, housing strategies, the need to diversify the local economy and provide community services (Taylor and McClintock 1984).

Before the early 1980s the social component of preliminary planning was largely limited to some community profiling and the identification of potential negative attitudes. A more participatory process of planning then emerged, and this approach was used most effectively by the Joint Centre (now Centre for Resource Management) which is an independent, university-based group carrying out teaching and research. In its contract research, the Centre has pioneered innovations in a participatory SIA methodology. At the same time, social monitoring for the major energy projects demonstrated further the importance of including public participation and community development throughout the SIA process.

SIA AND REFORM OF ENVIRONMENTAL ADMINISTRATION

In 1984, a re-instated Labour Government set out to tackle problems that emerged out of public criticism of the system of environmental management in New Zealand. These problems included a tendency towards a narrow definition of the "environment" and a failure to take an integrated view of social, economic and environmental change; a failure to carry out a process of decision making and analysis that accommodates national, regional and local perspectives; little public participation in decision making; and the fragmentation of environmental management among several government agencies.

Major changes were initiated in the system of environmental and natural resource management as the new government set out to implement its environmental and natural resource policy. This policy is summarized as follows:

Labour will implement a strategy to integrate conservation
and development so that:

1. We move to a sustainable economic base by shifting
    from the use of nonrenewable to renewable
    resources;

2. Those resources are used to achieve the ends of social
    justice;

3. Our trusteeship responsibilities for future generations are
    recognised;

4. Our remaining endangered species and ecosystems and
    representative examples of our full range of plants,
    animals and landscapes are protected. (Minister for
    the Environment 1984:10)

These general objectives could only be pursued by making changes to
the nature of decision making at all levels of government and in the private
sector. The primary need was to bring the key aspects of the environment--
physical, biological and social--to bear on all stages of planning.

Participants at an environmental forum held by the Government in
early 1985 to propose changes generally represented environmental concerns
and pushed hard for a major revamping of all the environmental and Crown
land agencies. In rebuttal, managers of Crown land and forests maintained,
with some justification, that they have always sought a balance of
conservation and development and of social and economic development.

All participants in the debate appeared to underestimate the
Government's determination for change and, especially, the strength of an
underlying ideology of neoclassical economics. Otherwise liberal, Labour's
new conservative "free-market" economic policy contrasted with the otherwise
conservative National government's intervention and direct involvement in
major energy projects. With Labour's current economic policy, central
government trading activities are being placed under publically owned
corporate structures to operate in "full-market" conditions. This restructuring
of the state sector is consistent with the removal of subsidy and regulation for
agriculture, export industries, and most other areas of the economy. A new
Ministry for the Environment and Parliamentary Commissioner with audit
functions were established in late 1986 and will be matched in 1987 with a
major new conservation agency to administer areas such as reserves and
national parks. New state corporations will operate Crown land, forests, coal

mines, and electricity production. Future decisions will cover the organizational structures for soil and water administration and town and country planning.

SIA Working Group and Network

A vital ingredient in the promotion of an effective SIA process as part of the reform of environmental administration is the national SIA Working Group and SIA network organized in late 1983. This body represents SIA practitioners from central government departments involved with social policy and social impact research, social planners from regional government--most importantly from regions where major projects were being built, academics, and people involved in practical aspects of community development. The group is informal in organization and variable in size (usually between 10 and 15 people collaborate on issues). These people reflect a strong degree of consensus about lessons learned in New Zealand and overseas. Moreover, they have shown an ability to effect changes in social policy and social planning in both central and regional government. They have been particularly important in promoting social policy as an integral part of the new set-up for environmental legislation.

Initially, the Working Group met to improve methods for mitigation and management of impacts arising from the major projects. An early focus was the mechanism for distribution of levies made against major developments under the Local Government Act (1974) to mitigate local and regional impacts. They concentrated on reviewing and proposing legislation for SIA and the refinement of the principles for an effective SIA process. This led to publication and wide distribution of *SIA in New Zealand: A Practical Approach* (Conland 1985). Secondary activity included networking and clearing of information. Recent concerns of the Working Group, with the near completion of several major energy projects and implementation of new economic policies, have included plant closures with industrial restructuring, changes in rural communities with new "free-market" agricultural policies, impacts of rapidly expanding tourism development, and introduction of new computerized technology in work places.

Since the various propositions for reorganizing central government agencies have been floated, the Working Group has been in a good position to argue for a social emphasis in resource management as a counter to the otherwise predictable emphasis on economic and biological-physical concerns.

TOWARD A SOCIALLY DRIVEN PROCESS

A greater role of social impact assessment in future New Zealand resource development will largely depend on further evolution of an "integrated approach" to planning, decision making, and management. Implicit in this emergence is that social analysis and social policy should not be subservient to economic analysis and policy but integrated with it, alongside analysis of biological and physical science components. While the past and present emphasis on economic analysis is often determined by the academic backgrounds of resource managers, it also reflects patterns of power and influence in natural resource agencies. Thus, also implicit for the successful emergence of an integrated approach is that these patterns will have to change as well.

At least four main orientations can be identified in the present implementation of social perspectives in public policy. These four perspectives can be conceptualized in terms of two main dimensions, as shown in Figure 1. The implications of these distinctions form the departure points for an integrated approach to SIA and public policy.

Technocratic Versus Participatory Philosophies

The first dimension is founded in the distinction between technocratic and participatory approaches. Some argue that futures can be predicted, planned for, and controlled. Others stress that SIA should involve "genuine" public participation, whereby people affected by change take part in the shaping of their own future. Technocratic approaches to development, which have been common in New Zealand to date, are centralized and focus on social planning and the management of impacts.

Cost/benefit analyses, as the scenario typically goes, are conducted by "experts" and appear in documents (as part of the "product" orientation) which provide the "official" rationale for decisions. Resource development is organized in a bureaucratic union of government and the private sector. Nevertheless, with sufficient demand from below, there is potential for a move toward more participatory approaches to planning. Serious questions should be posed about the frequent failure to involve local groups in impact assessments, so that community development becomes an integral part of the decisions being made and implemented. Different community sectors and local interest groups can be involved in an assessment, especially when expert practitioners work to facilitate their participation.

Many officials of central, regional, and local government, as well as managers in the private sector, distrust SIA. The process has a way of making values explicit and interjecting a degree of accountability in the setting of decision criteria. It has been said that every political decision is in fact an

116

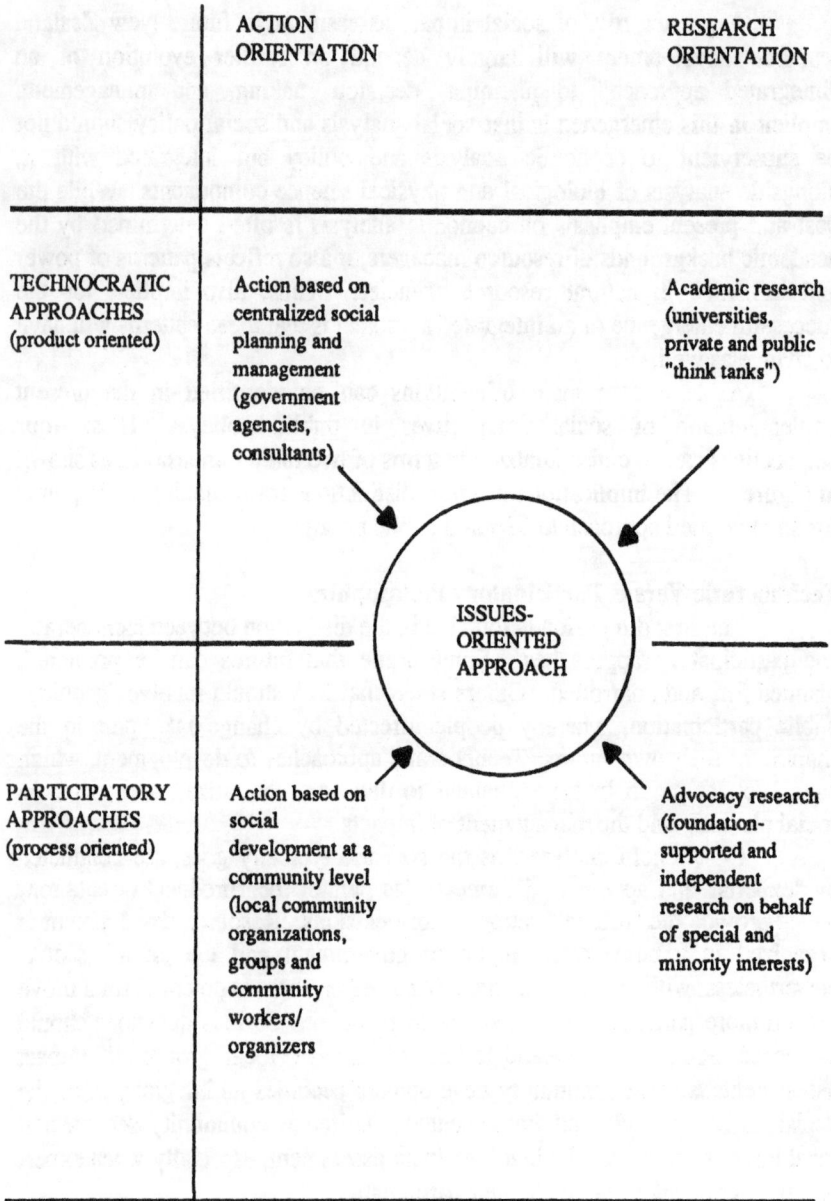

Figure 1 Orientations in the field of SIA

experiment in human behavior. But the outcomes and implications of such "experiments" are seldom clearly explored. The SIA process advocated here leads to this very type of examination, so it is no wonder that some politicians do not support what they see as a stripping of their prerogatives. In fact, the environmental assessment process in general should be designed to be an exercise in disclosure of information.

Perhaps one of the most difficult aspects about the setting of decision criteria is that their early and explicit statement makes it difficult for those with hidden values (agendas) to avoid exposure of self-interest. And that self-interest has often been tied up in the passing along of hidden costs to assumed benefactors of a project. For example, the construction of a reservoir for hydro-electricity generation has been "sold" to a community on the basis of job creation and increased economic vitality for the area. And the obvious benefits to electricity consumers, or to those whose business is engineering and construction, are considered legitimate. But what is not legitimate are the hidden costs to the community of the "boom and bust cycle" associated with the arrival and departure of a large, outside workforce. Real estate speculators make money, but young citizens looking for new homes in the community soon find themselves priced out of the market. The community is left to provide extra local revenue for expansion of community services (schools, recreation facilities, fire and police protection) and to engage in many hours of voluntary work bolstering inadequate social services. This scenario has been documented for several New Zealand cases of major resource projects (Taylor, Bettesworth and Kerslake 1983, Taylor and Sharp 1983). In the current case of Clyde dam on the Clutha River in the South Island, long-term benefits have been proposed in respect to a new tourism industry based on lake recreation when, in fact, the river has potentially more tourism value in its natural state. (New Zealand officials have sometimes been slow to recognize that overseas tourists have plenty of lakes but diminishing free-flowing river resources in their own countries).

It may well be that in the example cited the overall national benefits of hydro-electric power outweigh the costs. But the early setting of social and environmental decision criteria forces a careful accounting of costs and benefits before commitment to the project is made. Full and early disclosure of who gains, who loses, and by how much, makes for public debate and cost/benefit analysis leading to better decisions.

Research Versus Social Action Philosophies

The second dimension in Figure 1 embodies a distinction between an orientation towards social action and research in support of that action, or toward the generation of knowledge through research for its own sake. SIA, of course, is not a research process in the strict definition of the term. Formal hypotheses are not posed to see if they find support in the data. Instead, social futures are projected based on data and procedures that are sufficiently reasonable and convincing for others to agree on their plausibility. But these are futures about which one can never be sure, for the "future" will keep changing as people react to the project or plans in their attempts to enhance the outcomes and to minimize the costs for themselves and others.

The purpose of SIA, then, is to enable officials and agencies to make more socially responsible decisions, and in a very direct way to involve people to be affected by these decisions as part of this process. Though the generation of new knowledge about communities undergoing change and social processes underlying these changes may occur, the immediate goals are the best decision and best management, as described in Conland (1985), not the generation of new knowledge.

All this is *not* to say that academic research and theoretical perspectives guiding this research are omitted from this process. Ideally, the theoretical perspectives and research data derived from the social sciences should provide the basis and guidance for SIA, so that each new assessment is not part of the "new Columbus syndrome," a discovery of facts and perspectives that actually have already been established. But part of the problem with the SIA process is that established theoretical perspectives, methodologies and data often are not used effectively during an SIA. The reason may be that a qualified social scientist who has this knowledge is not available for the SIA, or that much of the social science literature has not been translated into terms which facilitate its use or ready applicability to the process. Ironically, there is an abundant literature on community, social structure, and social change in general (Hall *et al.* 1983) and specific to such topics as rapid industrialization (Taylor *et al.* 1983) that has often remained untapped for these purposes.

The quantification issue looms large on the research orientation part of the ledger. "Hard" social scientists sometimes keep their distance from those "soft, social action types" who do not have the "real data" (i.e., numbers) to support their advocacy. Indeed, precise units of measure facilitate validation. Numbers provide effective summaries of information, and numbers are integral to most methods of projection. Yet it is often those things that cannot be counted that are "counted most" by different social groups. Qualitative or narrative data, therefore, often focus on significant social issues. This has been especially the case in studies of the indigenous Maori people of New Zealand, where data are usually oral or narrative in nature, and obtained through tribal elders. The point is that there needs to be a blending of use of quantitative and qualitative data from both research and social action perspectives.

SIA should be an interdisciplinary endeavor, and a number of central and regional agencies and community groups should be involved in a coordinated way. An academic perspective is necessary because there has been a tendency to treat separate impact assessments as isolated cases with minimal accumulation of a fund of practical experiences and methods and a failure to recognize cumulative change. An analytical perspective is necessary because the focus of much data gathering for SIA, particularly data compiled in lengthy community profiles, has to be questioned. Many practitioners are not researching and clarifying issues that center around the major environmental and social concerns in question. It seems essential that the focus of an SIA should be *issue-oriented*. There is increasing recognition that in New Zealand, as in the U.S., useful SIAs are analytic rather than encyclopedic and issue driven rather than general. They should involve a mixture of research in terms of data collection and action by the assessor to see that that data results in improved policy or management, either from "above" or "below" or both.

DISCUSSION

It is necessary to consider means to obtain greater acceptance and effectiveness for SIA in New Zealand if SIA is to be the basis for a socially-driven process of decision making and management. Many politicians and government officials see SIA as a threat to their technocratic approaches to the decision process. Individuals and community groups, on the other hand, often see SIA as a tool of those in authority to prescribe their social future and undermine their potential contribution to planning. Academics can see advocacy research and the "grass-roots" sociology that it entails as threatening to their notions of "proper academic distance" and objectivity.

These common conflicts to be found in SIA usually result from people in different work environments adhering strongly to their own particular approaches and ideologies. The most obvious conflicts arise between technocratic (top-down) and participatory (bottom-up) approaches. For example, it is difficult for top-down oriented management to take a positive view of community development processes. It may not appear in the interests of government or industry to establish community development programs that could potentially assist a group to oppose particular developments or policies. Yet the changes proposed could be enhanced for all parties given a better context of social development. At the same time, a local interest group can be so embroiled in its advocacy role that it finds it very difficult to take part in a participatory process when a genuine opportunity to do so becomes available. Action and research orientations can cut across the technocratic and participatory orientations. In the technocratic approach, for example, there are common conflicts between action and research as demonstrated in consultancy and the control of the research setting by a funding agency, control which an academic might find unacceptable. There are further conflicts between academic and applied approaches to research as shown in the requirement of the academic setting to pursue publishing in "respectable academic journals," at the expense of "practical" approaches and solutions to planning problems.

There are also conflicts between action and research in participatory approaches. Whereas community action may demand data that supports a particular stance, there may also be conflicts between the pursuit of that stance and the research required to supply the data. In being drawn into the community action, the advocacy researchers may find themselves compromising the methods required to supply the data.

The experience of SIA in New Zealand shows the importance of work in the middle ground that does not have a narrow adherence to existing ideologies. The best prospects for practitioners of social impact assessment are embodied in moves by some away from the established stances and work environments such as when an academic works for government, or a government department becomes involved in community development. In the middle ground, the social impact assessment practitioner becomes a broker of information and a mediator among interest groups. It is fortunate that New Zealand has a number of people working in this middle ground. Their current activity demonstrates the need to move toward a new proactive process for social impact assessment, where social considerations are taken into account in the early formulation of resource policy and continue over the main periods of change in a given project or activity (Bryan and Taylor 1986).

REFERENCES

Bryan, C.H. and C.N. Taylor. 1984. "United States and New Zealand SIA: A Cross-Cultural View." In L.N. Wenner (ed.), *Issues in Social Impact Analysis: Interagency Symposium Proceedings.* Washington, D.C.: USDA Forest Service, Environmental Coordination. 70-73.

_____ 1986. "Proactive Social Science for Resource Management." Plenary paper presented to the National Symposium on Social Science in Resource Management, Corvallis, Oregon, 12-16 May.

Conland, J. (ed.). 1985. *Social Impact Assessment in New Zealand--A Practical Approach.* Wellington: Town and Country Planning Directorate, Ministry of Works and Development.

Fookes, W.T. 1981. *Intentions and Practice of the Monitoring Project: Monitoring Social and Economic Impact, Huntly Case Study.* Final Report Series, 9. Hamilton, New Zealand: University of Waikato.

Gilbert, J. 1986. "Environmental Assessment in New Zealand." *Northwest Environmental Journal* 2:85-105.

Hall, B., D. Thorns, and W.E. Willmott. 1983. "Community Formation and Change--A Study of Rural and Urban Localities in New Zealand." *Working Paper No 4*, Department of Sociology, University of Cantebury, Christchurch.

McPherson, J. 1985. "Social Impact Assessment in New Zealand." Paper presented at the International Association for Impact Assessment Special North American Conference Impact Assessment in Resource Development, 1920. Calgary, Alberta, September, 1985.

Minister for the Environment. 1984. "Environmental Administration in New Zealand: A Discussion Paper." Wellington: State Services-- Commission.

Morgan, R. K. 1983. "The Evolution of Environmental Impact Assessment in New Zealand." *Journal of Environmental Management* 16:139-152.

Taylor, C.N. and B. Sharp. 1983. "Social Impacts of Major Resource Development Projects: Concerns for Research and Planning." Discussion paper, Centre for Resource Management, University of Canterbury and Lincoln College.

Taylor, C.N., C.M. Bettesworth, and J.G. Kerslake. 1983. "Social Implications of Rapid Industrialisation: A Bibliography of New Zealand Experiences." Discussion paper, Centre for Resource Management, University of Canterbury and Lincoln College.

Taylor, N. and W. McClintock. 1984. *Rapid Growth and Resource Development: Social Issues and Strategies for Coping.* Wellington, New Zealand: Town and Country Planning Directorate, Ministry of Work and Development.

III

APPLICATIONS OF
SOCIAL SCIENCE

INTRODUCTION TO PART III

Marc L. Miller
Richard P. Gale
Perry J. Brown

The history of applied social science in natural resource management systems is a short one, covering only the last several decades. Throughout this period, researchers of many persuasions have served the public interest. Nonetheless, the social sciences are in something of a Kuhnian pre-paradigmatic state in matters of resource management. Continuing debate over such concepts and methods as social carrying capacity, optimum yield, multiple-use management, and social impact assessment reveals there is no solid consensus about what should count as research problems, how problems should be measured, or how results should be communicated.

The four articles in this section display some of the methods and types of findings which have proven useful in the management of natural resource systems. As introduction, we make the following brief remarks.

Socioeconomic Impact Assessment, Regional Integration, Public Participation, and New National Park Planning in Canada.

On this continent, it is Canada which has most systematically recruited the social sciences to a national park system. This follows from the Canadian policy that parks can only be developed (by federal-provincial agreement) if positive social, economic, and physical impacts are to be expected for the region in question.

In this case study, Erik Val describes how Canada's federal parks agency employed a private consulting firm to evaluate the socioeconomic consequences of a park proposed for Bruce Peninsula (Ontario). Analyses of park and no-park scenarios suggested that while the peninsula as a whole would benefit from a park, the two townships involved would be affected in opposite ways insofar as issues of tourism, land use, lifestyle, population, and municipal finance are concerned. In light of both public and government responses to the study, Val concludes that the Canadian system of park planning is especially appealing.

Visitor Activity Planning and Management in Canadian National Parks: Marketing Within a Context of Integration.

National park management is inherently difficult because the twin management goals of resource preservation and provision of recreational experience are so frequently incompatible. As we have noted above, the Canadian response has been to count on elaborate management programs and procedures, and on a pluralistic scientific community, for acceptable solutions.

In this article, Robert Graham, Per W. Nilsen, and Robert J. Payne disclose how the innovative Visitor Activity Management Process (VAMP) brought sociological analyses to assist in the consideration of a park proposal for the Mingan Archipelago (Quebec), and in the management of the Kejimkujik National Park (Nova Scotia). Although VAMP has its imperfections (the process has the potential to become a bureaucratic snowball; in addition, it could generate solutions which create zoning problems), the authors are encouraged by the way it and the Natural Resources Management Process blend with the National Park Management Process.

A Planning Approach to Social Carrying Capacity Research for Aravaipa Canyon Wilderness, Arizona.

The most difficult challenge facing applied social scientists in natural resource systems is to give meaning to the term "applied." Applied research often fares differently depending on whether it is reviewed within or outside academe. Resource agencies, industries, and publics have different perspectives on management than academically located scientists. This results in differing priorities concerning topics of research.

In this article, Steven D. Moore and Stanley K. Brickler examine the problems of research design when on-site wilderness managers contract for work with university scientists. The authors are persuasive in showing that the issue of making research relevant can be resolved by early and multiple collaborations between managers and scientists. Moore and Brickler emphasize that social scientists must take the responsibility to work with policy makers and people affected by policy to construe the right research questions.

Emotions in Environmental Decision Making: Rational Planning Versus the Passionate Public.

At a time in which natural resource policy processes are increasingly subjected to intense scrutiny by diverse and sophisticated interest groups, managers are pressed to comply with an array of legal requirements concerning public participation and input. In response, some agencies, notably the U.S. Forest Service and U.S. Army Corps of Engineers, have institutionalized procedures for eliciting public attitudes about policy. Such efforts have been largely organized on the assumptions that preference data are rather easily obtained and interpreted, and that emotions connected to rational arguments are best ignored.

In this article, Joanne Vining and Herbert W. Schroeder draw on recent theories of psychology which hold that emotions, rather than just playing interfering or benign roles in cognition, contribute to the ways people reason. Implications of preliminary studies by these authors suggest that resource agencies should revamp procedures so that affect is incorporated, instead of neutralized, in the measurement of public opinion.

8

SOCIOECONOMIC IMPACT ASSESSMENT, REGIONAL INTEGRATION, PUBLIC PARTICIPATION, AND NEW NATIONAL PARK PLANNING IN CANADA

Erik Val
Ontario Regional Office
Environment Canada, Parks Service

The development and operation of national parks in Canada is an effective instrument of public policy to protect and preserve natural and heritage resources of national significance. The National Park Management Planning Process used to establish and operate such federal parks, develops, proposes, and evaluates optimal development alternatives. The process also provides various opportunities for public participation in the planning process. Socioeconomic impact assessment (SEIA) is part of this process which not only identifies social and economic consequences of establishing a national park but also brings together public concerns related to parks development.

The purpose of this article is twofold: to discuss the role of SEIA and public participation in the National Park Management Planning Process in Canada, and to present the findings of a recently completed SEIA for a new park proposed for the Bruce Peninsula, a region located some 300 km (200 miles) north of Toronto, Ontario. This year-long study, undertaken by a Toronto-based consulting firm, included an extensive survey of permanent and seasonal residents in two lightly populated rural townships (Williams 1985). The assessment analyzed the lifestyle, demographic, tourism, land and resource use, economic, and financial/fiscal effects of the proposal both on the region and province.

The Bruce Peninsula case study is important because it was one of the first SEIAs completed by the Parks Service when preparing for a new park development. These results, in combination with the biophysical assessment findings, will be used in planning for the effective regional integration of the park into the Bruce Peninsula.

The article begins with an overview of the National Parks Management Planning Process and the role of the SEIA and public participation in that process. Next, the Bruce Peninsula SEIA case study is presented by first summarizing the research objectives and methodology; then follows a brief description of the proposal and the regional context of the study area. Next, the results of the analysis are presented. The importance of SEIA as an effective regional planning tool as well as a useful medium for public participation is discussed in a final section. This section also provides an update on the status of the proposed park.

NATIONAL PARK MANAGEMENT PLANNING AND SEIA IN CANADA

Overview
The Parks Service is committed to assessing the biophysical and socioeconomic impacts related to parks operations and development (Parks Canada 1982:12). The National Park Management Planning Process provides for this commitment to assessment.

This planning process is a procedure to establish, develop, and operate 31 national parks across Canada's 10 provinces and 2 territories (Parks Canada 1986). The process provides for each park the basic steps in setting planning objectives, establishing the scope and nature of planning, undertaking the various inputs, reviews, and approvals needed to study a park proposal, and documenting the required action for implementation, evaluation, and monitoring such parks.

The principles of the process involve integrated senior program management and planning; flexible and comprehensive planning; a multidisciplinary team approach; public participation; environmental impact assessment including SEIA; and continual plan review, evaluation, and adjustment. Figure 1 provides an overview of the process and side comments

```
┌─────────────┐   ┌──────────────┐   ┌──────────────┐
│SYSTEMS PLAN │   │CORPORATE     │   │REGIONAL      │
│    FOR      │   │PROGRAM PLANS │   │PROGRAM PLANS │
│NATIONAL     │   │              │   │              │
│   PARKS     │   │              │   │              │
└─────────────┘   └──────────────┘   └──────────────┘
```

provides comprehensive national level planning to ensure that all of 39 natural and 29 marine regions of Canada are represented; sets national level objectives and priorities

provides national program level direction on a rational and fair distribution of human and financial resources based on national and regional objectives

establishes regional priorities to satisfy the broader national corporate programs: priorities are set amongst National Parks, Historic Parks and Sites, and Heritage Areas such as Canals, Waterways, and Rivers

```
┌──────────────────┐
│PARK PURPOSE +     │
│AND OBJECTIVES     │
│STATEMENT          │
└──────────────────┘
```

states specific park purposes and objectives in the context of the national systems plan

```
┌──────────────────┐
│INTERIM           │
│MANAGEMENT        │
│GUIDELINES        │
└──────────────────┘
```

provides guidelines to a park superintendent to manage the park lands, resources and services until a Park Management Plan is developed and approved

PARK MANAGEMENT PLAN PRODUCTS

```
┌──────────────────┐
│TERMS OF REFERENCE│
└──────────────────┘
```

defines the responsibilities of the planning team to undertake the necessary research and planning to produce the Park Management Plan; included are objectives, priorities, schedule and timeframe, milestones, research inventory and goals, level and type of public involvement, team composition and resource levels, and environmental impact assessment (EIA) requirements including SEIA needs

```
┌──────────────────┐
│DATA BASE ANALYSIS│
└──────────────────┘
```

provides comprehensive information and database on natural and cultural resources, resource sensitivities, socio-economic characteristics of visitors and visitor activities, recreation and interpretation opportunities, land use relationships, and the results of public consultation; serves as the basis, in part, for SEIA; in total a 3 year part of the process.

```
┌──────────────────────────┐
│ALTERNATIVE PLAN CONCEPT(S)*+│
└──────────────────────────┘
```

based on the analysis of the database, formulates range of meaningful park development alternatives to provide park managers and public understanding of how the park could be operated and managed; alternate concepts must be guided by park purpose and objectives; EIA and SEIA are part of the analytical and synthesis process

```
┌──────────────────┐
│PARK MANAGEMENT   │
│PLAN AND PLAN     │
│SUMMARY** +       │
└──────────────────┘
```

based on the selection of the preferred alternative provides a statement of management objectives, and the means and strategies for achieving them; constitutes a comprehensive framework within which subsequent detailed planning for activities and areas will take place; the plan provides a comprehensive conservation, recreation and development zoning overview of the park, a statement of resource levels needed to develop and operate the park, and a statement on how public concerns and issues will be dealt with including regional integration; the Plan is a public document

```
┌──────────────────┐
│SUB-ACTIVITY      │
│PLANS             │
└──────────────────┘
┌──────────────────┐
│AREA PLANS+       │
└──────────────────┘
```

develops sub-activity plans for visitor services and interpretation; is part of a concurrent planning process called V.A.M.P. (Visitor Activity Management Process)

develops specific area plans involving the same process but applied at a specific detailed/smaller scale; such plans include townsite, campground, and facility/development

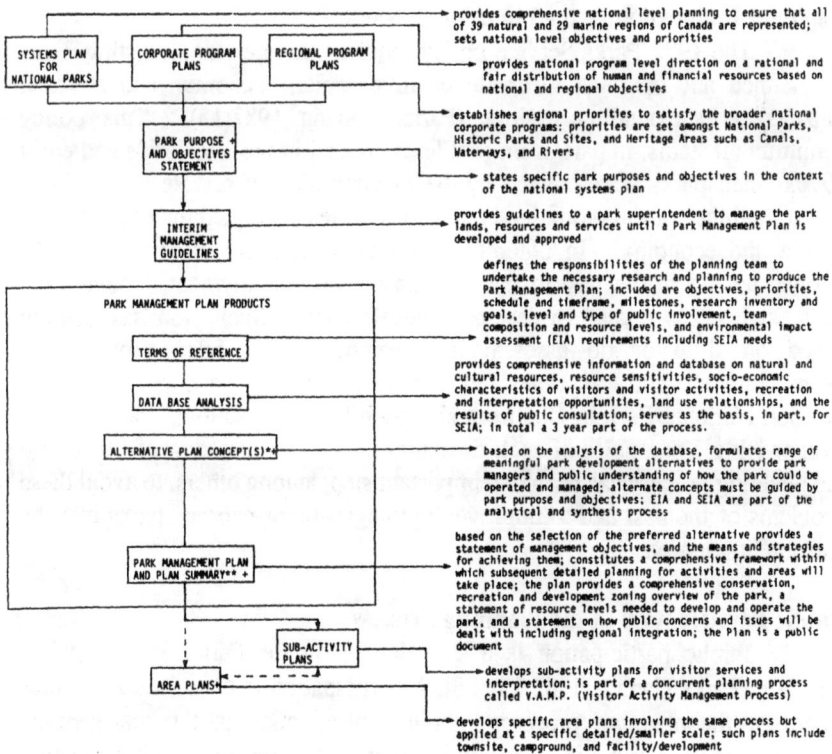

* Approved by the Assistant Deputy Minister of Environment Canada

** Approved by the Minister of Environment Canada

+ Stage at which public participation is requested

Figure 1   Park Management Planning Process

describing each major step of the process. The process is a typically hierarchical planning procedure starting from broad national level principles and objectives moving down through the process to finer levels of detail until specific visitor activity and park area plans are developed.

Another planning procedure, the Visitor Activity Management Process (VAMP), feeds into national park management planning at various stages by providing the necessary framework for park interpretation, visitor services, public safety and regional integration (Graham This Volume). The results of much of the research required for the park planning process including SEIA is used in VAMP planning.

Regional Integration in the Planning Process

The 1982 Parks Service policy requires that new and existing parks be planned and operated to create positive social, economic, and physical impacts on surrounding regions (Parks Canada 1982:15). This policy commitment stems, in part, from problems created in the late 1960s and early 1970s when parks were created by the expropriation of private lands. Such expropriations not only took land but also, at times, disrupted the regional way of life and economy. In order to offset these negative effects, the Parks Service tended in the past to over-emphasize the employment, income, and business benefits related to new park development. Such promises, usually based on little or no assessment research, created false expectations, disappointment and, at times, violent resistance to park establishment. Forillon National Park in Quebec and Kouchibouquac National Park in New Brunswick are examples of such difficulties. The introduction of SEIA into the planning process has been one important step, among others, to avoid these problems of the past and to improve the integration of national parks into the surrounding region.

Public Participation in the Planning Process

Public participation is a key element in the Parks Service policy mandate (Parks Canada 1982:13). Such participation is organized at various stages of the planning process: public introduction to the management planning program at the interim management guidelines stage, public reaction to the park development options at the alternative plan concept stage, and public input to the actual Park Management Plan (Figure 1). Public participation also occurs when required for the review of townsite or area plans, and during the Management Plan review every 5 years. The techniques used must ensure full disclosure of information to allow adequate opportunity for meaningful public response. Such techniques could include public information meetings, workshops, interviews, public hearings, seminars, publications, or advisory committees. The Parks Service is then committed to respond and provide feedback to the public as questions, comments, and issues are raised during the participation process. Public participation also helps to address the concerns and problems related to the regional integration of parks discussed in the previous section.

Socioeconomic Impact Assessment in the Planning Process

As provided for in the Park Management Planning Process, SEIA is required at the database analysis and alternative plan concept development stages (Figure 1). The assessment procedure requires an analysis of the expected negative and positive social and economic effects, and identification and implementation of a plan for appropriate mitigation or enhancement measures. A procedure is also required for the monitoring of major impacts to ensure that park development and operation impacts are minimized and benefits are maximized. Such an assessment analyzes the lifestyle, demographic, tourism, land and resource use, economic, and financial/fiscal effects of the park development locally and regionally. Techniques used in SEIA vary greatly and can include public surveys, cost/benefit analysis, forecasting and trend analysis, economic modeling, and other related methodologies (Parks Canada 1983).

Although theoretically separate in the Park Management Planning Process, SEIA and public participation do converge and overlap to the mutual benefit of both components of the process. Results of public forums, meetings, and workshops assist in defining the need for and scoping the content of an SEIA. Equally useful to the Parks Service in better understanding regional concerns are the results of a methodologically sound public opinion survey. Such a survey collects baseline socio-demographic data and specific information on people's attitudes and expectations related to new park development.

The inter-relationship between SEIA, regional integration, and public understanding and participation is well illustrated in the proposed Bruce Peninsula National Park case study. The balance of the article discusses this case study.

PROPOSED BRUCE PENINSULA NATIONAL PARK

Background

The SEIA prepared for the proposed Bruce Peninsula National Park is only one stage in a lengthy process of analysis, review, and public consultation. Active steps were taken by the federal government in 1980 in concert with provincial and local authorities to explore the possibility of establishing a national park on the Bruce Peninsula. In late 1981 Parks Canada undertook a public consultation process which included setting up a 12-member study committee appointed by the councils of Lindsay and St. Edmunds Townships, the two townships most affected by the proposal (Figure 2). Using this forum, a series of community meetings was held to inform the public and receive its feedback on the proposal. A short opinion survey questioning people's support for the proposal was also part of the public participation process. Concurrent with the study committee's consultation process, a separate lobby group against the proposal, People Opposed to the Park Proposal, was established. This group was primarily concerned about the impact of increased tourism on the rural lifestyle and the loss of control over local decision making. The formation of this opposition group showed that divisions existed within the two townships concerning support for the proposal.

In the fall of 1982, the 12-member study committee released its findings which included general support for the proposal subject to a series of conditions related to park operations, employment, access rights, resource use, municipal finance, compensation, and other matters. Early in 1983 this conditional approval was altered due to a change in municipal leadership in Lindsay Township. The Township now wished to make its approval conditional on the results of a SEIA. Complying with its own process and this condition, the Parks Service along with the two townships developed terms of reference for a SEIA. The consulting firm of Woods Gordon was retained to undertake the research.

The role of the consulting firm was one of an objective analyst assessing the positive and negative aspects of the proposal in a balanced and dispassionate manner. As this approach was required to maintain the credibility of the results, the Parks Service played an arm's length role in the preparation of the SEIA involving draft report reviews and the payment of the consultant.

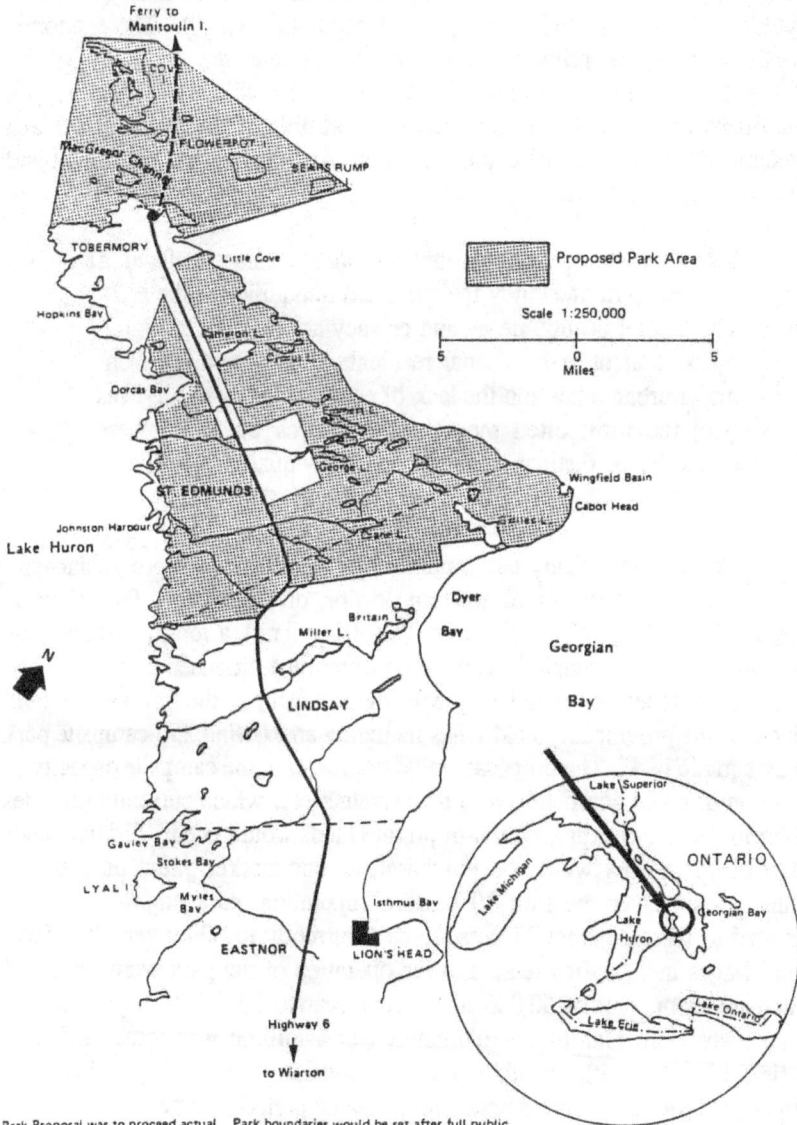

Figure 2 Proposed national park on the north Bruce Peninsula

The Region and the Proposal

The proposal is located on 270 square kilometers of North Bruce Peninsula in two lightly populated rural townships: St. Edmunds (1984 total population 2,750) and Lindsay (1984 total population 1,700). The economic base for Lindsay is primarily agricultural, whereas the economy of St. Edmunds is related to tourism and is focused on the village of Tobermory at the northern tip of the Peninsula. About two-thirds of the residents of each township consist of seasonal cottage owners. As noted by the consultant and based on the survey results:

> Many of the permanent and seasonal residents have a frontier spirit and enjoy the quiet and tranquility of the area. The natural beauty, peace and privacy are rated most highly by permanent and seasonal residents alike. Distance from major urban areas and the lack of economic opportunity was [sic] the most often mentioned negatives but these were noted by a distinct minority of individuals. (Williams 1985:5)

The region already has a number of municipal and provincial park facilities as well as the small western portion of an existing federal park, Georgian Bay Islands National Park. The Bruce Trail, a long province-wide hiking trail, threads through the eastern portion of the proposed park.

If a federal/provincial agreement is reached, the proposal would include all the provincially-held lands including an existing 250-campsite park and an aquatic park. The proposal would not increase the campsite capacity of the region to avoid competing with the private sector which currently provides some 550 sites. No expropriation of private lands would occur. Private lands within the park area would be purchased at fair market value on a seller-willing basis. Over the first 10 years of operation, park employment was estimated to increase from 11 person-years currently to 40 by year 10. Total annual wages and salaries related to the operation of the park were estimated to increase from some $250,000 in the first year to $900,000 in year 10. A capital investment plan of approximately $11.6 million was forecasted over the first 10 years with an additional $4.1 million spent on operations and maintenance for the proposed park over the same period of time.

Study Methodology

A number of consultative, fact-finding and research approaches were used in the study focusing on local official liaison and study review; survey of permanent and seasonal residents, businesses and landowners in the two townships; interviews with persons, organizations, and agencies affected by the proposal; the use of secondary sources of information from statistical banks, other studies and reports; and the use of standard analytical techniques including an age-cohort population forecast, an economic impact model and other related methodologies.

One of the key ingredients in the success of the study was the high response rates (approximately 40-80 percent) to the various surveys conducted, illustrating the keen public interest shown throughout the research. The survey was a fundamental tool in the public participation process as it insured a representative and unbiased sample of public opinion related to the proposal.

A typical impact assessment framework or model was developed and used by the consultant in analyzing the inter-related socioeconomic factors affected by the proposal (Figure 3). These factors include the national park proposal, tourism/visitors, land use, population/lifestyle, economy, and municipal finance. A basic no-park scenario and a park scenario were used to forecast change over a 10-year period from 1984-1994. The difference between the two scenarios constituted the net impact.

SEIA RESULTS

Tourism/Visitor Impacts

The Bruce Peninsula currently serves a destination and pass-through tourism market. The latter is particularly true as Tobermory at the north end of the Peninsula is the departure point for a ferry to Manitoulin Island, a popular tourist destination. Currently about 93,000 visitor parties come to or through the Peninsula area, of which 13,600 parties spend 31,300 nights in built accommodations, 31,700 groups camp for 72,900 nights in the area, and the remaining 47,900 or 51 percent of the tourists pass through the region (Figure 4-1). Assuming a modest growth rate of less than one percent based on the region's distance from the major urban centers of southwestern Ontario (Toronto-Hamilton-Windsor-Detroit) and intervening tourism/recreation opportunities, the no-park growth increase over the 1984-1994 period is projected at 10.5 percent, whereas with a park 18.0 percent was predicted. The incremental impact for North Bruce was estimated at some 7.5 percent.

Focusing on the proposed park study area within North Bruce region, the analyses showed that the current 38,500 visitor parties would increase over the 1984-1994 period by some 10 percent to 42,400 without a park and to

138

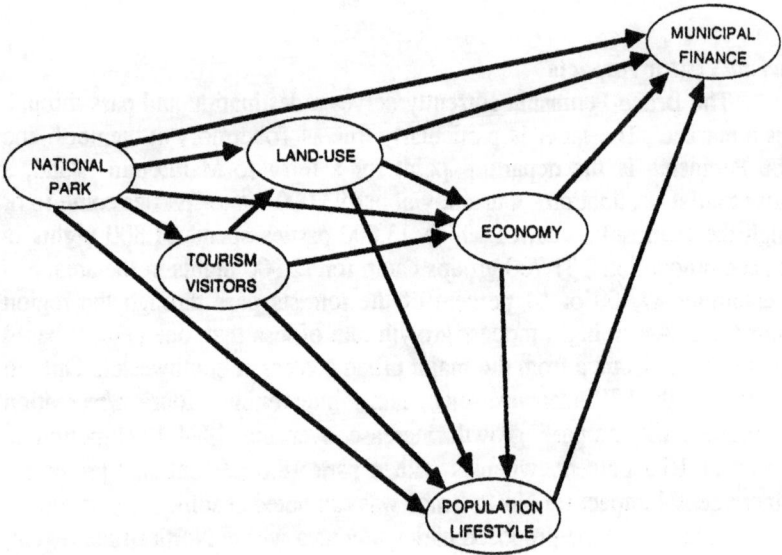

Figure 3   Influence diagram of impact beginning with a national park

4-1	Increase in Transient Tourists on North Bruce (Unique Visitor parties)			
		STAY OVERNIGHT IN NORTH BRUCE	PASS THROUGH NORTH BRUCE	TOTAL
IMPACTS	CURRENT (1984)	45,300	47,900	93,200
ON	No Park Increase (1994)	10.6%	10.4%	10.5%
TOURISM	With Park Increase (1994)	28.7%	7.9%	18.0%
IN AREA	Impact (1984-1994)	18.1%	-2.5%	7.5%

4-2	Increase in Park Visitors			
		VISITOR DAYS/NIGHTS	VISITOR PARTY DAY/NIGHTS	UNIQUE VISITOR PARTIES
IMPACTS	CURRENT (1984)	125,000	55,000	38,500
ON USE	PROJECTED NO PARK (1994)	138,700	60.600	42,400
OF PARK	No Park Increase	10.6%	10.2%	10.2%
FACILITIES	PROJECTED WITH PARK (1994)	212,500	90,800	56,500
	With Park Increase	69.5%	65.1%	46.8%
	Impact (1984-1994)	58.9%	54.9%	36.6%

Note: Excludes projected 102,900 visits to the two Visitor Reception Centres.

Definitions:

Visitor Day/Night — One person for one day use or one overnight use (e.g. one camper staying for 5 days and nights at Cyprus Lake is 5 visitor days/nights)

Visitor Party Day/Night — One group (usually a family) for one day use or one overnight (e.g. a family visiting Flowerpot Island during the day is 1 visitor party day/night)

Unique Visitor Party — One group (usually a family) visiting the area irrespective of how long they stay (e.g. one family camping at Cyprus Lake for a week is 1 unique visitor party)

Figure 4   Summary of tourism impacts on area and at park

56,500 with a park. The incremental impact for the proposed park area was estimated at approximately 37 percent (Figure 4-2). The majority of this increase is accounted for by fuller use of the current excess campsite capacity, and increased day and off-season use of the area as the proposed park would be operated year round. Translated into park use in terms of visitor days/nights, the incremental increase over the 10-year period of establishing the park would be some 59 percent. In sum, the primary effect of the proposed park would be to draw a small amount of new visitors and to retain some of the current pass-through tourist traffic.

Land-Use Impacts

Land uses in the proposed park area vary from small, cedar, wood-cutting to cattle-farming operations with a handful of residences and cottages. Much of the land, some 40 percent, is currently owned by either the local, provincial or federal levels of government. In addition, hunting and fishing is a prevalent use on both public and private lands.

The impact upon private landowners of establishing the park would be virtually non-existent as federal policy provides for land purchase on a fair market and seller-willing basis. The development of the park may prevent the establishment of an estimated 25-45 cottages if such private lands were sold. The new park would not significantly increase adjacent property values as the current rural and relatively undeveloped character of the region would remain unchanged with or without the park.

The major land-use impact concerns lost hunting opportunities as some one-third of the residents hunt on public lands. Private landowners within the park's boundaries could continue to hunt. An estimated 5,300 deer hunting days currently take place in the park area with some 1,400 of these used by local residents and the balance by seasonal residents and non-residents. No readily available alternate areas exist. Fishing would be essentially unaffected as Parks Service policy allows for this use in national parks.

Economic Impacts

Employment in person-years and income in wages, salaries, and business profits were the two economic indices used to measure economic impact. As the economic structure and diversity of the region is primarily resource based with some tourism service sector activity, the leakage of capital and operations and maintenance expenditures is substantial and the respending effects of income is limited. An estimated increase of 12 percent in direct and induced employment or 59 person-years would be generated by the establishment and operation of the park from 1984 to 1994. Direct and induced personal income and business profits would increase by some $1 million annually or 16 percent as a result of jobs and work created by the park (Figure 5).

Population Change Impacts

Because much of the hiring for the park would take place locally, the population change effects would be minimal. The change in population growth due to the park was projected at 7 percent and 12 percent for Lindsay and St. Edmunds Townships respectively (Figure 6).

The proposed park would more effectively stem the flow of out-migration from the region rather than draw newcomers. Such a situation would cause no threat to the existing social and political structure of the community.

The consultant does discuss the following point of interest:

> Of note is the fact that 23% of permanent residents in
> Lindsay and 17% in St. Edmunds said they would move out
> of the area if a Park was established. This seemed to be due
> to a strong desire for privacy and the assumption that there
> would be a large influx of tourists as a result of the Park.
> Since we only project a 7.5% increase in tourism, spread out
> over 10 years, we do not expect this exodus to materialize.
> (Williams, 1985:6)

Lifestyle Impacts

The detailed survey illustrated the correlation between the type of job an individual has or depends on and the person's perception of the park. Not surprisingly, St. Edmunds residents who depend on the tourism industry tended strongly to support the park proposal,whereas Lindsay residents who are more tied to the land and agriculture tended to take the opposite view. Therefore some 30 percent of St. Edmunds respondents said life would improve with the park, 41 percent said no change and 22 percent said life would worsen. The Lindsay Township results were almost the opposite with 17 percent indicating an improvement, 34 percent said no change and 40 percent said life would worsen with the park.

	Place of Business Lindsay St. Edmunds		Total Both Tosnwhips	Outside Area
PERSON-YEARS				
Current Employment (1984)	101	399	500	
No Park (Annual Average Years 1-10)	101	403	504	
With Park (Annual Average Years 1-10)	104	459	563	
(Annual Average in Year 11)	104	458	563	
Net Impact # % (Years 1-10)	+3 +3.0	+56 +14.1	+59 +11.8	14
PERSONAL INCOME (1984 $) (Wages, Salaries and Business Profits)				
Current (1984)			$6,233,000	
Net Addition due to Park: Average annual of Years 1-10			$1,005,900	$239,400
Impact %			+16.1%	
Year 11 $			$ 932,500	
Impact %			+15.0%	

Figure 5 Economic impacts of establishing the park (1984-1994)

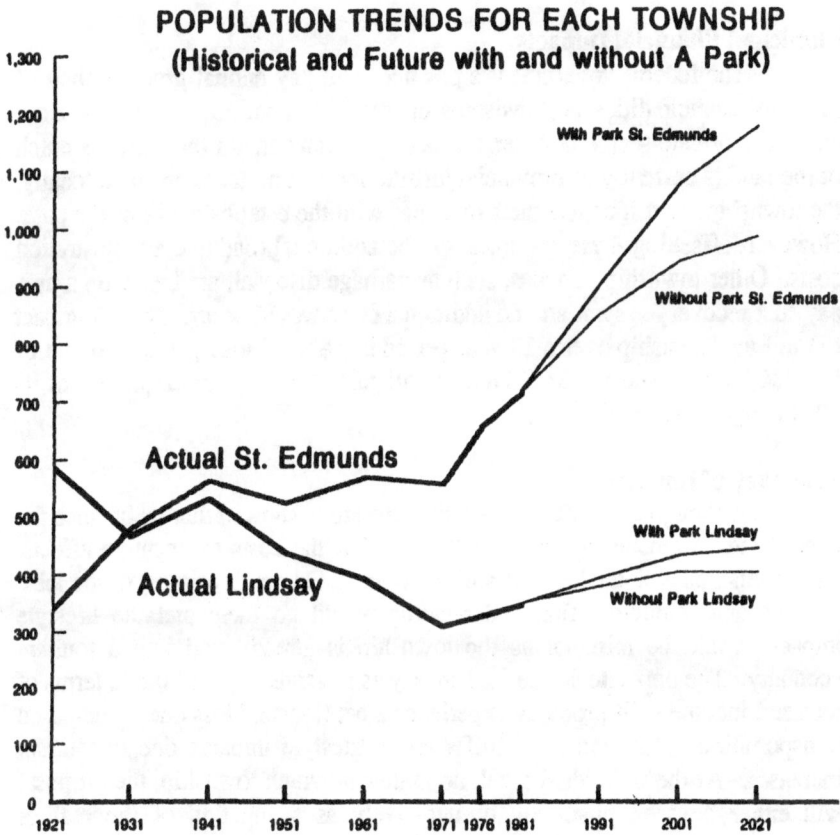

POPULATION TRENDS FOR EACH TOWNSHIP
(Historical and Future with and without A Park)

Figure 6   Economic impacts of establishing the park (1984-1994)

In sum, the research indicated that more employment would increase the standard of living, shopping opportunities would improve due to year round food and fuel services, some loss of privacy would occur, hunting opportunities would be lost affecting some one-third of the local residents, and recreational opportunities would increase.

Municipal Financial Impacts

The federal government's practice is to pay annual grants-in-lieu of taxes to municipalities or townships on property obtained for a park from either the private sector or other levels of government. In this case, as much of the land is currently in provincial jurisdiction and no taxes are paid locally, the townships will increase their revenues with the establishment of the park. However, offsetting these revenues will be additional road and administration costs. Other township services, such as garbage disposal, are based on a user pay cost recovery system and no additional costs would occur. The net impact to Lindsay Township over a 10-year period is a $3,000 loss or 0.07 percent of its 1984 budget, whereas St. Edmunds will gain $270,500 or 3.2 percent of its 1984 budget (Figure 7).

Summary of Impacts

Although difficult to generalize, the study showed that on balance the overall regional benefits appeared to outweigh the costs or negative effects. At a township level, the benefits split favored St. Edmunds as most of the jobs, income, and municipal financial benefits would go there and the lifestyle impacts would be minimal as the township is already tied into a tourism economy. The opposite is true for Lindsay as it stands to gain little in terms of jobs and income, will probably experience a net financial loss due to increased transportation costs, and may suffer some lifestyle impacts due to tourism increases. At the individual level, no matter in which township, the proposal will either be seen positively or negatively as a function of the real or perceived personal gain or loss derived from the park.

PUBLIC REACTION TO THE SEIA AND THE PROPOSED PARK

Before the study was finalized, the SEIA was presented to the townships' councils for review, comment, and amendment. On the whole, the study was relatively well received without major objection from Lindsay Township. The Township did not, however, agree with the modest tourism increase projections and felt that municipal finance impacts could be greater.

	LINDSAY (1984 $)	ST. EDMUNDS (1984 $)
ADDITIONAL EXPENSES	- 24,000	- 125,000
ADDITIONAL REVENUES	+ 21,160	+ 395,510
NET IMPACT	- 2,840	+ 270,510
1984 BUDGET (EXCLUDING OTHER LEVELS)	386,642	845,011
NET IMPACT - ANNUALIZED AS % OF 1984 BUDGET	- 0.07%	+ 3.2%

Figure 7   Municipal financial impact of establishing the park
(Total over 10 years 1984-1994)

St. Edmunds Township responded generally favorably and supported the conclusions. Both townships felt that the findings were objective and the study was appropriately conducted. The spilt in support between the two townships was not surprising given the allocation of positive and negative effects. Since the completion of the study the Township of Lindsay has, by plebiscite, rejected the proposed park. Before the completion of the SEIA, the township did not perceive the proposal in its best self-interest and SEIA confirmed that Lindsay stood to gain little from the park development. However, the SEIA also showed that the extreme negative effects of increased tourism feared by the township are not likely to occur.

The Minister of Environment, responsible for the Parks Service, responded to the township's wishes by removing the 25 percent of the proposal which is located in the Township. In this way, the Township will not be directly impacted, but given the road network into the region, some indirect minor effects of increased tourism may still be felt. Even with this withdrawal, the Township cannot be totally isolated from park development effects.

In fall of 1986, the Minister announced that federal/provincial negotiations were underway to finalize an agreement to establish a national park on the Bruce Peninsula in late 1986 or early 1987.

CONCLUSIONS

The study has shown the importance of SEIA in planning for the regional integration of parks. Results of the study showed that on a township level the benefits and negative effects were not allocated equitably. The role of the SEIA in affecting Lindsay Township's rejection of the proposed park is difficult to assess as the Township was not completely supportive from the outset. The SEIA did substantiate the Township's concerns and allowed the Parks Service to plan for the park accordingly. This study shows that national park planning and regional integration has come a long way since the troubled days of the 1960s and early 1970s.

In addition, the SEIA for the Bruce Peninsula park proposal has served interchangeably as an analytical tool to identify and assess socioeconomic change as well as an instrument of public participation. The survey upon which much of the study was based served as a forum to gauge a cross-section of public opinions and attitudes to the proposal.

The document was useful in promoting better understanding of the consequences of the proposal, and showing that neither the extreme positive effects (many jobs and income) nor extreme negative impacts (vast social disruption due to increases in tourism) held true. Rather, a more moderate range of social and economic benefits and costs was identified.

In conclusion, SEIA and properly conducted public surveys are effective techniques to measure public concerns as the methods used are generally reliable, representative, and unbiased. Other public participation techniques such as public meetings and workshops tend to, when controversy exists, draw out the extremes in public reaction thereby often muting the moderate view. The use of survey research as a public involvement technique has also been identified in the Canadian and U.S. experience as a useful tool for resolving resource conflicts (Jaakson 1985, Wellman and Farmy 1985).

ACKNOWLEDGMENTS

The opinions expressed in this article are those of the author and do not represent the views of the Parks Service of Environment Canada.

REFERENCES

Jaakson, R. 1985. "The Role of Surveys in Social Impact Assessment." In R. Jaakson, and V. Maclaren eds., *Environmental Impact Assessment; The Canadian Experience*. Toronto: University of Toronto Press. 191-225.

Parks Canada. 1982. *Parks Canada Policy*. Ottawa: Minister of Supply and Services Canada.

_____ 1983. *Management Directive 2.2.1*. Socio-Economic Analysis in Management Plans for National Parks. Ottawa: Parks Canada.

_____ 1986. *Management Directive 4.2.1*. National Parks Management Planning Process. Ottawa: Parks Canada.

Wellman, J. and P. Farmy. 1985. "Resolving Resource Conflict: The Role of Survey Research in Public Involvement Programs." *Environmental Impact Assessment Review 5:363-372*.

Williams, M. and J. Linton. 1985. *Socio-Economic Impact Assessment of the Proposed National Park on the Bruce Peninsula*. Toronto: Woods Gordon Management Consultants.

9

VISITOR ACTIVITY PLANNING AND MANAGEMENT IN CANADIAN NATIONAL PARKS: MARKETING WITHIN A CONTEXT OF INTEGRATION

Robert Graham
Department of Recreation and Leisure Studies
University of Waterloo

Per W. Nilsen
Department of Recreation and Leisure Studies
University of Waterloo

Robert J. Payne
Department of Geography
Wilfrid Laurier University

The legislated mandate of Environment Canada, Parks[1] is to protect for all time those places which are significant examples of Canada's national and cultural heritage and also to promote public understanding, appreciation and enjoyment of heritage in ways which leave the park or heritage site unimpaired for future generations (Parks Canada 1979a). The mandate is implemented through a network of national parks, historic parks, heritage canals, co-operative heritage areas and heritage rivers. There are currently 32 terrestrial national parks consisting of approximately 140,000 square kilometers (1.3 percent of the Canadian land mass). A policy to guide the implementation of National Marine Parks in 29 marine areas in the Arctic, Atlantic, Pacific and Great Lakes environments was recently approved (Environment Canada, Parks 1986).

Care of the physical, biological, cultural and historic resources in a national park is the primary concern or mandate of Parks. Among Canadians there is strong support for the continuation of national park programs and the mandate of Parks, but familiarity and use of national parks are not nearly as broadly based a phenomenon as was previously expected (Parks Canada 1984e). A recent government analysis (Neilsen Task Force Report 1986) recognizes the importance of these programs but suggests changes in the quantity and quality of service to the public. Concerns about the visitor, support facilities and related social and economic impacts are becoming significant as concerns about the resource. In 1983, socioeconomic analysis in management plans for national parks became an integral part of the park planning process (Parks Canada 1983, and Val This Volume). The socioeconomic analysis includes the effects of social and economic factors on visitor use, traditional use and regional integration which are relevant to the park's management plan. Examples of social and economic factors include population growth, mobility, recreation patterns, employment, income and economic base of the protected area undergoing either designation as a new national park, development of a management plan, or a 5-year review of an existing management plan.

The requirement in the mandate to protect heritage resources led Parks Canada to develop substantial objective data about natural and cultural resources within park boundaries but little about the dimensions and nature of human use. Canadian national park planning has reflected that protection bias with the result that issues related to the mix of opportunities, activities, services and facilities were neither well analyzed nor taken seriously. In practical terms, management action in national parks suffered. Facilities were located where they should not have been; mixed messages were sometimes given to visitors; facilities were sometimes too large or too small. Visitor activities evolved and Parks reacted without managing the explosive growth in recreation and leisure (Parks Canada 1982, 1984f, 1985a and b, Payne and Graham 1984, and Payne, Graham and Nilsen 1986).

A reawakening to the requirements of the mandate to consider both visitor issues and protection of heritage resources led to the development of the Visitor Activity Management Process (VAMP) (Parks Canada 1984b). VAMP provides a framework to ensure that visitor understanding, appreciation and enjoyment of the resources--the other side of the mandate--is just as carefully and systematically considered in the selection of new national parks or review of management plans for existing parks as protection for the natural resources. It is important to state that VAMP does not stand alone.

VAMP operates within a strong planning and management context as it represents how social science data are integrated within the National Parks Management Planning Process (Parks Canada 1986a) in Canada.

By connecting visitor opportunities and demands within the context of National Park Policy (1979) and National Marine Park Policy (1986), VAMP identifies the appropriate mix of opportunities, activities, services and facilities which may be provided in a national park. The VAMP framework is an appropriate response to the agency's mandate and strives to end the myth that a park can be all things to all people.

In the sections that follow, we briefly introduce Environment Canada, Parks' VAMP, illustrate its application through two case studies and conclude with a discussion which raises questions about aspects of VAMP's implementation in Canadian national parks.

VISITOR ACTIVITY MANAGEMENT PROCESS

Evolution of the Process

In the late 1960s and for some years afterwards, Parks Canada, like many national protected-area agencies, underwent tremendous growth (Harrison et al. 1982). During this growth period there appeared to be little need or time to manage the tension between the resource and the user. Most of the person-years and budget allocations were directed to expansion of the national park system. Meanwhile, non-governmental organizations and academics had turned their attention to the need for a planning system which would rationalize the policy objectives of preservation and use with operational management in the parks. Parks Canada had begun the development of Provisional Master Plans to describe existing and possible future park situations. These plans were dependent on natural resource information with little or no emphasis on the social sciences. Moreover, during this era, provincial and local tourist agencies began to advertise the natural splendor of national parks and the underlying theme that a park could meet all the needs of a complex public.

Parks' staff professionals began to openly express the feeling that the classic approach of educating the masses was not effectively presenting the agency's mandate, image and messages. Beginning in 1970, and culminating in 1975, a federal-provincial task force on interpretation attempted to answer the question: "What is wrong with interpretation and visitor services in parks?" The task force recommended a communications strategy based on marketing. Product definition was expressed in terms of resource values; market segmentation was based on definition of potential users, their behaviors and their needs; and organization/agency resources were based on mandates, management systems, staffing and finances. It was urged that:

> ... we must identify market segments, so that we can design communication systems that will reach each visitor segment before, during and after they [sic] have enjoyed parks (Federal-Provincial Parks Conference 1975:11).

At the same time, Parks Canada developed an Interpretation Planning Process. Unfortunately, the direction established by the federal-provincial task force was overlooked, and there was no attempt to link interpretation and visitor services directly to the agency's proposed Park Management Planning Process (Parks Canada 1975).

Subtle organizational changes within Parks Canada slowly began to reflect both sides of the policy mandate. Some of these changes included the emergence of the Socio-Economic Research Division, the creation of a Natural Resource Conservation Division which began the development of a framework for analysis and management of the natural resources and formulation of the Natural Resources Management Process (Parks Canada 1978a), the development of a rational basis for additions to the parks system (Parks Canada 1972), the three-year effort to clearly define a Park Management Planning Process (1975-1978), and a 15-year effort to answer the question of how best to respond to the need for the mix of opportunities, activities, services and facilities required by visitors.

In 1970, at the Federal Provincial Parks Conference, John Farina, one of Canada's early leisure researchers, made the statement that "parks people were out of touch with the general population--while parks are for people, what people have priority?" (1970:3). He suggested that parks were only one opportunity for the public's leisure activity and that parks agencies were competing with other public/private organizations for discretionary time. Moreover, he felt that if a park agency's mandate was not clearly communicated, parks would lose their traditional public support permanently. Parks Canada was described by Farina as "inward-oriented," "traditional" and "with no vision of the future in respect to leisure and recreation." Throughout the next 9 years, internal functional reviews, program reviews and task forces continually asked: "What is Parks Canada's business" and "how is the agency's business reflected in its planning and management?" Reviewers gradually realized that visitor services staff within the parks were operating and maintaining facilities rather than managing visitor opportunities, facilitating interpretation and encouraging public understanding, appreciation and enjoyment of natural and cultural heritage. Interpretation, and Visitor Services, in conjunction with the Socio-Economic Research Division, began a series of approximately 120 projects, studies, reviews of literature and meetings to formalize the visitor management component of the overall park management planning process. In an agency seemingly overloaded with management processes, another process was not greeted with open arms.

In 1979, Parks Canada selected a consultant to develop a senior management perspective on the issues related to visitor management (Brooks 1980). In the same year, Parks Canada's senior management approved and implemented a system, Project Initiation Planning System (PIPS), that required managers and planners to justify and substantiate the relationship between "ad hoc" projects and management planning (Parks Canada 1979b). Based on the 1980 Brooks report and subsequent approvals by the Program Management Committee, four draft versions of a management process for visitor activity were developed and tested to the point that nationwide staff training could begin in 1985. To date, three national training workshops and numerous regional and park-specific training efforts have been completed. An implementation strategy within current financial and human resources has been prepared.

VAMP is not a process by itself. It is a way to respond to the policy mandate and to senior management's vision of the need to be accountable and professional in decisions related to the development of recreation opportunities for heritage enjoyment. It also enables the manager to judiciously consider efficiency and effectiveness in terms of visitor opportunities and the selected markets they serve.

Generic Model

Parks' management planning program employs a traditional approach involving six steps: (1) objectives, (2) terms of reference, (3) database analysis, (4) concepts/options, (5) recommendations, (6) approval and implementation. This sequence is repeated for each planning cycle from new park proposals to operating park service plans (interpretation, visitor services, public safety, operations, etc.). The generic model for VAMP is depicted in Figure 1.

It must be emphasized that the VAMP model is bureaucratic in that it outlines a series of steps which must be followed and checked by management. VAMP has yet to develop the mechanisms which give a planning framework such as the Recreation Opportunity Spectrum (ROS) its power and internal coherence (USFS 1981, Clark and Stankey 1979, Driver and Brown 1983, Manfredo, Driver and Brown 1983).

The generic model has three components. The series of steps within which issues are identified and options advanced to deal with issues are supported by a database as well as management policy and directives.

154

Figure 1
GENERIC REPRESENTATION OF VAMP

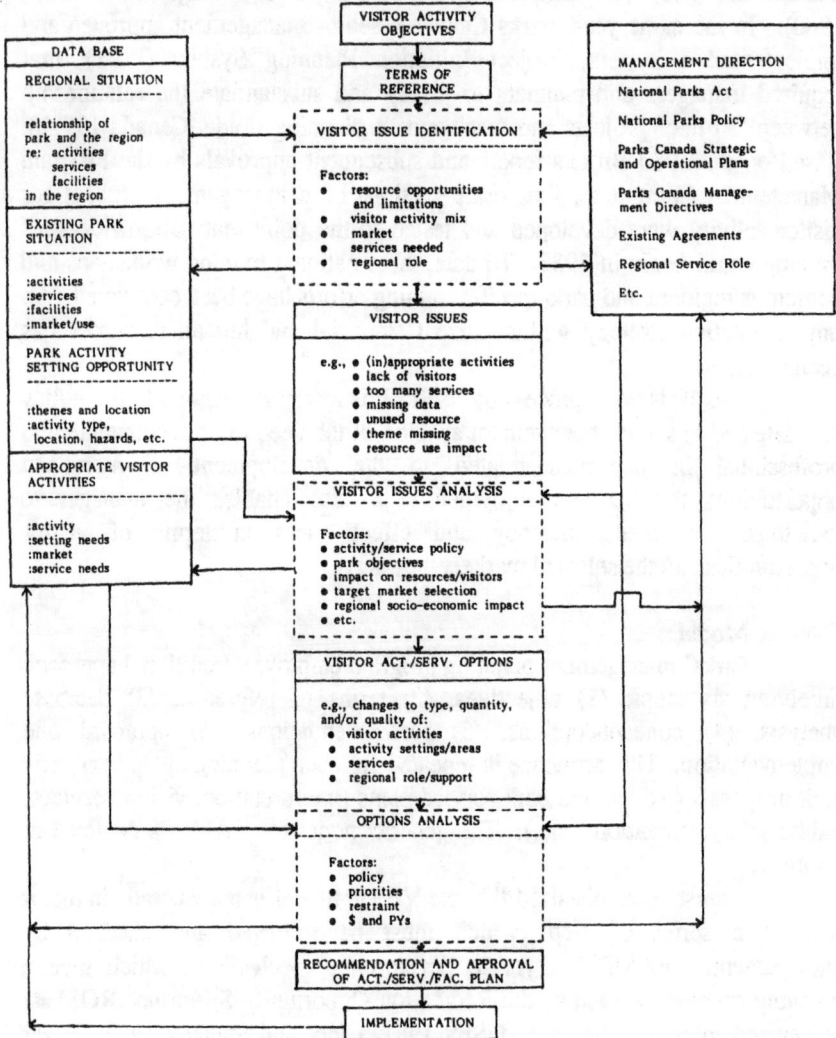

VISITOR ACTIVITY
OBJECTIVES

TERMS OF
REFERENCE

DATA BASE

REGIONAL SITUATION
----

relationship of
park and the region
re: activities
     services
     facilities
in the region

EXISTING PARK
SITUATION

:activities
:services
:facilities
:market/use

PARK ACTIVITY
SETTING OPPORTUNITY

:themes and location
:activity type,
 location, hazards, etc.

APPROPRIATE VISITOR
ACTIVITIES

:activity
:setting needs
:market
:service needs

MANAGEMENT DIRECTION

National Parks Act

National Parks Policy

Parks Canada Strategic
and Operational Plans

Parks Canada Manage-
ment Directives

Existing Agreements

Regional Service Role

Etc.

VISITOR ISSUE IDENTIFICATION

Factors:
• resource opportunities
  and limitations
• visitor activity mix
• market
• services needed
• regional role

VISITOR ISSUES

e.g., • (in)appropriate activities
      • lack of visitors
      • too many services
      • missing data
      • unused resource
      • theme missing
      • resource use impact

VISITOR ISSUES ANALYSIS

Factors:
• activity/service policy
• park objectives
• impact on resources/visitors
• target market selection
• regional socio-economic impact
• etc.

VISITOR ACT./SERV. OPTIONS

e.g., changes to type, quantity,
and/or quality of:
• visitor activities
• activity settings/areas
• services
• regional role/support

OPTIONS ANALYSIS

Factors:
• policy
• priorities
• restraint
• $ and PYs

RECOMMENDATION AND APPROVAL
OF ACT./SERV./FAC. PLAN

IMPLEMENTATION

This point VAMP begins to exhibit its capability to specify for managers the requirements for both supply and demand information. For information about visitors and use, it is logical to begin with what is known and what can be easily determined (e.g., the regional situation). Experiential, informal and indigenous knowledge all play an important part in the process. After determining what is known about the regional situation and existing use of the (proposed) national park, information on potential visitor activity markets is compiled. Natural and cultural resource information collected through the Natural Resources Management Process is inventoried and assessed to identify resource opportunities and constraints. The inclusion of such information in VAMP helps achieve an integration between visitor use and resource protection.

The bureaucratic basis of VAMP is illustrated clearly through the role of management. Management ensures that activities are compatible with national park policy. Moreover, critical decisions are made about the level of support that activities should receive in the national parks. The importance of management direction cannot be over-emphasized: it is to VAMP what carrying capacity is to the Recreation Opportunity Spectrum (ROS).

Management Contexts for Implementing VAMP

VAMP is currently being implemented in both new park proposals and in existing national parks. Implementation of VAMP in New Park Proposals (Figure 2) provides a statement termed Preliminary Evaluation of Visitor Activities (A.1). This preliminary analysis provides an understanding of the proposed park's visitor opportunities, associated market segments, local and regional socioeconomic issues and suggests preliminary development scenarios to be reviewed in a Social and Environmental Impact Assessment. By comparison, implementation of VAMP in existing national parks yields a more detailed discussion of issues and presentation of options (Figure 3). In turn, these options guide the selection of target markets, specify the public and private mix of recreation opportunities, activities, services and facilities, and guide the design and development of programs, services and facilities.

The accompanying figures also illustrate how VAMP is integrated with natural resource information by means of the National Park Management Planning Process (Parks Canada 1986a). An important component in each of the management contexts illustrated in Figures 2 and 3 is the Park Data Plan for visitor activities. It presents a specific program for the collection and updating of required relevant visitor activity data. In the past, visitor-use data were marked by confusion, inconsistent data collection procedures, and missing definitive user data, with no linkages to management planning.

156

Figure 2

NEW PARK PROPOSAL

Visitor Activity Management Process: Relationship To New Park Proposal Development and Other Management Processes

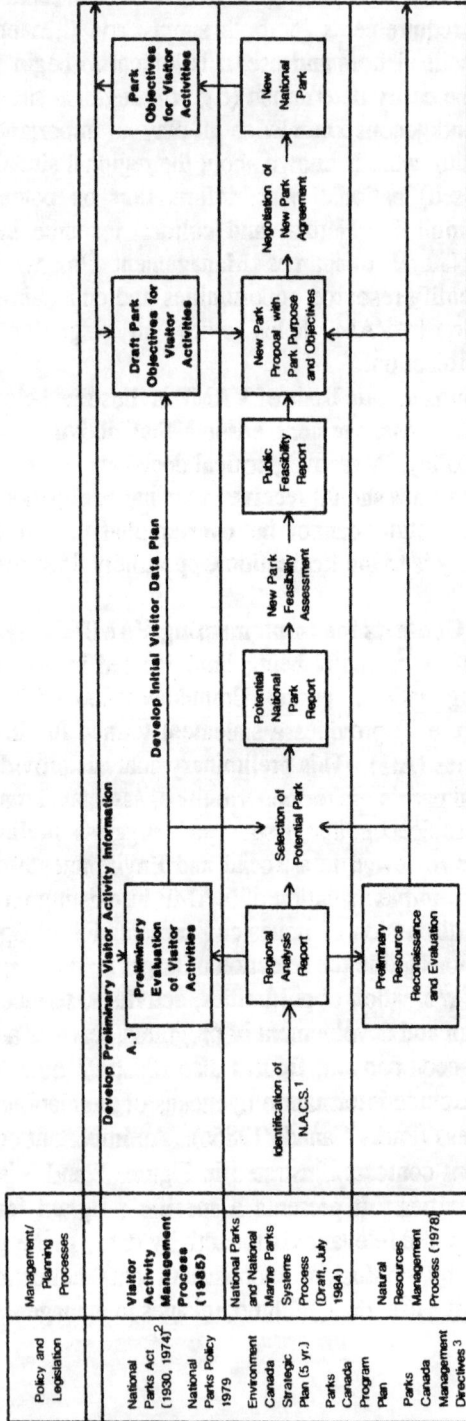

Policy and Legislation	Management/ Planning Processes

Develop Preliminary Visitor Activity Information

Develop Initial Visitor Data Plan

National Parks Act (1930, 1974)[2]

National Parks Policy 1979

Visitor Activity Management Process (1985)

Environment Canada Strategic Plan (5 yr.)

National Parks and National Marine Parks Systems Process (Draft, July 1984)

Parks Canada Program Plan

Parks Canada Management Directives[3]

Natural Resources Management Process (1978)

A.1 Preliminary Evaluation of Visitor Activities

Identification of N.A.C.S.[1]

Regional Analysis Report

Preliminary Resource Reconnaissance and Evaluation

Selection of Potential Park

Potential National Park Report

New Park Feasibility Assessment

Public Feasibility Report

Draft Park Objectives for Visitor Activities

New Park Proposal with Park Purpose and Objectives

Negotiation of New Park Agreement

Park Objectives for Visitor Activities

New National Park

1   N.A.C.S. Natural Area of Canadian Significance

2   Office Consolidation. National Parks Act, 1974 (R.S.,cN-13). Ministry of Supply and Services, 1978.

3   Parks Canada, 1983. Socio-Economic Analysis in Management Plans for National Parks. Management Directive 2.2.1. April. The completion of a socio-economic analysis is an integral part of the development of a New National Park Proposal.

A.1 Refers to a section in the Visitor Activity Management Process Manual (1985). Parks Canada.

157

Figure 3

ESTABLISHED PARKS WITH A PARK MANAGEMENT PLAN DEVELOPED
WITHOUT VISITOR ACTIVITY MANAGEMENT PROCESS INPUT

Visitor Activity Management Process: Relationship To Other Management/Planning Processes

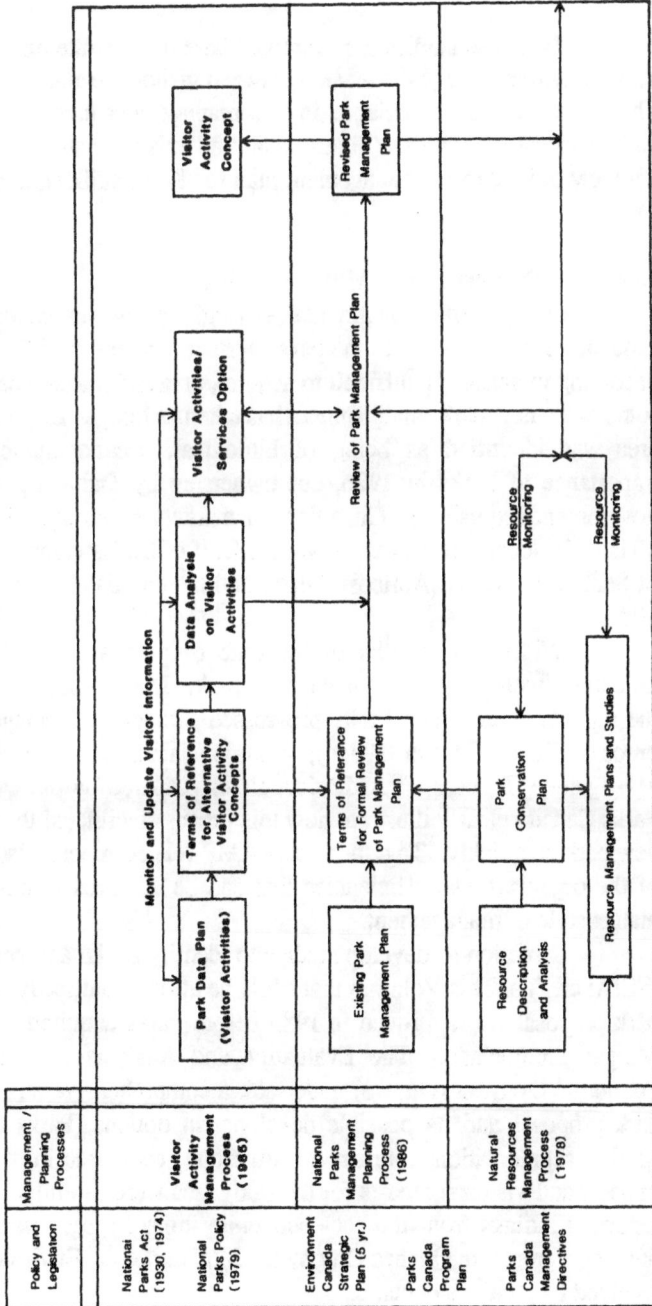

CASE STUDIES

Two case studies are presented here to illustrate how VAMP enables Parks to better manage the tension between visitor use and resource protection. The cases draw on experience in two management contexts: a new national park proposal for Mingan (Figure 2) and an existing national park undergoing a review of its current management plan for Kejimkujik National Park (Figure 3).

New Park Proposal: The Mingan Archipelago

One of the fundamental strategic problems facing Parks is the acquisition of new areas to the parks system. In an era of fiscal restraint it is becoming increasingly difficult to acquire, plan and manage new additions. In some cases new park establishment has taken as long as 15 years. The Mingan area was identified as being of biological, oceanographic and historical importance to Parks in 1926, but ownership by Dome Petroleum inhibited government acquisition. Changing oil markets encouraged Dome to sell the 40 islands, located in a chain along the Gulf of St. Lawrence north shore, east of Sept Iles between Anticosti Island and the mainland, to the government in 1983.

Within 18 months of the date of purchase, interim management guidelines were approved for the new park. Many variables were related to the rapidity with which Parks progressed through its management planning process (Parks Canada 1984c); a major factor was the Visitor Activity Management Process. VAMP documents prepared by the Quebec region of Parks Canada clearly illustrate how this process facilitated the planning of the new park so quickly. Together, the VAMP-related reports also illustrate some of the organizational efficiencies that can be acquired through the use of a matrix style of management.

Direction to develop studies to identify social and economic impacts (SEIA; cf., Val This Volume) that could be attributed directly or indirectly to a park proposal was approved in 1983 before Parks acquired ownership of the Mingan archipelago. The Evaluation and Analysis Branch of the Socio-Economic Division (Ottawa) undertook a comprehensive analysis of the new park proposal and its possible development options (Parks Canada 1984d). Market segmentation, tourism infrastructure, economic impacts, community impacts and visitor forecasts for the study area were carefully developed in the report. Findings from the socioeconomic impact assessment presented at a press conference in Quebec City by the Minister of the Environment were well received by local residents.

SEIA data and additional research required by the VAMP framework took the analysis to another level of specificity. A series of important firsts for a new park proposal was achieved with the utilization of SEIA data and the VAMP approach. These included a marked reduction in the size and number of visitor services and facilities suggested in the preliminary report for the proposed park, removal of proposed park services from within park boundaries to mainland areas, increased local support from native persons and residents of coastal communities, and identification and signing of tourism and regional development institutional arrangements and co-operative strategies before the park reached a concept stage. The VAMP approach also contributed to longer planning horizons and perspectives than previous new park proposal documents had. Scenarios for interpretation, visitor services, public safety and an initial park data plan for visitor activities were developed as part of the VAMP documentation.

In this management context (New Park Proposal), VAMP gave rise to a new awareness of the need for social science research to complement natural science data. The Mingan case is both unique and encouraging as undoubtedly in the future Parks will have occasion again to respond quickly to opportunities to establish new national parks. This application of VAMP sets the stage for subsequent park management planning and detailed service planning.

Existing Park Management Plan Review: Kejimkujik National Park
Kejimkujik is located in central, southwestern Nova Scotia. Its 380 square kilometer area was designated as a national park in 1967 to protect and manage a natural area of Canadian significance representing important features of the eastern Canadian Atlantic Coast Uplands. The gentle rolling landscape with numerous lakes interconnected by rivers provides excellent canoeing and backcountry camping opportunities. In addition, semi-serviced camping, group tenting, picnicking, winter camping and cross-country skiing opportunities attract approximately 210,000 visitors per year.

The Park Management Plan for Kejimkujik was completed in 1978 (Parks Canada 1978b). A major drawback of the plan was the lack of direction provided to guide the management of visitor use. Until the pilot work for VAMP was initiated (1982-1986) managers and planners had little knowledge about such matters as visitor socio-demographics, recreation behavior, program and activity preferences of visitors, motivations and levels of satisfaction, user perceptions of issues related to crowding, impacts and conflicts or the extent of customary use of the park.

The pilot work on visitor activities was completed in two phases. Phase I concentrated on the development of the visitor activity profile concept (Tayler 1981).   Activity profiles were developed from a summary and synthesis of existing theoretical and empirical literature and site-specific, informal knowledge.   The profiles represent a compilation of data which describes the participant (socio-demographics, expectations, preferences, motives and market segments), the activity (setting requirements, safety, equipment requirements, definition), market trends (existing and potential for growth, societal trends, activity trends), infrastructure requirements (levels of service for facilities, information requirements and setting requirements for on-site support services), strategic direction (Parks' policy, Park Management Plan, management directives, budget), management by other agencies and the private sector (who services what markets now and in the future), appropriateness of the activity (the profiles are tied to the policy mandate and the biophysical resources of the park), research requirements (what additional information needs to be collected), and sources of information (annotated bibliography, list of contacts and related information).

Detailed profiles on 26 park activities were subsequently prepared, initially from secondary analysis (library sources and existing data bases, e.g., Tourism Canada Research) and long-term park staff's experiential knowledge. Mullen (1982) argues that much of the value of profiling lies in the Park staff's involvement in the process, leading to increased understanding of the activities themselves and the Park's publics. The activity profiles themselves do not enter the decision-making process. Rather, each park and its management planning team decide what is appropriate for that park based on its resource capability, current use and the park's role in the regional recreation and tourism industry. This enables each park to match levels of service with its target markets and to downscale, retrofit or develop the appropriate levels of information and service to match specific user groups or target market requirements.

Phase II of the pilot work involved confirming what the final product of the project (a summer session Visitor Services Plan) would include, defining the process required to develop the strategy and identifying the research needed to complete the plan.

The major achievement of this pilot project was the definition of an activity-package concept for the national park. An activity package includes the identification of selected park specific visitor services (mix of opportunities, activities, services and facilities) designed to provide a certain segment of the park visitor population with a satisfactory experience.

This approach required segmentation of the total potential visitor population and definition of the major characteristics of significant target markets (Robertson and Wright 1983, Market Facts 1984). An activity package was then suggested for each segment that the park might serve subject to National Parks Policy, the Park Management Plan and other management directives.

The application of VAMP in this management context has provided Park staff with a more comprehensive understanding of the range of existing visitor activities and priorities for future management action. Additional requirements relating to visitor services for specific target markets were also summarized and options to address them were suggested. Finally, additional social and natural science information needs to guide future research were identified. The park undertook a regional visitor demand analysis in the summer of 1986 to assess its potential market and to address issues related to identified markets.

DISCUSSION

Canadian national park planning and management has been substantially improved by the recognition through VAMP that social science, the techniques of marketing for non-profit agencies, and management information systems aid in understanding, communicating and serving the public. As a management process, VAMP assists in streamlining data collection, identifying revenue potential, specifying opportunities for volunteer involvement, reappraising scale of development, communicating more effectively with publics, and improving visitor satisfaction. However, some reflections seem appropriate.

VAMP remains a new management framework with only limited application in Canadian national parks. A series of organizational and technical barriers may impede the implementation of VAMP in national park planning.

The framework is bureaucratic in nature, a fact which might result in VAMP becoming an end in itself, merely used to justify the design and development of services, programs, infrastructure and facilities. While such justification is an important consideration on economic grounds, VAMP must also be integrated effectively with the other management process, the Natural Resources Management Process (Parks Canada 1978a) and with the existing National Parks Management Planning Process (Parks Canada 1986a and b). Neither VAMP nor the Natural Resources Management Processes are planning frameworks. They are management processes which identify and acquire social and natural science data required by the National Parks Management Planning Process. In effect, the two management processes support a planning framework for national parks. The tradition that the life sciences, archaeology, history, and earth science dictate park and protected area planning is a historic bias within Environment Canada, Parks which must be overcome if the VAMP framework is not to create additional problems for park planning and management.

At present, VAMP remains a framework, a skeleton in need of further development to establish a technical capability. The absence of a technical capability has created uncertainty and problems for planners and managers in the national parks, especially in those parks such as Kejimkujik which have been established for some time and are undergoing management plan reviews. The development of a technical capability is clearly required, but currently poses considerable organizational problems for Parks.

Surprisingly, VAMP is seen by senior Canadian national park management as going farther than the ROS framework. In using marketing concepts and techniques, especially in the development of service plans (interpretation, visitor services and public safety), VAMP offers progress in areas where difficulties have been encountered when ROS has been applied. However, differences in the two frameworks (ROS and VAMP) are rather more subtle than this obvious difference. There is a need to review and examine their similar roots in theoretical and empirical literature, and the connections between them.

Implementing VAMP will present Parks with technical and organizational problems with respect to the current preservation and use zoning system. No capability exists, at present, in the Park Management Planning Process to reconcile VAMP input with park zones. Activities identified by VAMP may lead to environmental impacts not identified by either the Natural Resources Management Process or the planning process. Impacts which threaten the heritage values of the park will require a review consistent with the current Canadian Environmental Assessment and Review Process.

CONCLUSION

In conclusion, VAMP offers the potential to integrate social science and natural science data in national park planning and management. That potential is illustrated in this paper by case studies which indicate how, in the case of Mingan, a proposal for a new park was enhanced by the data developed by the VAMP framework. In the case of Kejimkujik, an existing park, VAMP's role has been to more precisely identify visitors' motivations and recreation behavior, necessary changes in levels of service for the park's publics, and future research needs of the park. VAMP helped remedy a major data gap in the existing park management plan.

As favorable as these results are as testimony to VAMP's potential, it must be pointed out that a number of serious problems have yet to be overcome. The requirement to reconcile VAMP input with the existing zoning system, the need to develop a technical capability for the framework and the danger of further entrenchment of VAMP as a bureaucratic process unto itself are major obstacles to an effective integration of social and natural science data in Parks' management planning process for Canadian national parks.

ACKNOWLEDGMENTS

We wish to acknowledge the helpful comments on an earlier draft of this paper by John Carruthers, Liaison Officer, Heritage Resources Centre, University of Waterloo; Grant Tayler, Head of Interpretation, Environment Canada, Parks, Ottawa; Scott Meis, Chief, Socio-Economic Information, Environment Canada, Parks, Ottawa, and Dave Redekop, Acting Chief, Evaluation and Analysis Division, Environment Canada, Parks, Ottawa. Our special thanks go to Pam Schaus who produced the figures and Jo-Anne Horton, Pam Fawcett and Karri Deckert who typed (and re-typed) the manuscript. The information base on which this paper was developed includes comments, interviews and discussions related to supported work by Environment Canada, Parks. This paper was not prepared for Environment Canada, Parks. Any errors or omissions are those of the authors alone.

NOTES

1. During the summer of 1986, Parks Canada officially changed its name to Environment Canada, Parks.

REFERENCES

Brooks, L. 1980. *The Role of National Parks*. Internal Document. Ottawa: Parks Canada.

Clark, R.N. and G.H. Stankey. 1979. *The Recreation Opportunity Spectrum: A Framework for Planning Management and Research*. General Technical Report. PNW-98. Portland, OR: U.S. Department of Agriculture, Forest Service, Pacific Northwest Forest and Range Experiment Station.

Driver, B. and P.J. Brown. 1983. "Contributions of Behavioral Scientists to Recreation Resource Management." In J. Altman and J.F. Wohlwill (eds.), *Behavior and the Natural Environment*. New York: Plenum Press. 307-339.

Environment Canada, Parks. 1986. *National Marine Park Policy*. Ottawa: Parks Canada.

Farina, J. 1970. "Parks and Leisure Behaviour." In *Proceedings: Federal Provincial Parks Conference*. Ottawa: Parks Canada. 3-9.

Federal-Provincial Parks Conference Proceedings. 1975. *Task Force Report on Interpretation*. Ottawa: Parks Canada.

Harrison, J., K. Miller and J. McNeeley. 1982. "World Coverage of Protected Areas: Development Goals and Environmental Needs." *Ambio* 11:238-246.

Manfredo, M.J., B.L. Driver, and P.J. Brown. 1983. "A Test of Concepts Inherent in Experience-Based Setting Management for Outdoor Recreation Areas." *Journal of Leisure Research* 15:263-283.

Market Facts. 1984. *Kejimkujik Visitor Survey: Summer, 1982*. Socio-Economic Branch, Headquarters, Ottawa: Parks Canada.

Mullen, E. 1982. Final Report: Recreation Activity Planning Project, Kejimkujik National Park. Halifax: Wildland Associates.

Neilsen Task Force. 1986. *Environment: Improved Program Delivery.* Ottawa: Government of Canada.

Parks Canada. 1972. *National Parks System Planning Manual.* Systems Planning Branch, Ottawa: Parks Canada.

_____ 1975. *A Proposal for Park Management Planning.* Ottawa: Parks Canada.

_____ 1978a. *Natural Resources Management Process.* Ottawa: Parks Canada.

_____ 1978b. *Management Plan: Kejimkujik National Park.* Atlantic Region, Halifax: Parks Canada.

_____ 1979a. *Parks Canada Policy.* Ottawa: Parks Canada.

_____ 1979b. *Project Initiation Planning System.* Ottawa: Parks Canada.

_____ 1982. *Roles and Responsibilities (1979-1982).* Internal Report, Parks Canada. Ottawa: Parks Canada.

_____ 1983. *Directive 2.2.1; Socio-Economic Analysis in Management Plans for National Parks.* Ottawa: Parks Canada.

_____ 1984a. *National Parks and National Marine Parks Systems Process.* Draft. Ottawa: Parks Canada.

_____ 1984b. *Management Process for Visitor Activity.* Draft. Ottawa: Parks Canada.

_____ 1984c. *Mingan: Park Feasibility Studies.* Quebec Region, Quebec: Parks Canada.

_____ 1984d. *Impact Socio-Economique Local et Regional de la Creation d'un Parc National en Minganie.* Ottawa: Parks Canada.

_____ 1984e. "Canadians' Familiarity and Involvement with National Parks." Paper presented at the 9th Annual Meeting of the Canadian Association of Applied Research. Learned Societies Conference. Guelph, Ontario. Ottawa: Parks Canada.

_____ 1984f. *A Based Review*. Internal Report. Ottawa: Parks Canada.

_____ 1985a. *Internal Organizational Management Study (1982-1985)*. Internal Report, Parks Canada. Ottawa: Parks Canada.

_____ 1985b. *Management Information Framework (1979-1985)*. Internal Report, Parks Canada. Ottawa: Parks Canada.

_____ 1986a. *National Parks Management Planning Process Manual*. Ottawa: Parks Canada.

_____ 1986b. *In Trust for Tomorrow: A Management Framework for Four Mountain Parks*. Western Region, Parks Canada. Calgary: Parks Canada.

Payne, R.J. and R. Graham. 1984. "Towards an Integrated Approach to Inventory, Planning and Management of Parks and Protected Areas." *Park News* 20(4):20-32.

Payne, R.J., R. Graham and P.W. Nilsen. 1986. *Preliminary Assessment of the Visitor Activity Management Process (VAMP)*. A Technical Report prepared for Parks Canada Interpretation and Visitor Services. National Parks Branch. Ottawa: Parks Canada.

Robertson, S. and A. Wright. 1983. *Kejimkujik Visitor Survey*. Atlantic Region, Parks Canada. Halifax: Parks Canada.

Tayler, G. 1981. *A Management Process for National Parks Visitor Activities*. Ottawa: Parks Canada.

U.S. Forest Service (USFS). 1981. *Recreation Opportunity Spectrum User's Guide*. Washington, D.C.: U.S. Department of Agriculture.

10

A PLANNING APPROACH TO SOCIAL CARRYING CAPACITY RESEARCH FOR ARAVAIPA CANYON WILDERNESS, ARIZONA

Steven D. Moore
School of Renewable Natural Resources
University of Arizona

Stanley K. Brickler
School of Renewable Natural Resources
University of Arizona

Social scientists and natural resource managers often belong to two different professional communities, each with separate values, different reward systems, and different languages. Scientists value the sanctity of scientific endeavor; are judged and rewarded on the technical merit and originality of their publications; and speak and write in a language of theoretical, methodological, philosophical, and statistical jargon. Managers, on the other hand, value the mandates of the people; are judged and rewarded by their success in juggling legal and political imperatives; and speak in the practical lingo of field application.

With these differences, the two groups often have difficulty communicating with each other. Each group is motivated to view resource management issues from different perspectives: scientists view issues as interesting topics for research and thus focus on theoretical aspects of the problem; managers, who are on the "front lines" of resource management, view issues as hurdles that potentially complicate successful site management, and thus they focus on immediate, practical solutions. Because of these divergent perspectives, applied social science research often yields unsatisfactory results in the manager's perspective: the data and analyses produced simply do not address pertinent management questions and concerns.

Collaborative efforts during the research process, particularly during formative stages, can help overcome this problem. In this article, using social carrying capacity (SCC) and wilderness management as the focus of our discussion, we emphasize the need for collaborative efforts in designing applied research on natural resource issues. First, we examine how requirements for SCC determinations in wilderness management plans may cause managers to seek the assistance of researchers. Next, we discuss how that assistance may or may not be beneficial to managers and suggest an approach to research that helps integrate the diverse interests of scientists and managers. Finally, we present our efforts at applying this approach to ongoing SCC research at Aravaipa Canyon Wilderness in Arizona.

ROLE OF SCC RESEARCH IN WILDERNESS MANAGEMENT PLANNING

SCC plays a key role in wilderness management planning--a role, however, that often bewilders resource professionals. Based on a simple concept--the "level of recreational use an area can withstand while providing a sustained quality of recreation" (Wagar 1964:3)--SCC tantalizes resource managers wishing to set scientifically defensible limitations on recreational use in wilderness areas facing overcrowding or overuse. So tantalizing has the concept been that most federal agencies responsible for wilderness management require carrying capacity determinations for their areas.[1] Consequently, SCC, or a derivative,[2] is the focus of many wilderness management plans. Management of visitation levels is often regarded as a paramount concern by wilderness managers.

Unfortunately for those involved in wilderness management planning, SCC determinations are exceedingly complex. Research over the past 20 years has demonstrated no simple relationship between recreational use and many measures of wilderness quality (Graefe *et al.* 1984). Rather, numerous factors have been uncovered that may be considered in determining SCC. First, and probably most important, wilderness quality, as with beauty, is only in the mind of the beholder. Visitors bring to wilderness areas very individualized standards of what constitutes a quality recreation experience.

Consequently, determination of a level of use that sustains a certain quality of wilderness recreation depends on who is doing the recreating.

Second, "quality" may be defined in a number of ways. It could mean enjoying a certain degree of solitude, meeting pleasant people, not encountering a lot of trash while hiking, or seeing lots of wildlife. Any environmental factor that can be influenced by people can become a variable in a SCC determination. Finally, perceptions of quality and tolerance of impacts by the beholder are influenced by the activity being pursued, by the season of the year, and by location within the wilderness area.

Accordingly, the wilderness manager must integrate a complex array of user-impact relationships in arriving at a SCC determination. Because of the individual nature of perceptions of wilderness quality, value laden judgments must also enter into this determination. Faced with such complexity and challenged by divergent user groups competing for access to a wilderness area, the wilderness manager may be reluctant to make a SCC decision. Indeed, Washburne (1981) reports that in a recent survey of resource professionals in the National Wilderness Preservation System, 46 percent felt unable to estimate capacities for their areas. Only 16 percent of the managers responding to the survey had calculated capacities.

Managers may respond to the challenge of determining SCC by turning to social scientists for technical assistance. Social scientists, by investigating the factors that influence SCC, can play a key role in facilitating and influencing wilderness management planning. The information, analyses, and recommendations provided by researchers can significantly influence development of capacity limits for a wilderness area.

The extent of this influence, however, should be carefully circumscribed. Establishment of carrying capacities is "always an issue for politics, not a matter for decision by science" (Burch 1984:494). Thus, the manager should not regard research assistance as the final answer on a carrying capacity limit. Research is but one input into a planning process that should include input from the public and from within the managing agency itself. One alternative is for the researcher to divorce him or herself from the policy component of the carrying capacity decision and simply "describe the social and ecological consequences of alternative use levels...", and not "supply answers about what the carrying capacity of a site is or should be" (Stankey 1979:52). At the other end of the spectrum is the alternative role of the researcher as policy-maker, conducting research and making recommendations that will become policies themselves.

We believe in a balanced perspective between these two extremes. The researcher should be more than a passive provider of information requested by management. On the other hand the researcher should not assume a role that usurps managerial prerogatives. Manager and researcher should work together to develop a research program that addresses the diverse inputs that enter into a SCC decision. Care should be taken to ensure that (a) the researcher is providing valuable input into the process, and (b) that the manager is getting the information he or she needs. One way of achieving this balanced perspective is to follow a planning approach to social carrying capacity research.

A PLANNING APPROACH TO DESIGNING SCC RESEARCH

A typical approach to applied social research in natural resource settings involves minimal researcher-manager interaction. The managing agency identifies a need for research to address some management concern. A call for proposals is issued. Proposals outlining in detail a research theory, design, and methodology are prepared and submitted for review. The managing agency then selects a proposal and research is initiated. When the research is completed, a report is submitted to management. Few substantive contacts occur between the researcher and the manager during this process. The scientist assumes that he or she knows what the manager wants and can deliver the needed information.

Lack of coordination and communication between the researcher and manager, particularly during the formative stages of research, can lead to discrepancies between results desired and results obtained by the manager. A significant drawback to the research process depicted above is that the research problem may not be well formulated in the minds of managers when the call for proposals is issued. A need for research is felt but, often, the specifics are not worked out. The manager relies on the experience and judgment of the researcher to interpret his or her felt need appropriately and to come up with a relevant approach to conducting research.

Too often, however, the researcher is well separated from the management situation. The research institution may be situated away from the study site. The researcher may have only visited the site a few times, if at all, before designing the research. Contacts with management personnel, except with the individuals coordinating the proposal effort, may have been brief or nonexistent. Unfamiliar with the details of on-site management, the researcher may misinterpret or miss altogether pertinent management issues, challenges, and logistics and come up with a research design that looks good to the manager, but does not address the entire realm of the management problem.

A planning approach to research design can overcome some of these difficulties. Incorporating a planning structure into the formative stages of research is a good way of promoting coordination and communication between researchers and managers. By use of the term "planning approach," we mean incorporation of a formalized process for facilitating interaction between researchers and managers after the contract has been awarded but before field research has begun. Thus, much like the public participation stages of agency planning processes, coordination and collaboration are built into the research process.

This approach to applied social research, which has been termed "action research," has four basic characteristics (Ketterer, *et al.* 1980):

1. A problem focus. The research is designed to address specific problems faced by managers of a social system. "Unlike traditional research, action research...seeks out social problems and issues that can serve as the context for continuing research, action, and evaluation activities." A theoretical perspective is not lost by this focus; the practical situation is viewed as situs for developing and testing theory.

2. Collaboration between researchers and managers. Action research attempts to bridge the gap between researchers and managers. Consequently, managers become involved in nearly every aspect of the research effort: design of the research, selection of the variables to be studied, determination of the types of field techniques to be used, and evaluation of the types of data analysis to be attempted.

3. Development of scientific and practical knowledge. Five types of knowledge are produced by action research. First, scientists and managers, working together, try to make sense out of confusing or complex managerial problems or social phenomena. New ways of looking at such problems or phenomena may be the output of this process. Second, descriptive information is produced that has direct managerial value. Third, through research, factors are identified that influence delivery of social services (e.g., wilderness experiences) to clients (e.g., wilderness visitors). Fourth, prescriptive guidelines for managerial action (e.g., implementation of a management plan) are generated from action research. Fifth, research methods and analytical tools are developed that can be applied in other settings.

4. Promoting use of research. Steps are taken to ensure that the research is actually used by management. First, collaboration between researchers and managers promotes a stewardship role on the part of both parties. The researchers develop a true affinity for managerial problems and a sense of responsibility toward their ultimate solution. The managers feel that they are part of the research team and work to apply the results of their efforts in the field. Second, the research effort is broadly defined so as to incorporate a spectrum of managerial concerns. Third, feedback is continually provided to managers by researchers about the research process and about preliminary results of data collection. In this manner, over time, the manager becomes comfortable with conceptualizing, and possibly applying in stages, research findings. Finally, the results of the research process are presented clearly and unambiguously. This further eases field application.

AN APPLICATION

During 1985 and 1986, we had the opportunity to apply this planning approach to SCC research. In 1985, the School of Renewable Natural Resources at the University of Arizona (UA) entered into a cooperative agreement with the Bureau of Land Management (BLM), Safford District, to determine the recreational carrying capacity of Aravaipa Canyon Wilderness (ACW), Arizona. Because Aravaipa Canyon has long been regarded as a significant ecological as well as recreational resource, a use limitation of 50 persons at any one time and a permit and reservation system was implemented over 10 years ago. The use limitation was based on a qualitative hunch; no systematic evaluation had ever been made in arriving at the limitation. With wilderness designation in 1984 and consequent need for development of a management plan, the BLM became interested in a scientific evaluation of its use limitation.

The first year of this ongoing, 3-year effort was oriented primarily toward planning and coordinating activities. This section of the paper addresses only those activities that took place during this first year. Many activities and tools were employed during the year which aided establishment of an atmosphere of coordination and collaboration, most of which are common in applied research settings: phone conversations, meetings, and quarterly reports. One activity which proved to be helpful to the research was a formalized, issue identification process.

Issue identification is a typical first step in rational planning processes. Its purpose is to draw out (typically from the public) any concerns or problems that deserve attention in the planning effort. We incorporated issue identification as the first step of our research process. (Other planning steps--formulation of research goals and objectives, and development of a research design--which were also accomplished during the first year of the research project will not be discussed in this paper.) Taking approximately six months to complete, the issue identification step used four tools: field reconnaissance, review of agency documents, attendance at public scoping sessions, and agency review and comment.

Field Reconnaissance
We visited ACW on numerous occasions to familiarize ourselves with the resource, to observe visitors, and to have informal conversations with visitors and on-site personnel. On many trips BLM administrative staff joined us to offer their impressions of social carrying capacity issues and to facilitate formation of a researcher-manager partnership. Observations from our field experiences as participant-observers were compiled and organized into a set of fieldnotes.

The knowledge gained from field reconnaissance fell into three general categories: familiarity with the recreational setting, visitor behavior patterns and attitudes, and administrative procedures.

1. Familiarity with the recreational setting. Located within the Lower Sonoran Desert, ACW features a unique riparian ecosystem that supports an unusual diversity and abundance of plant and animal life. Cottonwoods, sycamores, Arizona walnuts, mesquite, and box elder line Aravaipa Creek and inhabit the nine side canyons of Aravaipa Canyon, providing cover and food for 25 mammal, 35 reptile, 9 fish, 6 amphibian, and 202 bird species (BLM 1979). A number of the plants and animals inhabiting ACW are threatened or endangered. Standing in contrast to the verdant riparian system of the canyon bottoms is the Sonoran Desert landscape of the canyon walls and rocky slopes. Saguaro, cholla, barrel cactus, gila monsters, desert bighorn sheep, and other plants and animals of the desert manage a living there. This contrast and the other desirable characteristics of this 7,000-acre wilderness area create a unique setting for recreation, attracting more than 3,000 visitors annually.

As social scientists, we felt it imperative to get to know the recreational value of ACW from the perspective of a visitor. Accordingly, we participated on numerous occasions in the various activities available there: hiking, backpacking, birdwatching and other wildlife observation, swimming, horseback riding, and rock climbing. Admittedly, participation in these activities was an enjoyable aspect of the research effort. Without such participation, however, development of our survey instrument and other measurement tools might not have been as relevant to on-site conditions.

Our observations, combined with information gained through interactions with visitors, allowed us to make some preliminary judgments of which natural attributes are important to visitors: the abundance of perennial water, outstanding scenery, a relatively unimpacted setting, and excellent opportunities for viewing wildlife. We also got a general feel for the typical wilderness clientele: small groups of friends, some families, many organized groups, a few hunters, and a large number of wildlife observers.

2. Visitor behavior patterns and attitudes. Conversations with visitors on-site and with management personnel uncovered some regularities in visitor behavior patterns. Most visitors restrict their stays to the 11-mile-long canyon corridor. Many visitors interviewed during field trips were either unaware of opportunities available outside of the canyon corridor or were reluctant to travel out of the corridor because of the hazards (real or imagined) involved. One scout leader commented that he restricted his troop to the corridor because of danger from rattlesnakes in the side canyons. Only more adventurous visitors visit the nine side canyons of ACW. Because of limited access from the corridor, few visitors use the rimlands above the canyon. Hunters who access the zone via jeep trails to the wilderness boundary appear to be the primary users of the rimlands.

In light of these regularities, we divided ACW into three recreation opportunity zones: corridor, side canyon, and rimlands. Visitor use of and attitudes about these zones were identified as significant management issues. Instrumental to establishment, implementation, and monitoring of management standards will be understanding visitors' affective and behavioral responses to conditions encountered in the three opportunity zones. Research in many settings has demonstrated relationships between contact with various social and environmental conditions and visitors' ratings of the quality of their recreational experience (cf., Lee 1975). Thus, an important affective response we might investigate at ACW would be the perceived influence of human presence on wildlife populations and viewing opportunities. Behavioral responses worthy of study might include actions taken by visitors to correct perceived deficiencies in their environment: migrating to other zones of the wilderness, complaining to rangers, or ceasing to visit the area altogether.

3. Administrative Procedures. BLM activities influence visitors' recreational experiences by modifying setting attributes and thus modifying recreation opportunities in the wilderness area. The BLM manipulates setting attributes in ACW by controlling use levels, by allocating recreation opportunities among competing users through its permit and reservation system, and by its presence on-site. Controlling use levels controls the frequency of social contacts visitors can have and, to a certain extent, determines how much environmental impact is evident. Allocating recreation opportunities controls the types of social contacts visitors can have. Contact with a ranger on patrol, depending on the viewpoint of the visitors, provides either a positive or negative contribution to the social setting.

During our field visits, we found visitors to be generally satisfied with the social and environmental conditions they had found at ACW. Some people, however, complained that the area was too crowded. Most visitors appeared to support the permit and reservation system. Few seemed to respond negatively to the presence of rangers (although this response was not observed many times).

Review of Agency Documents

Office files were made available to us by the BLM. Examination of this in-house data source helped us develop a historical perspective on characteristics of the recreational setting at ACW. In particular, useful insights came from a 15-year file of trailhead register sheets, a newspaper and magazine clippings file, visitation data, and research reports on the biological components of ACW. From visitation data we observed seasonal and spatial patterns of use, and trends in annual visitation rates. From the register sheets, we were able to note qualitative changes in visitors' comments over time. The clippings file yielded magazine and newspaper stories dating back 30 years. Reading these stories provided us with an important base for understanding influences that form public opinion regarding ACW. Finally, from available reports on the biology of ACW, we came to a basic understanding of the ecological functioning of the wilderness resource, particularly the function of seasonal and catastrophic floods in renewing the canyon bottoms.

Attendance at Public Scoping Sessions

BLM policy requires public input into wilderness management planning (BLM 1984). The BLM used scoping sessions (informal question and answer periods) to fulfill this requirement. We were fortunate to have these sessions fall within our issue identification step. Attendance at and participation in these sessions both as concerned citizens and as researchers provided us with valuable insights. Critical concerns voiced during the scoping sessions included (a) conflicts between local residents and wilderness users as use levels increase, (b) hazards to visitors from hunting within Aravaipa Canyon, and (c) danger and annoyance to visitors and wildlife from military training flights over the wilderness.

Agency Review and Comment

A formal, agency review and comment process was used to arrive at a consensus regarding issues for research. The information obtained from previous efforts (combined with a literature review) was compiled into a document and submitted to the BLM. In turn, the BLM distributed the document for internal review by resource area personnel, the district recreation staff, field scientists, and an anthropologist. A meeting was then held between representatives of the BLM and the UA research team to clarify and discuss the issues, and to arrive at a preliminary consensus on key issues. The BLM then compiled the written responses of its reviewers and submitted them for review by the UA. A final meeting achieved a consensus on the issues.

The review and comment process was the most fruitful of the issue identification steps. Both the BLM and the UA gained a substantial education as a result. The BLM, who had originally viewed carrying capacity research as a technical, but straightforward, process leading to a single capacity figure, became familiar with the true complexities involved. After learning about the breadth of the proposed research, they became very enthusiastic about the value to their management mission of the information they would be obtaining. UA researchers, who had previously been acquainted with the BLM on only a superficial level, quickly learned about BLM policy, mandates, operating procedures, and external pressures.

This process of mutual education succeeded primarily because of the opportunities for interaction that the review and comment process provided. The issues document became the basis for phone conversations and meetings in which the participants began to understand and speak each other's language. Having done this, future efforts in the research design phase were facilitated.

DISCUSSION

None of the tools explained above are new to either the applied research or resource management fields. Many readers of this article probably apply or have applied these tools on research projects. Some, having faced more complex situations, have probably applied more sophisticated tools.

Our message, then, is simple and well known, but one that cannot be repeated too often: the basic task in applied research is to facilitate the flow of communication between researchers and management personnel. The best way of improving communication is for each participant in the research project to assume, to a certain degree, the role of the other participant. Each participant thereby becomes committed to the success of the other and the four benefits of action research described previously can be achieved: addressing and solving real management problems, bridging the gap between researchers and managers, developing scientific and practical knowledge by looking at problems in new ways, and promoting utilization of the research findings.

Our research, to date, has already enjoyed these four benefits. By working closely with the BLM for an extended period of time, we have discovered management problems and concerns that were not apparent when we initiated the research project. We have come to understand each other's language. We believe that, through collaborative efforts, we have developed a research approach that will address practical field problems while contributing new scientific knowledge. Finally, and very importantly, we have already influenced the BLM to look at its management challenges in new ways, setting the stage for better utilization of our research findings.

CONCLUSION

Coordination, communication, and collaboration during the formative stages of research can facilitate development of a research approach that accommodates the divergent values and reward systems of social scientists and resource managers. Various tools are available to achieve this accommodation. We found the issue identification process to be particularly useful. The substantive dialogues between researchers and managers that these tools promote can bridge critical language gaps--gaps that can block field application of research findings by managers.

Commitment to a planning approach to research requires investments of time and effort that might not be required otherwise, but that invested effort pays dividends. The researcher and manager become partners in research, each partner contributing specialized knowledge to help define the research problem. This partnership, if developed properly, can last and continue to pay dividends to each partner long after the final report has been prepared.

NOTES

1. Forest Service regulations require carrying capacity determinations for wilderness areas (Federal Register 1979). Bureau of Land Management regulations require use capacities and limits of acceptable change (see note 2 below) to be determined as part of wilderness planning efforts (BLM 1983). The National Park Service was mandated by the National Parks and Recreation Act of 1978 (P.L. 95-625) to identify and implement carrying capacities for all park units. The Park Service has recently embarked on a program to design a methodology for accomplishing that task (Loomis 1985). The Fish and Wildlife Service, which typically has biological rather than sociological constraints on recreational use of its wilderness areas, directs managers   to manage recreational activities to "ensure high quality experiences."(USFWS 1985, 8 RM 1.1).

2. Alternatives to SCC have been proposed. Most prominent of these is the limits of acceptable change (LAC) system for wilderness management planning (Stankey et al. 1985).   This alternative improves on SCC by changing the focus from a preoccupation with use levels to a concentration on determination of acceptable levels of resource and social change. We consider the LAC system a derivative of SCC because it incorporates SCC concepts at key steps in the process. The LAC system is gaining widespread acceptance with federal land management agencies; most notably with the Forest Service in its application at the Bob Marshall Wilderness (McCool 1986) and with commitments to conduct the LAC process in BLM wilderness areas (BLM 1986a, BLM 1986b).

REFERENCES

Burch, W. R., Jr. 1984. "Much Ado About Nothing--Some Reflections on the Wider and Wilder Implications of Social Carrying Capacity." *Leisure Sciences* 6:487-496.

Bureau of Land Management (BLM, U.S. Department of Interior). 1979. *Aravaipa Canyon: Wilderness Draft Environmental Statement.* Phoenix: Arizona State Office.

_____ 1983. *Manual 8560: Management of Designated Wilderness Areas.* Washington, D.C.: Washington Office.

_____ 1984. *Manual 8561: Wilderness Management Plans.* Washington, D.C.: Washington Office.

_____ 1986a. *Draft Wilderness Management Plan: Paiute and Beaver Dam Mountains--Arizona-Utah.* St. George, UT: Arizona Strip District Office.

_____ 1986b. *Draft Wilderness Management Plan: Table Rock Wilderness--Oregon.* Salem, OR: Salem District Office.

Federal Register. 1979. "Rules and Regulations: National Forest System and Resource Management Planning." 44(181).

Graefe, A. R., J. J. Vaske, and F. R. Kuss. 1984. "Resolved Issues and Remaining Questions about Social Carrying Capacity." *Leisure Sciences.* 6:497-507.

Ketterer, R., R. Price, and P. Politser. 1980. "The Action Research Paradigm." In R. Price and P. Politser (eds.), *Evaluation and Action in the Social Environment.* New York: Academic Press. 1-15.

Lee, R. G. 1975. *The Management of Human Components in the Yosemite National Park Ecosystem.* Yosemite, CA: The Yosemite Institute.

Loomis, L. 1985. "Park Crowds are Pushing the Limits, NPCA has a Plan." *National Parks* 59:13-17.

McCool, S. F. 1986. "Putting Wilderness Research and Technology to Work in the Bob Marshall Wilderness Complex." In R. Lucas (compiler), *Proceedings--National Wilderness Research Conference: Current Research.* General Technical Report INT-212. Ogden, UT: Intermountain Research Station. p. 525.

Stankey, G. H. 1979. "A Framework for Social Behavior Research--Applied Issues." In W. R. Burch, Jr. (ed.), *Long Distance Trails: The Appalachian Trails--A Guide to Future Research and Management Needs.* New Haven: Yale University. 43-53.

Stankey, G. H., D. N. Cole, R. C. Lucas, M. E. Petersen, and S. F. Frissell. 1985. *The Limits of Acceptable Change (LAC) System for Wilderness Planning.* USDA Forest Service General Technical Report INT-176. Ogden, UT: Intermountain Forest and Range Experiment Station.

U.S. Fish and Wildlife Service (USFWS, Department of Interior). 1985. *Refuge Manual.* Washington, D.C.: Division of Refuge Management.

Wagar, J. A. 1964. *The Carrying Capacity of Wildlands for Recreation.* Forest Science Monograph 7. Washington, D.C.: Society of American Foresters.

Washburne, R. F. 1981. "Carrying Capacity Assessment and Recreational Use in the National Wilderness Preservation System." *Journal of Soil and Water Conservation* 36:162-166.

11

EMOTIONS IN ENVIRONMENTAL DECISION MAKING: RATIONAL PLANNING VERSUS THE PASSIONATE PUBLIC

Joanne Vining
Institute for Environmental Studies
University of Illinois

Herbert W. Schroeder
North Central Forest Experiment Station
Chicago, Illinois

Public participation in resource management decisions, mandated by law, has been institutionalized by all land management agencies. Public involvement programs can enhance planning decisions in two important ways. First, the public has an opportunity to influence planning decisions, presumably increasing the chances that a mutually acceptable option will be followed. Second, if public input is obtained and properly interpreted and incorporated, confusion and protest may be averted.

However, understanding the attitudes and reactions of the public and interpreting their responses are not easy tasks. A complex array of factors, such as the political climate, publicity, and the demographic characteristics of the target population, may influence the outcome of judgments and decisions made by individual citizens. One factor generally acknowledged to be important, but not previously examined systematically, is the emotion[1] involved in making decisions about environmental problems or issues. In this

article we will present a rationale for considering emotions as valid input to
public decision-making processes. In the first section we will discuss the
problems that emotion may pose for interpretation of public input in resource
management decisions. In the second section we will review some of the
psychological theories of emotion, and in the third section we will present
recent empirical evidence regarding the interaction between emotions and
knowledge in the public's reactions to environmental decision problems. In
the fourth and final section we will summarize our discussion and recommend
directions for further research.

RATIONALITY VERSUS PASSIONATE ADVOCACY

Since the seventies, communication between resource managers and
their constituents has become increasingly adversarial. One possible reason
for this adversary relationship is that the emotional responses of the public
may be ignored or misinterpreted by management professionals. In this
section we argue that the public's emotional responses to environmental
problems are important, but poorly understood by professional managers and
planners because of flaws in public input gathering and interpretation
processes.

Professional planners operate in a legal and scientific milieu in which
decisions and judgments must be defensible, logical, and traceable (Alterman
and Page 1978, Zube 1980). For instance, managers obtain advice from
planning staffs which are composed predominantly of technicians and
scientists whose professional standards are objective and logical. In addition,
over the past two decades, public opposition to some planning decisions has
increased the frequency of litigation concerning controversial decisions (Dana
and Fairfax 1980:306, Lucas 1976). In anticipation of legal challenges,
planning decisions must be defensible by the logical criteria of the legal
system, which require that management goals, policies and regulations be
explicit, traceable, and public.

Thus it behooves the professional decision-maker to make decisions
and judgments that can, at least in retrospect, be justified logically,
objectively, and unemotionally. This is not to say, of course, that
professionals do not have emotional responses to environmental problems. On
the contrary, most resource managers ·and environmental planners have
selected their professions out of concern and affection for the environment.
However, the legal and scientific context in which decisions are made strongly
encourages professionals to eliminate subjective content such as emotion
when decisions are presented to other professionals and to the public. This
process may increase the gap of understanding between professional decision-

makers who must rationally justify their decisions and members of the general public who may be as emotional in their decisions as they wish. Ultimately, some planning and management professionals may come to view emotion as undesirable and inadmissible to environmental decisions. For example, Gardiner and Edwards (1975) developed methods explicitly designed to eliminate emotional considerations, or "passionate advocacy" as input to resource management and environmental planning decisions.

In this way the public involvement process itself may become a source of interpretation error. Public hearings and surveys may encourage expression of objective, logical thought processes while inhibiting the expression of emotions, which are difficult to verbalize. Hammond (1981) proposed that analytic thought processes are more likely when well-organized information is presented unambiguously, and when the decision required is a choice between a small number of well-defined alternatives. He further characterized analytic decisions as highly traceable, justifiable, and readily verbalized. Conversely, subjective processes, such as emotion, are associated with complex and ambiguous conditions, and are difficult to trace and verbalize.

The usual format of a public participation program is to present a brief series of alternative plans, each with carefully and objectively described advantages and disadvantages. The participant is then asked to choose one of these alternatives, and occasionally asked to justify a response. But he or she is seldom asked to describe the process by which the judgment was made. Moreover, at public involvement sessions the alternatives are usually presented by authoritative professionals and "experts." In the face of this authority, the average individual may find public involvement sessions a difficult place in which to experience or to express emotions. These conditions are likely to foster analysis and objectivity and actively inhibit the expression of emotion. Conversely, the decision-making context outside the public involvement process, for example discussing an environmental problem with concerned friends, may enhance rather than discourage emotional content in decisions.

Even if public involvement procedures do not inhibit emotions, the methods commonly used to gather information from the public make it unlikely that planners will gain an adequate understanding of public emotions and values. Public involvement programs typically place a greater emphasis on producing a final decision than on comprehending the process by which such a decision is made. For example, many survey forms instruct respondents to choose one of several alternatives without indicating the reasons for the choice, or the amount of conviction reinforcing the decision.

Understanding the thoughts, feelings and experiences which lead to a decision, however, may be as important or more important than observing the decision itself.

For example, in a study of conflict and perceived importance of environmental management goals, Schroeder (1981) found that some respondents gave the goal of maintaining scenic beauty low importance ratings, not because they thought it was intrinsically unimportant, but because they had already given a high importance rating to wilderness preservation and thought that this would also ensure scenic beauty. Also, Anderson (1981) studied variations in perceived attractiveness of forested scenes and found that the landscapes were rated differently depending on whether respondents had been told they were wilderness areas or commercial timber stands. These examples indicate that a final decision outcome, such as a preference or importance rating, can only be adequately interpreted in light of the emotions, attitudes, and beliefs that produced the decision.

To summarize this section, it seems likely that the emotional content of public opinions and decisions will not be recognized by professional decision-makers who operate in the logical, scientific planning tradition. Even worse, emotions may be dismissed as illogical or immaterial. In addition, the emotional content of everyday decisions and judgments regarding environmental issues may not be revealed by the usual public involvement techniques, and may actually be inhibited by the formal objectivity of the public participation process. These factors may explain why the public response to environmental planning decisions is often poorly interpreted and under-utilized.

THEORIES OF EMOTION

Although many researchers have proposed that individuals can be trained to make consistent, unemotional decisions (e.g., Gardiner and Edwards 1975, Hammond *et al.* 1975), it is probably neither feasible nor desirable to train members of the general public to do so. A better approach would be to encourage resource planners and managers to accept and try to understand the emotional processes that may arise in natural resource decision problems. In recent years the study of emotion has enjoyed a resurgence of interest by psychologists, and a number of theories have been proposed which should shed some light on the interpretation and communication dilemmas faced by resource managers.

For several decades researchers have acknowledged that emotion is a large and meaningful part of overall thought. Miller, Galanter and Pribram (1960) estimated that only about 25 percent of mental functions are strictly logical. The remainder are evaluative, and consist of value judgments which incorporate emotional content to various degrees. Moreover, Newell and Simon (1972:53) stated that "problem solving situations in which...emotion is not aroused would...seem austere surroundings in which to study psychology."

A growing body of psychological evidence suggests that cognitive functions such as memory or problem solving may interact with emotions. There is substantial empirical evidence for at least two such interactions (Bower 1981). First, people tend to pay more attention to events that match their emotional state. For example, someone distressed about development of a natural area near their home may selectively perceive distressing attributes of information presented in other development proposals. Second, recall for an event is enhanced when an individual is in the same mood as was experienced during the original event. For example, a person who becomes angry at a public hearing may be likely to recall events and information that occured on past occasions when he or she experienced anger.

To explain these interactions, Bower (1981) proposed that emotions are part of the overall associative network by which memory is organized and items retrieved. According to this theory, memory for an event may trigger an emotion congruent with the original event. Conversely, and perhaps more importantly, an emotional experience may increase the accessibility of memory for events experienced in similar mood states. This explains why, for example, an individual who once became intensely angry about a particular wilderness preservation case may later experience similar emotions when considering similar cases.

Others have argued that the interaction of emotion and cognition has important adaptive significance. Abelson (1963) theorized that emotion, or hot cognition, contributes a useful evaluative function to overall cognition. Similarly, Ittelson (1973) proposed that the evaluative or emotional response to environmental stimuli is the precursor to "colder" cognitive appraisals. Zajonc (1980) provided empirical evidence that the affective mode of thought can be primary in cognition, while the colder objective modes, such as memory, are secondary. Thus, in contrast to previous theories of emotion which postulated that emotions are formed in response to cognitive evaluations of situations or stimuli, these theories propose that emotion may precede and in some cases determine the cognitive response. More importantly, emotion is increasingly being viewed as an inseparable and meaningful component of overall cognition.

Recently, the logic and objectivity of normative, or prescriptive models of human judgment and decisions, such as those recommended by Gardiner and Edwards (1975), has met with some criticism. As one critic noted, "if we're so dumb, how come we made it to the moon?" (Nisbett and Ross 1980:249), meaning that human decisions and problem-solving strategies, emotions and all, must somehow be adaptive and functional or the species would not have survived. As March (1978:593) noted:

> [I]f behavior that apparently deviates from standard procedures of calculated rationality can be shown to be intelligent, then it can plausibly be argued that models of calculated rationality are deficient not only as descriptors of human behavior but also as guides to intelligent choice.

STUDIES OF THE INTERACTION OF INFORMATION AND EMOTION

Certainly if emotional processes are integral to cognition and serve a useful function, then there is a need to understand the effects of passion before attempts are made to eliminate it. Unfortunately, there has so far been little systematic research on the public's emotional responses to natural resource decision problems.

In two recent studies we have begun to examine the interaction of emotion with other characteristics of the environmental decision-making process. Vining (1987) studied college students' responses to manipulations of the kind, quantity, and context of information that was provided in descriptions of a resource management problem (the proposed expansion of a ski area). Information regarding the proposed development was focused on four primary issues: expansion of the ski area might bring economic and recreational benefits, but it also could damage a pristine environment and possibly violate the rights of local Indian tribes to practice their religion on nearby sacred sites. The number of paragraphs of information on these four issues (economics, recreation, wilderness, and Indian religion) was varied so that each description of the problem had a greater depth of information on one of the four issues. For example, a description would have a general introduction and conclusion, a one-paragraph treatment of each of three issues, and three paragraphs on the remaining fourth issue.

Each of these issue emphasis conditions was then written in both a dry, factual (cold) style, and in a vivid emotional (hot) style. Thirty-four subjects were randomly assigned to read one of the resulting eight descriptions and then wrote a description of how they thought the problem should be resolved. They rated their decision about the issue on a linear scale ranging from complete development of the proposed expansion of the ski area to complete preservation of the environment in its natural state.

Subjects' decisions were influenced by the issue which was emphasized, but not by the style in which the descriptions were written. Decisions to preserve the environment resulted when more information was presented on preservation issues (e.g., wilderness), and decisions to develop the ski area resulted when more information was presented on development issues (e.g., economics). Subjects' written descriptions of their decisions were scored by independent judges for the emotional vehemence expressed in the writing. These ratings of expressed emotion were higher for descriptions written by subjects who read the problem scenarios written in the hot, or emotional, style than for those who read the texts written in the colder style. In addition, subjects who read emotionally-written problem descriptions wrote longer descriptions of their decisions, possibly indicating a deeper involvement in expressing opinions or justifying decisions.

A series of 42 emotion scales adapted from Izard's (1982) Differential Emotion Scale were used to evaluate subjects' emotional states during problem resolution. These scales consisted of an emotion descriptor, such as joy or anger, and a 0 to 10 rating scale. A factor analysis of these ratings yielded eight well-defined emotion factors (angry, distressed, happy, nervous, alert, fatigued, afraid, and surprised). Scores for these eight factors were used for further analysis. A multivariate analysis of variance indicated that subjects' ratings of their own emotions, as measured on a series of scales, were not significantly affected either by the issue emphasized or by the style in which a description was written. The subjects' self-rated emotional state did, however, account for 20 percent of the variance in decisions in a stepwise multiple-regression analysis. Although this proportion of explained variance might seem small, it is impressive considering the large number of other factors that probably influenced subjects' responses to this complex decision task. Negative emotions such as anger, fear, and distress were associated with decisions to preserve the environment. Development decisions were characterized by happiness, and a relative lack of negative emotions.

A third general variable in this study was the context in which subjects made their decisions. Half of the subjects made and described decisions prior to completing the emotion scales; the other half completed the emotion scales first, then made and described their decisions. Even though both groups were instructed to report the emotions they experienced while evaluating the problem descriptions, subjects who evaluated their emotional state prior to describing their decisions reported significantly more negative emotion. Anger, distress, fear, and nervousness were all higher for these subjects, and happiness was lower. This suggests that the final step of making and verbalizing a decision may help to resolve and reduce some of the negative and stressful emotions experienced during the decision task.

To summarize, the results of this study indicate that decisions were significantly influenced by a relatively subtle manipulation of the amount of information presented on particular issues. Also, there was a strong indication that decisions result from an interaction between information about an environmental problem and the emotions experienced by the subjects. Higher levels of negative emotions were reported by subjects who made preservation decisions, and by those who had not yet described their decision in writing.

To explore these findings further, Vining, Schroeder and Terry (1986) studied the interaction between information and emotion in an urban forestry setting. Descriptions of proposed plans for commercial development of an urban forest area were written with an emotional pro-development bias, a vivid pro-preservation bias, and with a neutral, unemotional style. Conflict between urban nature and economic development goals was manipulated in a map of the proposed development area. The high conflict condition consisted of a map with an existing natural wooded area located in an ideal place for commercial development. In the low conflict condition the wooded area was adjacent to a cemetery, in a location unsuitable for commercial development. The scarcity of urban nature was manipulated with a single sentence in each problem description. High scarcity was indicated by a statement that similar wooded natural areas were not available in surrounding neighborhoods; low scarcity was indicated by a statement that similar areas were plentiful.

Twenty-five subjects were randomly assigned to read and evaluate one of 12 possible combinations of the three variables described above (total N=300). Subjects then responded to a series of questions, including the emotion rating scales described in the study above (Vining 1987). A three-way multivariate analysis of variance was conducted on the eight emotion factors. Higher levels of anger were experienced by subjects in the high conflict condition, and higher levels of anger, distress, and alertness were experienced by subjects in the high scarcity condition. In addition, anger was significantly higher, and a trend for higher distress was found for subjects reading descriptions with the pro-preservation bias.

These results are consistent with the association between negative emotions and preservation-oriented decisions observed in the earlier study, and additionally suggest that anger and distress are significantly heightened in contexts which emphasize scarcity of natural resources and threats to their preservation.

DISCUSSION

The association of preservation-oriented issues, information, and decisions with negative emotions was found in scenarios of management problems in both urban and natural settings. Perceptions of conflict and resource scarcity were also associated with negative emotional arousal in these studies. These emotions may represent a very general defensive response which is triggered by the threatened loss of valued resources. In many cases, the development or exploitation of a natural environment may be perceived as an irreversible loss, so it is not surprising that it would evoke strong negative emotions. These kinds of defensive emotional responses have played an important role in the survival of the human species throughout its history, so it is unreasonable (and perhaps dangerous!) to attempt to exclude them from environmental policy decisions. Clearly, however, more work is needed to learn how emotions can be constructively integrated into resource decision making and public involvement.

The manipulations in both studies described here were relatively subtle, consisting of minor differences in the order in which questions were answered, slight changes in wording or quantities of information, and subtle differences in illustrative maps of the planning problem. In addition, the problems were presented in a laboratory situation, and in the case of the urban forestry experiment were hypothetical as well. Yet these subtle differences presented in laboratory experimental situations resulted in differences in decisions and levels of emotion registered by subjects. Planners and decision-makers must therefore realize that the precise manner in which they present information to the public may have important and unanticipated effects on public response. It seems likely that differences even greater than those we observed would be seen for actual resource management problems, where individuals have access to information from many sources, some of which may present issues in a flagrantly biased manner.

An important issue for future research is the behavioral consequences of emotional involvement in resource management problems or issues. It seems likely that high levels of emotion contribute to such actions as writing irate letters, placing indignant phone calls to resource managers, or possibly instituting legal challenges of management actions. A high level of negative emotion combined with a high level of energy may provide the necessary impetus for such actions.

In conclusion, based on the research and theory presented here, we would argue that natural resource managers and researchers should be more concerned with understanding the emotional processes of the public. There is growing evidence that intelligent, adaptive behavior does not strictly follow the laws of logic or objectivity, and in many cases may be based on emotional reactions to events and information. Emotion, in fact, may predominate and precede other thoughts and behaviors in "real" environments (Ittelson 1973, Zajonc 1980), and has a very positive role to play in motivating individuals to be concerned about their environment. Therefore, emotions should be viewed as an appropriate component of natural resource decision making. This is a fact which is likely to be overlooked in the public participation process, in part due to the rigors of the process itself, and also to the logical standards under which professionals commonly evaluate and incorporate public input. Misunderstanding or ignoring emotions is likely to result in protest and challenge of professional resource management and environmental planning decisions. On the other hand, by understanding and responding to the public's emotional concerns, natural resource managers may be able to enlist "passionate advocacy" in support of intelligent resource management.

NOTES

1. The term emotion has a wide variety of referents, and an emotional state can range from a relative mild feeling of preference for one object or event over another to an all-consuming passion. Emotion may be transient or enduring. In this paper we refer to what Berscheid (1982) termed "hot emotions," or those conscious subjective events which are characterized (and distinguished from other cognitive events) by an increased arousal of the endocrine and autonomic nervous systems the experience of which is interpreted with constructs such as anger, fear, or joy.

REFERENCES

Abelson, R.P. 1963. "Computer Simulation of Hot Cognition." In S.S. Tomkins and S. Messick (eds.), *Computer Simulation of Personality.* New York: John Wiley and Sons. 67-98.

Alterman, R. and J.E. Page. 1978. "The Ubiquity of Values and the Planning Process." *Plan* 13: 13-26.

Anderson, L.M. 1981. "Land Use Designations Affect Perception of Scenic Beauty in Forest Landscapes." *Forest Science* 27:392-400.

Berscheid, E. 1982. "Attraction and Emotion in Interpersonal Relationships." In M.S. Clark and S.T. Fiske (eds.), *Affect and Cognition.* Hillsdale, NJ: Lawrence Erlbaum Associates. 37-54.

Bower, G.H. 1981. "Mood and Memory." *American Psychologist* 36:129-148.

Dana, S.T., and S.K. Fairfax 1980. *Forest and Range Policy: Its Development in the United States.* New York:McGraw-Hill.

Gardiner, P.C., and W. Edwards. 1975. "Public Values: Multivariate-utility Measurement for Social Decision Making." In M.F. Kaplan and S. Schwartz (eds.), *Human Judgment and Decision Processes.* New York: Academic Press. 1-38.

Hammond, K.R. 1981. *Principles of Organization in Intuitive and Analytical Cognition.* Center for Research on Judgment and Policy Report Mo. 231. Boulder, CO: University of Colorado.

Hammond, K.R., T.R. Stewart, B.' Brehmer, and D.O. Steinman 1975. "Social judgment theory." In M.F. Kaplan and S. Schwartz (eds.), *Human Judgment and Decision Processes.* New York: Academic Press. 272-312.

Ittelson, W.H. 1973. "Environment perception and contemporary perceptual theory." In W.H. Ittelson (ed.), *Environment and Cognition.* New York: Seminar Press. 1-19.

Izard, C.E. 1982. *Patterns of Emotion: A New Analysis of Anxiety and Depression.* New York: Academic Press.

Lucas, A.R. 1976. "Legal Foundations for Public Participation in Environmental Decision Making." *Natural Resources Journal* 16:73-102.

March, J.G. 1978. "Bounded Rationality, Ambiguity, and the Engineering of Choice." *Bell Journal of Economics* 9:587-608.

Miller, G.A., E. Galanter, and K.H. Pribram. 1960. *Plans and the Structure of Behavior.* New York: Henry Holt & Co.

Newell, A., and H.A. Simon. 1972. *Human Problem Solving.* Englewood Cliffs, NJ: Prentice-Hall.

Nisbett, R., and I. Ross. 1980. *Human Inference: Strategies and Shortcoming of Social Judgment.* Englewood Cliffs, NJ: Prentice-Hall.

Schroeder, H.W. 1981. "The Effect of Perceived Conflict on Evaluations of Natural Resource Management Goals." *Journal of Environmental Psychology* 1: 61-72.

Vining, J. 1987. "Environmental Decisions: The Interaction of Emotions, Information, and Decision Context." *Journal of Environmental Psychology.* In Press.

Vining, J., H.W. Schroeder, and C. Terry 1986. *Perceived Conflict, Resource Scarcity, and Emotionality in Environmental Decision Making.* Final Report, Cooperative Agreement No. 23-84-07, Chicago: USDA Forest Service North Central Forest Experiment Station.

Zajonc, R.B. 1980. "Feeling and Thinking: Preferences Need no Inferences." *American Psychologist* 35: 151-175.

Zube, E.H. 1980. *Environmental Evaluation: Perception and Public Policy.* Belmont, CA: Brooks/Cole.

IV

ANALYSES OF INSTITUTIONS

INTRODUCTION TO PART IV

Marc L. Miller
Richard P. Gale
Perry J. Brown

The most typical products of social science in natural resource management systems (e.g., impact assessments, analyses found in management plans) are intended to be of rather immediate use in the crafting of natural resource policy. In this research, the social phenomena of substantive interest predominantly concern the lives of people affected by resource decisions.

The three articles in this section discuss research designed more to comment on the policy process than to inform specific management decisions. Thus, these illustrate how social scientists have investigated social change within the bureaucratic element, rather than the industrial or public elements, of natural resource management systems. The application of this kind of work will be found in new ways of structuring the policy process. As before, we introduce these articles with a few observations.

Off-Road Vehicle Policy and Arizona National Forests.
Controversies concerning the use of off-road vehicles (ORVs) on federal lands illustrate how the mere existence of policy directives is no guarantee of effective recreation management. In this article, Stephen R. Dennis notes that a plethora of laws, regulations, and guidelines are in force to control ORV use. Unhappily, these rules are inconsistently implemented and only weakly enforced by U.S. Forest Service managers at the local level.

Citing successes in the regulation of hunting, Dennis suggests that better control of ORVs would result from increased involvement of user groups by means of education, vehicle registration, and other management programs. Currently, the USFS rule permits ORV use of any land unless specifically designated as off-limits. Dennis concludes that revising this rule to allow ORVs only on designated lands would greatly improve enforcement.

The Spruce Budworm Spray Controversy in Canada: Foresters'
Perceptions of Power and Conflict in the Policy Process.
In Canada, where 94 percent of forest lands are owned by the Crown, forest policies are ultimately established by provincial authorities after

consideration of the recommendations of the forest industry, publics (including the environmental community), and professional foresters (situated in ministries, universities, and institutes). Under this system, foresters have struggled to convey to policy makers the scientific opinion that insecticide spraying is a solution to problems caused by the spruce budworm.

In this provocative article, Jeremy Rayner and David Peerla infer the political theories of foresters and find these to incompletely explain the forest management process. The conclusion is that a keener understanding of politics would make foresters, and other resource constituencies, more effective in the management arena.

Forest Planning: Learning with People.

Natural resource management bureaucracies such as the U.S. Forest Service have been challenged to balance agency legacies of professional top-down management with the intensifying demands of diverse publics to become involved in the resource management process. Thus, the planning methods of the USFS have undergone change due to general and agency-specific legislation such as the National Environmental Policy Act of 1969 and National Forest Management Act of 1976. The general thrust of this law has been to simultaneously increase the complexity of resource planning and the requirements for public participation.

The research reported in this article by Margaret A. Shannon provides a detailed glimpse of how individual national forests develop forest plans in ways which incorporate affected publics in the planning process. Central to the behavior of the different forests studied is the management style of the forest supervisor. Shannon concludes that participatory management style is most responsive to the concerns of different natural resource constituencies.

12

OFF-ROAD VEHICLE POLICY AND ARIZONA NATIONAL FORESTS

Stephen R. Dennis
Department of Recreation and Parks Management
California State University, Chico

Off-road vehicle recreationists are predominantly dependent on access to public lands to pursue their activity. The federal government has recognized off-road vehicle use as an accepted recreational activity (USDI 1971), and has actually stimulated the use of ORVs by providing free access to public lands. But the costs of their environmental effects are not being borne by the ORV users themselves (Rosenberg 1976). Thus, federal land managers have been operationalizing policies in a paradox of recreation benefits and resource costs.

To reduce the detrimental effects of off-road vehicles, myriad policy statements have been issued. Off-road vehicle policy has been defined through executive orders, statutes, the *Code of Federal Regulations*, the *Forest Service Manual*, and state and management unit off-road vehicle plans. These statements provide the framework for Forest Service management of ORV recreation.

To scrutinize U.S. Forest Service off-road vehicle policy, this article presents an analysis of ORV policy as implemented on Arizona National Forests. Section one presents a brief overview of the benefits and costs of ORV recreation on federal lands. The second section describes the principal policy statements used by managers of ORV recreation on national forest lands. Section three describes a survey of recreation managers on Arizona national forests, focusing on problems faced in local implementation of ORV policy. The final section is a discussion of survey findings, with implications for future management of off-road vehicle recreation.

BENEFITS AND COSTS OF ORV RECREATION

The use of off-road vehicles gives pleasure to millions of people, and supports an entire industry of off-road vehicle manufacturers, retail and repair outlets, and on-site providers of services to ORV recreationists. Descriptions of the social benefits of ORV use abound (Hope 1972, Malo 1972, Schade 1980, Watson, *et al.* 1980). Off-road vehicle users point to their activity's positive recreational benefits, strengthening of family ties, appreciation of nature, and increased access to otherwise inaccessible terrain. They recognize the detrimental image presented by "bad apples" (Dunn 1970, Kockelman 1983), and ORV groups frequently volunteer their services to Forest Service managers to help offset the negative view.

The physical and social impacts of off-road vehicles have been extensively documented over the past 20 years. Baldwin (1970), Lodico (1973), Webb and Wilshire (1978, 1983), and Sheridan (1979) contain solid bibliographies on the subject. Off-road vehicle impacts vary considerably depending upon the style of usage, user density and frequency, and susceptibility of the resource to ORV-caused degradation. In principle, ORV impacts can be categorized as to their effects on (1) soils, (2) vegetation, (3) wildlife, and (4) other forms of outdoor recreation.

The rise in outdoor recreation has greatly increased human presence on public lands managed for multiple use. As a result, recreationists find themselves competing for limited space in their efforts to realize positive and beneficial experiences. All users claim a right to pursue their style of activity on public lands. Arbitration is left to resource managers who prefer dealing with the ORV issue through proactive planning rather than reactive disciplining. Jacob and Schreyer (1980:378) noted the necessity for effective ORV planning:

> Once recreationists have allied themselves with interest groups and causes, conflict resolution becomes a costly political and legal process over which the resource managers may have little control.

POLICY STATEMENTS ON ORV RECREATION MANAGEMENT

Policy statements directing the management of ORV recreation appear in a variety of forms:

Executive Orders

In February, 1972, Richard Nixon issued Executive Order 11644, calling upon federal land-managing agencies to begin to cope with the ORV problem in a systematic manner. The Order required agencies to designate specific areas and trails to be open to ORV use, and to designate areas in which ORV use was not permitted. Use regulations were to be formulated with concern for resource protection, safety, and reduction of user conflicts. Specifically, the Order required that ORV areas and trails be located to minimize (1) damage to soil, watershed, vegetation, or other resources of the public lands; (2) harassment of wildlife or wildlife habitats; and (3) conflicts between off-road vehicle use and other recreational uses of the same or neighboring public lands. Additionally, the Order prohibited off-road vehicles from designated wilderness areas, and required agencies to monitor the effects of ORVs in order to take appropriate future management actions.

In implementing E.O. 11644, the Forest Service continued its traditional policy of allowing the national forests to remain open to ORV use unless designated as closed. This led to the practice of placing restrictive signs on areas closed to ORV use, and leaving open areas unsigned. One direct result of this signing strategy was the unofficial "opening" of areas by the tearing down and vandalizing of signs (Rosenberg 1976). The use of the term "minimize" in E.O. 11644 led to the Order being interpreted as allowing ORV use with reduction of ORV effects to the smallest degree feasible short of elimination (Reames 1980). Sheridan (1979) reported that when the supervisor of Washington's Olympic National Forest proposed to close the entire Forest to cross-country ORV use, he was reminded by the regional forester that "restrictions and closures are to be used only as a last resort."

Executive Order 11644 provides a foundation for reducing environmental degradation caused by off-road vehicles. However, the Order does not eliminate the use of ORVs on federal lands, and agencies have failed to take advantage of the opportunity to develop effective ORV regulatory schemes (Rosenberg 1976).

Five years after Executive Order 11644, Jimmy Carter issued Executive Order 11989, effectively amending E.O. 11644 to a more powerful ORV management stance. Executive Order 11989 gave agencies the power to "immediately close" areas where ORV use "will cause or is causing considerable adverse effects on the soil, vegetation, wildlife, wildlife habitat or cultural or historic resources of particular areas."

Once again, the language of the Executive Order left much room for interpretation. No guidelines were released as to what constituted a "considerable adverse effect" nor were standards developed for closures (Reames 1980:144). Sheridan's 1979 ORV report to the Council on Environmental Quality quoted an Interior department employee as saying:

This issue is a political hornet's nest. The Executive Order
refers to 'considerable adverse effects', that's the operative
phrase, but what does it mean really? You can bet the BLM
and Forest Service are going to interpret it very narrowly
until they get clear signals to the contrary. In other words,
not much has changed.

Statutes

Congressional input to land management agencies regarding ORV
regulation has been very general and has been frequently ignored by land
managers (Sheridan 1979). Legislation indirectly relating to Forest Service
ORV management includes the Multiple-Use and Sustained Yield Act (1960)
and the National Forest Management Act (1976). Both of the Acts authorize
and provide guidelines for the Forest Service to manage the national forests
for multiple use of their various resources, and to protect those resources to
meet the present and future needs of the American people. However, neither
of these Acts makes specific reference to the management of off-road vehicles.
A more obscure 1974 law, known as the Sikes Act represents Congress' first
official acknowledgement of ORVs as a special land management issue. The
Act calls upon the secretaries of Interior and Agriculture to "develop, in
consultation with state agencies, a comprehensive plan for conservation and
rehabilitation to be implemented on public land." In such planning, the Act
requires "the control of off-road vehicle traffic." However, the cooperative
planning efforts conducted under the Sikes Act have produced no evidence to
indicate the "control" of ORV traffic (Sheridan 1979).

The most powerful congressional limitation on ORV use on national
forests is the 1964 Wilderness Act which effectively excludes all ORVs from
designated wilderness areas by prohibiting the "use of motor vehicles" and
other forms of "mechanical transport." The national debate on ORV use
centers on management of non-wilderness, or multiple-use lands.
Nonetheless, reassignment of lands to the National Wilderness Preservation
System must be considered the most effective, although indirect, means of
excluding ORVs from the national forests.

Code of Federal Regulations and Forest Service Manual

Specific federal regulations, and guidelines within the *Forest Service
Manual* provide additional policy statements regarding ORV management.
Forest Service ORV management requirements in the *Code of Federal
Regulations* issued pursuant to Executive Order 11644 "are a diluted form of
those set forth in the Executive Order..." (Rosenberg 1976). Though very
specific with regard to safety conditions, licensing and public participation in

planning, the *Federal Register* contains little additional guidance to assist ORV managers in dealing with the use-protection paradox. Regulation language uses ambiguous terms such as "minimization of use conflicts," "creating excessive damage," and "will be monitored" in describing how ORV management should take place while accomplishing "all of the other resource objectives for National Forest System Lands" (U.S.CFR 1975).

The *Forest Service Manual* (USFS n.d.), Chapter 2355, provides guidelines for ORV recreation management. The *Manual* is a service-wide document that serves as a framework for more specific regional and forest-level management directives. A massive set of values, the *Manual* is often very explicit in its instructions. In other cases, where local conditions are a strong contributing management variable, the *Manual* provides leeway for on-site management discretion. Such is the case with *Manual* directions for ORV management.

The *Forest Service Manual* contains numerous directives that leave ORV management essentially to the discretion of on-site managers. Two general instructions are clear: (1) ORV recreation is an acceptable use of national forests, and (2) ORV use will be managed to reduce impacts and conflicts. Chapter 2355, section 03 (Policy) reads:

1. Off-road vehicle travel is an acceptable recreation use of National Forest System lands, when managed to a level as identified in the Forest Land Management Plan. Managers will provide a diversity of off-road vehicle recreational opportunities when that use is compatible with established land management objectives.

2. Off-road vehicle use will be managed while recognizing the different impacts of specific vehicle types, to provide user enjoyment, to protect the resources of the lands, to promote public safety, and to resolve conflicts among the various uses of National Forest System lands.

In Section 05 (Definitions) the *Manual* tries to clarify "minimize ORV effects," defining this phrase as follows:

To reduce ORV effects to the smallest degree feasible short of elimination, consistent with the specific management direction and practices established for the area as determined by economic, legal, environmental and technological factors.

Additionally, the *Manual* (2355.05,10) defines adverse effect as the result of ORV use that does not meet the standards of maintenance for (1) long-term productivity of the land, (2) air and water quality, (3) wildlife and habitat, (4) other potential forest uses, and (5) preservation of cultural and historic resource values.

These policy statements provide guidance to the forest manager, yet retain only two specific criteria: (1) ORV recreation is to be allowed, and (2) ORV use is to be managed in accordance with local forest conditions. Even when the *Manual* lists planning criteria (2355.12), the language is unspecific: "Promote user enjoyment. Minimize damage to soil...Minimize harassment of wildlife...Minimize conflicts...Promote the safety of all user(s)..."

Sections of the *Manual's* ORV policy are well detailed and adequately specific. Guidelines for inventory, public participation in ORV planning, issuance of permits for organized events, and corrective action (land reclamation) are all complete for management purposes. Finally, the *Manual* gives teeth to forest supervisors in defining "considerable adverse effects" (2355.05,11) as "any adverse effect...(which) may become irreparable due to the impossibility or impracticality of performing corrective or remedial measures." Planning section 2355.1 allows the forest supervisor to temporarily close areas suffering "considerable adverse effects" for up to one year without public participation.

Through the *Manual's* delegation of ORV management to local forest service practitioners, federal ORV policy appears to mandate local discretion for managing ORV use as required by on-site conditions. These localized policy directives are issued in various regional, state, and forest plans.

Arizona National Forest ORV Management Plan

The six national forests in Arizona compiled a statewide ORV management plan in 1975 and 1976 under authority of the *Code of Federal Regulations* (36 CFR 295).

> These regulations direct the Forest Service to establish, through the continuing resource planning process, designated specific areas and trails for off-road vehicle use, use restrictions, and closures to any and all types of such use (USFS 1976:5).

The statewide ORV planning effort was conducted as a specific component of the forest planning process, and included 34 meetings with attendance of 1,385 people, and receipt of more than 1,000 written comments. The purpose of this planning effort was to implement restrictions where necessary to manage for adverse ORV effects. The language of the plan reflected a philosophical bent toward minimal restriction of ORV use:

> The traditional policy of the Forest Service is that the National Forests should be open for public use and enjoyment; therefore, we made an effort to close the minimum amount of area necessary to deal with the protection of public safety, the minimization of conflicting uses and the protection of our natural resource base (USFS 1976:5).

The plan resulted in closure to ORV use on 62,584 acres, and restriction of ORV use on 435,100 acres. This translates to the implementation of ORV management on approximately five percent of the Forest Service managed land in Arizona not closed or restricted prior to 1976. The 1976 ORV restrictions brought the total amount of Arizona national forest land closed or restricted to ORV use to approximately 15 percent. It should be noted here that the remaining 85 percent of Arizona national forest land is not necessarily accessible to ORV use. Rough topography and dense vegetation provide natural closures in some areas. Further, passage of the Arizona Wilderness Bill on August 24, 1984, closed an additional 658,540 acres to ORV use (U.S. Code 1984).

Forest Land Management Plans and Other Directives

Arizona's six national forests are presently updating their Land Management Plans. Drafts were released for initial review in spring, 1985. Each Forest Land Management Plan contains a section on the management of off-road vehicle use, and within the framework of federal regulations, specifies management according to local conditions.

Off-road vehicle management directives are occasionally issued by the regional forester, forest supervisors and district rangers. These orders most often involve site-specific management actions such as emergency closures, enforcement, maintenance, reclamation, and planning.

Beyond these written policies, ORV management becomes a task of on-site actions implemented to meet the requirements set forth by the varied levels of the federal government. Realization of agency objectives is the duty delegated to Forest Service personnel at the field level. The ability to succeed in this endeavor is the subject of the following sections.

ORV POLICY ON ARIZONA NATIONAL FORESTS

This section reports a study conducted to assess the effectiveness of off-road policy as perceived by Forest Service managers in Arizona. The purpose of the study was to determine whether the multitude of policy directives regarding ORV management are being implemented as perceived by field-level personnel on Arizona national forests.

Data Collection Method

Questionnaire information was collected from 41 Forest Service personnel in the six supervisor's offices and 31 ranger districts in Arizona, and from the Southwestern Regional Office in Albuquerque, New Mexico. Telephone interviewing allowed for attention to specific details within the questionnaire, and for qualification and comment on individual queries.

Interviews were conducted during November, 1984, and averaged 15 to 20 minutes in length. Participants were selected by interviewing the recreation and lands staff officers at the six forest supervisor's offices and requesting the names of recreation and lands staff officers serving at the district level. If a recreation officer was not employed at the district office, or was unavailable, the interview was conducted with a manager assigned to recreation responsibilities or with the district ranger (Table 1).

Findings

The participants in this study had considerable experience as Forest Service employees. District office personnel averaged 15 years with the Forest Service, and supervisor's and regional office managers averaged 20 years of Forest Service experience. The number of years managers had served in their present capacities averaged seven for those from the supervisor's and regional offices, and five for those at district offices.

Of the 41 managers interviewed, 37, or roughly 90 percent, considered the use of ORVs to be a problem on their management unit. Four districts responded that ORV use was not a problem and based this on infrequency of ORV use and lack of public attention to the issue. Participants were asked to rate the magnitude of the ORV problem from one (slight problem) to five (major problem) in light of its impact on their management unit. Responses averaged 2.45, or roughly midway between a slight and major problem.

Table 1   Position titles of respondents.

Title	Frequency
Regional Ass't. Director for Rec. & Wilderness Mgm't.	1
Forest Recreation and Lands Staff Officer	5
Forest Lands Officer	1
Forest Landscape Architect	1
Ass't. Forest Recreation & Lands Staff Officer	1
District Recreation and Lands Staff Officer	22
District Ranger	6
District Resource Staff	2
Fire Management Officer & Recreation Staff	1
Public Affairs Specialist	1

N = 41

Management techniques to reduce ORV impacts include closure and restriction, informal methods to inhibit access, and planned ORV user education programs. This study found that 27 of the 31 ranger districts in Arizona have closed areas to ORV use (87 percent). The use of informal actions has occurred on 23 of the 31 districts (74 percent). Although respondents noted that enforcement of closures is weak at best, the most commonly used method is signing, followed by patrol using field personnel, physical barriers, and maps outlining closed areas. Less frequently mentioned were the use of fencing and patrol by county sheriffs. One manager stated that their closures were not enforced at all. Informal actions to reduce ORV access are not enforceable, but nevertheless can be effective. Managers principally relied on physical barriers (some called "tank traps"), followed by suspension of maintenance to access routes, fences, and natural topographical barriers.

Educating ORV users through planned programs has been attempted on half of Arizona's ranger districts, and through four of the six supervisor's offices. Respondents noted that the most common method of user education is through field contact, followed by dissemination of information through newspapers and brochures, and through scheduled meetings. One district had contacted ORV shops and another had made use of local TV air time.

Participants were asked to identify the policy directives they utilize in ORV management. The question was open-ended, and responses were tallied by specific document(s) and by management level. The *Forest Service Manual* and state and forest ORV plans stood out as the principal sources of ORV policy used by participants in this study. To a lesser extent, Executive Orders and the *Code of Federal Regulations* were cited, noted principally by supervisor's and regional office staff. A number of respondents said that administrative directives were another source of policy, indicating that specific management directives are used to supplement the *Manual* and Forest Plans (Table 2).

Table 2 Policy directives used in ORV management

Source	% District Staff n=32	SO & RO Staff n=9	Total n=41
Executive Orders	9	44	17
Code of Federal Regulations	9	33	15
Forest Service Manual	44	56	46
Forest & State ORV Mgm't. Plans	50	67	56
Washington Office	16	0	12
Regional Office	19	11	17
Supervisor's Office	28	11	24
District Office	19	0	15

Managers were asked if existing policies are adequate to effectively manage ORV use. This question frequently drew additional comment and qualification, but was answered soundly in the affirmative by 33 of the respondents (80 percent). Of the 33 managers who stated that ORV policies are adequate, 29 of them (88 percent) qualified their response, stating that although written policies are sufficient, the ability to enforce them is not. This group further revealed that funding and manpower are insufficient to properly implement written policies. Several respondents stated that policies are unclear, and a number of others remarked that policies are only effective if implemented with a good "on-the-ground-plan."

When asked what policy improvements are needed, most respondents reiterated the need for funding and manpower, but were not specific in suggesting appropriate levels. Most respondents felt that policy statements on paper were conducive to effective management. Several managers stated that they would like to see a policy emphasis toward ORV user education, feeling that this method has not been promoted. A variety of other policy improvements mentioned included increased emphasis on the ORV issue, closure of all areas except road and trail systems, reducing the formality of the planning process, and taxing ORV equipment to develop a funding pool for ORV management.

In order to compare public input from pro-ORV and anti-ORV interests, managers were asked if they had been contacted by individuals or representatives of these groups. Off-road vehicle users had made contact with 23 of the managers (56 percent). These contacts average about seven annually, and 75 percent are made by organized groups. Individual ORV users account for only 25 percent of the contacts with forest managers.

Managers are more frequently contacted by people opposed to ORV use. Anti-ORV interests had made contact with 30 of the respondents (73 percent). Contrasting with pro-ORV contacts, 71 percent of the contacts in opposition to ORV use are made by individuals. An average of 28 anti-ORV contacts are made annually, indicating that managers are four times more likely to be contacted by anti-ORV interests than by those in favor of their use. Frequently, these contacts are complaints expressed by recreationists and residents adjacent to national forest lands.

The methods used to contact forest managers appeared to be evenly divided among both groups. Common methods include planned public participation programs, personal visits, letters, and telephone calls. These systems for communicating with forest personnel appeared to be used with nearly equal frequency by pro- and anti-ORV interests.

At the end of each interview, respondents were asked if they had any additional comments. Many of these comments were clearly policy-oriented and could be considered as suggestions for future management practices. The most frequent comment was that the policy of leaving forests open, unless marked closed to ORV use, should be reversed. In this way, signing would provide a positive message telling the ORV user that an area is accessible, while simplifying the basic rule of closure. Several respondents suggested that special ORV areas should be set aside for concentrated use. Others noted the cyclic nature of public attention to the ORV issue, suggesting that public input to the controversy has been ebbing recently. A number of managers expressed concern over conflicts with enforcing ORV prohibition in areas recently designated as wilderness under the Arizona Wilderness Bill.

The second most frequent comment offered was a statement that three- and four-wheeled all-terrain vehicles are presently causing the greatest adverse effects among ORV types. Managers noted that ATV use is rapidly increasing, and their associated detrimental effects can occur in areas that are inaccessible to motorcycles and four-wheel drive vehicles because of the ATV's ability to negotiate rough terrain.

In summary, the ORV problem is judged to be moderate on Arizona national forests. ORV effects are greatest on forest lands near urban areas. Present management strategies are not particularly successful, principally due to a lack of current agency emphasis. Written policy statements are considered adequate for ORV management purposes, but the actions that will promote their implementation are not.

DISCUSSION

Management of off-road vehicle recreation on Arizona national forests suffers from discrepancies between written policy statements and field-level implementation. A foundational policy permitting ORV use on forest lands has perhaps fostered resistance to regulation among segments of the ORV-using public. Additionally, the "forests are open unless closed" policy has created the expectation that ORV recreationists will have access to public lands for ORV recreational opportunities. Closures and restrictions, therefore, are considered by ORV users as an infringement on their "rights" to public lands access. This foundational policy has forced managers to implement ORV policy statements in a manner reflecting a minimal amount of field-level regulation.

Policy, defined by Anderson (1984), focuses "attention on what is actually done as against what is proposed or intended." He further states that "policy involves what governments actually do, not what they intend, or say they're going to do." Forest Service policy regarding off-road vehicle use in Arizona cannot be determined by focusing on executive orders, statutes, federal regulations, the *Manual*, or land management plans. It is the interpretation of these statements and their implementation at the field level that reflects current agency policy.

Field level managers on Arizona national forests noted the difference between policy directives and field implementation when stating that they were unable to adequately enforce ORV regulations. Forest Service personnel interviewed in the study were genuinely concerned with the management of ORVs, yet felt that agency attention to the issue had waned. The study findings suggest the Forest Service has opted for a least-regulatory interpretation of a detailed, but negotiable legal framework for ORV management.

Forest Service managers explained that enforcement capabilities were reduced by lack of funding and manpower. This is a common response to agency inadequacies. In truth, ORV management is conducted in a socio-political environment that has (1) recognized the legitimacy of ORV use on public lands; (2) bent to pressure from ORV interest groups, manufacturers and industry; and (3) seen environmental interest group attention shift to other resource management issues. If the government chooses to further restrict ORV use on Forest Service lands, managers would be equipped with the necessary legal and enforcement tools. At present, the issue is not perceived to warrant more than remedial management actions.

The off-road vehicle issue, however, is anything but dead. Managers noted that attention to the issue has shifted, but not the problem itself. Participation in ORV recreation continues to rise, as technological improvements in vehicular design are peddled from overseas to an expanding U.S. market. Too, associated issues have surfaced, such as safety of three-wheel all-terrain vehicles and wilderness access requests from off-road bicyclists.

Future management of off-road vehicle recreation must break from the free-access, accommodating policies of the past. Off-road vehicle recreation provides benefits to users that are exacted from a public lands resource. It is appropriate to shift this cost burden to the user. Regulations are inherently incongruous with the outdoor recreation experience (Lucas 1982), and have been generally ineffective in reducing the resource costs of ORV use. An ORV management system approach may prove more successful.

A management system to control off-road vehicle use on public lands requires cooperation among federal and state agencies, industry associations, and user groups. This system is ideally structured by the following components:

1. Changes the regulatory scheme to mandate lands as closed to ORV use, unless designated as open.

2. Excise taxes and/or vehicle registration fees on ORV equipment.

3. User education and ORV licensing procedures.

4. Cooperative "adopt-a-trail" programs involving ORV groups.

Some, but not all, of these system components have been implemented by certain states, agencies, and ORV groups with successful results. Effective ORV management will require cooperative implementation of each of the system's components.

Hunting has evolved as a national form of outdoor recreation to include group-sponsored hunter safety courses, licensing of hunters, excise taxation, and agency regulation to conserve the wildlife resource and promote safety. Off-road vehicle recreation should be managed in a similarly responsible manner. Twenty years of experience have demonstrated that land managing agencies cannot effectively control ORV recreation alone. Responsibility for the ORV experience must be shared by federal, state, and local government, and by users of the public recreation resource.

REFERENCES

Anderson, J.E. 1984. *Public Policy Making*. New York: Holt, Rinehart and Winston (third edition).

Baldwin, M.F. 1970. *The Off-Road Vehicle and Environmental Quality*. Washington, D.C.: The Conservation Foundation.

Dunn, D.R. 1970. "Motorized Recreation Vehicles...on Borrowed Time." *Parks and Recreation* July:10-14,46-52.

Hope, J. 1972. "Invasion of the Awful ORVs." *Audubon* 74(1):36-43.

Jacob, G.R., and R. Schreyer. 1980. "Conflict In Outdoor Recreation: A Theoretical Perspective." *Journal of Leisure Research* 12:368-380.

Kockelman, W.J. 1983. "Management Concepts." In R.H. Webb, and H.G. Wilshire, *The Environmental Effects of Off-Road Vehicles.* New York: Springer-Verlag.

Lodico, N.J. 1973. *Environmental Effects of Off-Road Vehicles.* U.S.D.I. Office of Library Services. Bibliography Series No. 29.

Lucas, R.C. 1982. "Recreation Regulations - When Are They Needed? *Journal of Forestry* 80:148-151.

Malo, J.W. 1972. *All-Terrain Adventure Vehicles.* New York: Macmillan.

Reames, D.S. 1980. "Off-Road Vehicle Use As a Management Challenge." In R.N. Andrews, and P.F. Nowak (eds.), *Off-Road Vehicle Use: A Management Challenge.* Ann Arbor: University of Michigan Extension Service. 143-147.

Rosenberg, G.A. 1976. "Regulation Of Off-Road Vehicles." *Environmental Affairs* 5:175-206.

Schade, G.A., Jr. 1980. "Four-Wheel Vehicle User's Perspective." In R.N. Andrews, and P.F. Nowak (eds.), *Off-Road Vehicle Use:A Management Challenge.* Ann Arbor: University of Michigan Extension Service. 139-142.

Sheridan, D. 1979. *Off-Road Vehicles on Public Land.* Washington, D.C.: Council on Environmental Quality.

Watson, S.W., M.H. Less, and J.B. Reeves. 1980. "The Enduro Dirt-Bike Rider: An Empirical Investigation." *Leisure Sciences* 3:241-255.

Webb, R.H., and H.G. Wilshire. 1978. *A Bibliography of the Effects of Off-Road Vehicles on the Environment.* U.S. Geological Survey Open File Report 78-149.

_____ 1983. *Environmental Effects of Off-Road Vehicles.* New York: Springer-Verlag.

United States Code Congressional and Administrative News. 1984. 98th Congress, 2nd Session. (P.L. 98-406). "Arizona Wilderness Bill." October. St. Paul: West Publishing Company.

U.S. Forest Service (USFS). 1976. *Arizona National Forest: Environmental Analysis of the Off-Road Vehicle Management Plan.* Washington, D.C.: U.S. Department of Agriculture.

_____ *Forest Service Manual.* Title 2300. Chapter 2355. Washington, D.C.: U.S. Department of Agriculture, Forest Service.

U.S. Department of the Interior (USDI). 1971. *Off-Road Recreation Vehicles: Department of the Interior Task Force Study.* Washington D.C.: Government Printing Office.

United States Code of Federal Regulations. 36-295 (1975). Washington, D.C.: National Archives and Records Service, GSA.

13

THE SPRUCE BUDWORM SPRAY CONTROVERSY IN CANADA: FORESTERS' PERCEPTIONS OF POWER AND CONFLICT IN THE POLICY PROCESS

Jeremy Rayner
Department of Political Studies
Lakehead University

David Peerla
Sociology Board of Studies
University of California-Santa Cruz

On one fact there is general agreement: the Canadian forest industry is in a state of crisis (Reed 1978, Canadian Forest Congress 1980, Environment Canada 1981b, Marchak 1983, Swift 1983). Over the last decade, representatives of the forest industries, the federal and provincial governments, and professional foresters have all agreed that the severity of the problems facing Canadian forestry demands a coordinated effort from the major actors. They have, of course, disagreed over many of the details, particularly over attributing responsibility for the crisis and apportioning the costs of overcoming it. What follows is a study of one such disagreement, the controversy over the aerial spraying of eastern Canadian forests to protect against the spruce budworm. The point of view is that of one of the major actors, the professional foresters.[1] It is a study of how foresters, seeking to give an opinion on a technical matter within their field of professional competence, have been drawn into political controversy over the formulation of public policy.

The objectives of this article are twofold: first, to explore the ways in which foresters conceive of power and conflict in the Canadian political system, and, second, to determine how their understanding of their own role, and those of business and government, have promoted or hindered their attempts to intervene in forest policy. The first section briefly outlines the most important models of the political process used by political scientists, and draws attention to the distinctive conceptions of power involved in each model. The background to the forestry crisis and the special salience of the insect control issue are described in the following two sections. The fourth section considers the political assumptions of the first major report on the spruce budworm epidemic (Baskerville 1976), and the fifth section analyzes attempts by foresters to commit governments to a consistent policy on the use of insecticides. In the last section, the foresters' assumptions about power and conflict are compared with the political scientists' models; finally, the prospects for greater professional involvement in the forest policy-making process are assessed.

MODELS OF POWER AND CONFLICT IN POLITICAL SCIENCE

In comparing recent theories in political science, Alford and Friedland (1985) have drawn attention to the different conceptions of power which underwrite the three major theoretical models. These are summarized in Table 1.

Models of the political system based on a one-dimensional conception of power focus on overt conflict between the preferences of groups versus individuals where the outcome is a decision with observable winners and losers. Power is simply the observable ability to get what one wants. On this view, politics is characterised by free competition between individuals and groups. This conception also includes the view that a persistent imbalance to one set of preferences which are not supported by a societal consensus reflects restrictions on free competition which are analogous to market failures identified by economists. Such distorted outcomes are highly unstable and will require the visible coercion of disappointed groups.[2]

Theorists whose models are underwritten by a two-dimensional conception of power stress that, in addition to overt conflict over policy preferences, political scientists need to consider *covert* conflict, especially those decisions and "nondecisions" that determine which policy options will be the subject of overt. In their view, politics is largely concerned with negotiation among organizational elites to decide what will appear on the political agenda. An imbalance in policy outcomes, therefore, reflects the different organizational capacities of those elites.[3]

Table 1   The three dimensions of power (after Alford and Friedland 1985)

DIMENSIONS OF POWER	LOCUS OF CONFLICT	MODEL OF POLITICS	REASONS FOR BREAKDOWN
one dimension; overt	contested decisions by groups and persons	free competion for influence	market failure
two dimensions; overt and covert	agenda setting and "nondecision making"	negotiation between elites	bureaucratic disorganization
three dimensions; overt, covert, and latent	institutional practices shaping preferences	disguised conflict between structural interests	structural contradictions

In the most complex view, power is three dimensional so that conflict may be *latent* within the institutional practices of a society as well as observable in overt and covert conflicts. What appears on the policy agenda will be in part determined by the ways in which society shapes people's preferences. Such shaping affords a source of latent power for some groups and individuals. Indeed, the very existence of political conflict may be disguised because the structural advantages possessed by a particular group are sufficient to render opposing preferences illegitimate. The failure of political "markets" to produce a consensus and the inability of organizational elites to reconcile the demands of their clients may both be traced to deep contradictions in the institutional practices of a society.[4] More generally, whereas the one- and two-dimensional conceptions of power focus on *conflicts* (whether overt or covert), the three-dimensional conception introduces the notion of *constraints* latent in the values and institutions of any society.

This study is conducted under the assumption, which cannot be defended here, that social scientists' theories differ in degree rather than in kind from those used by ordinary agents in conduct. Theories in the social sciences are (or ought to be) more transparent in their assumptions and implications than the mainly pre-articulate theories of everyday life. Nevertheless, if power can be analyzed into these three competing conceptions, each supporting a theory of politics, the conceptions and their accompanying theories will also inform agents' everyday conduct. The task of the social scientist is to exploit the superior transparency of his own theories to explain how the less transparent versions hinder or promote the objectives of those who use them.

FORESTRY CRISIS: BACKGROUND AND HISTORY

Meeting in 1979, the Canadian Council of Resource and Environment Ministers (CCREM) agreed on a target for growth in Canadian forest output to be used as the basis for future forest policies. Using the Food and Agriculture Organization estimate of a 2.1 percent annual increase in world demand for forest products, the Council called for a 40 percent increase in Canadian output by the year 2000, or about 1.8 percent per annum (Environment Canada 1982). The sobering reality behind talk of a crisis in the industry is that the annual allowable cut (AAC) for softwood will be exceeded in the early 1990s (Reed 1986). Since the AAC is the maximum theoretically sustainable harvest, by the mid-1990s Canada will have turned its forests into a non-renewable resource. Moreover, the hypothetical surpluses which exist at present not only disguise serious local problems of accessibility and quality, but also the continuous downward revision of the AAC from 256 million cubic meters in 1978 to 203 million cubic meters in 1986, of which only 165 cubic meters is softwood.

The reasons for this critical state of affairs are not controversial. Part of the blame for the slow reaction of the forestry community lies with overly optimistic pictures of the available stocks. Early estimates failed to distinguish between economically accessible and inaccessible stands, or between the balance of age classes, which partially dictates how much wood must be cut if stands are not to become over-mature. But the main reasons for declining AAC have been known for a number of years, and are, to some extent, avoidable. According to Reed (1986:336) they are "past neglect of forest renewal, heavier than expected losses from fires and insects, the establishment of parks, wildernesses and other reservations, and the application of environmental guidelines to logging."

The neglect of reforestation has always been seen as a major problem by the forestry profession. In 1983, the Canadian Institute of Forestry (CIF) informed the Macdonald Commission that, even with the most optimistic assumptions about natural regeneration, less than one-third of the annual harvest between 1975 and 1979 had regenerated satisfactorily (CIF 1984).[5] In addition, a total wood volume equal to nearly twice the annual harvest was lost to fire and insects every year, creating a situation where annual withdrawals from the productive forest have been exceeding renewal by 450,000 hectares (Honer and Bickerstaff 1985). Little has changed since the critical comments by Reed (1978) noting that Canada was still at the exploitation stage in its forest lands while its major competitors were already practicing intensive forest management.

· Foresters, industry and government all assign part of the blame for poor reforestation to Canada's land-tenure system. In contrast to the United States or Sweden, where roughly three-quarters of forest land is privately owned, the proportion in Canada is about 6 percent (Macdonald 1985). Most of the rest is administered by the provincial governments in right of the Crown, and they lease the timber rights to corporations in return for an extraction fee known as stumpage. Foresters note that until World War II provincial governments were so eager to obtain the tax revenues generated by the forest products industry that they granted timber licenses without setting conditions for regeneration. When governments became more aware of their responsibililties during the 1950s and 1960s, their contributions were often limited to fire and insect control programs (CIF 1984). It was not until the 1970s, that the forestry profession and others successfully pressured provincial governments to change the terms of timber licenses, offering corporations increased security of tenure in return for an enforceable commitment to regeneration.

SPRUCE BUDWORM IN EASTERN CANADA

Seen against the background of a declining AAC and predictions of a wood supply shortfall, together with a growing public debate about forest policy, the significance of insect control is thrown into high relief. The most serious threat by far during the past decade has come from the spruce budworm.[6] The budworm, a defoliator whose preferred food source is actually balsam fir rather than spruce, has taken advantage of over-mature softwood forests in eastern Canada. The entire area has recently experienced the most extensive budworm outbreak of the century (Bellyea et al. 1975). The budworm is especially difficult to combat because it occupies a clearly-defined ecological niche in the spruce-fir forest. As records show, budworm populations explode every 60 years or so, destroying the mature forest and making way for new growth; the epidemic itself collapses when the food source is exhausted. Intervention in this natural cycle of renewal inevitably

alters the symbiotic relationship between the budworm and its host forest, and
budworm epidemics have been occurring more frequently and lasting longer.
The province of New Brunswick has endured a major epidemic in most of its
productive forest for over 30 years.

As foresters have been among the first to point out, it is the practice
of applying insecticides at strengths which preserve the foliage without
completely eradicating the pest, which is largely responsible (Blais 1974).
Thus, once spraying begins it seems probable that it will have to continue for
many years. Provincial politicians, who authorize and pay for spray programs,
have become increasingly worried because of claims that annual spraying
poses unacceptable long-term risks to the environment. However, the
alternative seems equally unpalatable. With Canadian commercial forests so
close to the limits of sustainable yield, industry spokesmen have been
particularly concerned that remaining stands not be damaged or destroyed
before they can be harvested.

Professional foresters have agreed. They are aware that the intensive
forest management which they have been proposing as the solution to the
forestry crisis must include an option to protect against insects. It makes no
sense at all to invest millions of dollars (2 billion dollars was the estimate of
the CIF) only to feed the spruce budworm. Moreover, high-yield forestry also
requires herbicides to check competing species, thus linking the herbicide and
pesticide issues. Foresters were at first puzzled and later outraged by the
apparent refusal of politicians to accept their assurances that properly
registered insecticides and herbicides pose no hazards to the environment.
Foresters have come to understand that spraying the budworm is, above all, a
political problem; thus, they have become increasingly vocal lobbyists on the
insect control issue. In the process, they have revealed their assumptions
about how the Canadian political system works.

CONSTRAINTS ON POLICY MAKERS: THE BASKERVILLE REPORT

The first significant attempt by a forester to treat the budworm as a
problem with a political dimension came in New Brunswick in 1976. Not
only was the important pulp and paper industry experiencing serious wood
supply problems, but New Brunswick had been carrying out aerial spraying
against the budworm almost continuously since 1952.[7] Concerns were raised
not only about the expense of the program, but also about its environmental
consequences. *The Report of the Task Force for Evaluation of Budworm
Control Alternatives* (referred to as Baskerville [1976] after its author) was
intended to present the provincial governments with a cost/benefit analysis of

the full range of alternative policies, including the immediate suspension of spraying. The report, written by a forester from the University of New Brunswick, concluded in favor of continued spraying on the grounds that nothing less could sustain the levels of harvest required by industry, but it also argued that reliance on spraying could be reduced by better forest management.

To arrive at this conclusion, Baskerville (1976:128-129) identified three constraints on policy-makers' freedom of action. They are worth quoting in full.

1. The policy must permit the maintenance of full
    employment in the forestry sector. No public
    decision-maker will make a decision the known
    result of which is a reduction in the number of jobs.

2. The policy must improve the forest in the long run. It is
    clear that no decision-maker will consciously decide
    on a policy that will fail to give any long-term
    improvement in the forest.

3. The policy must reduce the reliance on current spraying
    tactics. No decision-maker will consciously opt for a
    policy where continued extensive use of broad
    spectrum chemical insecticides is the expectation
    indefinitely.

Despite the considerable advance in political sophistication over treatments of insect pests as a forestry problem, or even as a purely entomological problem, Baskerville's analysis remains flawed. Policy-makers do act under constraints that may force them to take actions which are, from a forest management point of view, second best, but are they the constraints which Baskerville identifies?

On closer inspection the first constraint, which is intended to be an economic one, is confused. While it is possible to talk of full employment in an entire economy, i.e., a job for everyone who wants one, what does this mean in a sector of the economy? In the second sentence, the constraint is redefined as not reducing the current level of employment. This at least makes sense, but it is incomplete. Whereas no New Brunswick politician wants to be known as the man who created unemployment by causing mills to close for want of wood, relating employment directly to wood supply ignores the role of the market. Forest products companies will only employ workers if it is profitable for them to do so. The constraint on the policy-maker is that he cannot opt to reduce the short-term profitability of the industry without risking a flight of capital, and jobs, to more profitable areas. Wood supply is only one part of this equation.

Elsewhere, Baskerville is aware that the objectives of the forest products industry are not always easy to reconcile with those of the forest manager. The pursuit of a particular historic level of return on capital can contradict policies designed to reduce the long-term susceptibility of the forest to budworm infestation and to improve its yield. As Baskerville (1976:192) says, "in terms of the host forest, New Brunswick needs to decide whether it wants to be in the pulp, paper and lumber business or in the forestry business." The assertion that the two businesses are prone to conflict is a significant one, pitting the forester against industry. But Baskerville blunts the force of his statement with his use of a personification. By saying that "New Brunswick" needs to decide what business it wants to be in, he ignores the political process by which such a decision is made. This is a particularly clear example of a "one-dimensional" conception of power, in which a whole province is personified as an actor capable of taking a decision. The individuals or groups actually responsible for policy making, and the possibility that such a choice might never appear on the political agenda at all, are ignored.

The second constraint identified by Baskerville is also ambiguous. The claim that no decision-maker will consciously opt to degrade the forest, quite apart from contradicting the history of Canadian forestry, assumes that there is a generally agreed upon, value-neutral definition of the "good forest." The significance of this assumption is that, if it were true, the professional forester would be entitled to a special place in decision making as a technical expert. However, as one forester remarked in the context of the AAC, "the allowable cut, or rate of harvest, should be a dynamic thing, subject to economics, politics, the pressure of society and management input... You have to decide what you are sustaining to" (Mackay 1985:217). To acknowledge that the forester's goals are influenced by "economics, politics, the pressure of society and management input" is to deny that there could be a single definition of what counts as degrading the forest. The criteria lie outside the forester's control, and will be the object of social and political conflict between competing interests. Baskerville (1976:3,4,121) and other foresters may not share these criteria, but to assert that it is mere shortsightedness which privileges short-term exploitation over long-term management is an over-simplification. If the exploitation mentality has created the crisis and continues to exacerbate it, foresters need to consider why their own input into the policy process has not been able to convince decision-makers of the superior rationality of management goals. In terms of the three models of politics, has the political "market" broken down or is it a problem of bureaucratic disorganization? Could it be a question of structural contradiction between the foresters' goals and those of other prominent actors?

The third constraint, that any policy must reduce the reliance on current spraying tactics, looks like an environmental one. However, Baskerville objects to spraying on the grounds that it is an extremely blunt instrument when more sophisticated tools are available. With their aid, reliance on spraying can be reduced, though not entirely eliminated. Spraying should be seen as "buying time" to implement the goals of forest management (Baskerville 1975). But in order to achieve these goals, Baskerville is adamant that foresters must have a greater share in the formulation of forest policy. Politicians will have to resist both the industrial and the environmental lobbies, and here he is pessimistic: "It is clear that if no policy exists that satisfies all three of these conditions, then the third can be relaxed and, if necessary, the second, but any policy, to be acceptable, must meet the first one" (Baskerville 1976:129). In short, he recognizes the contradiction between industrial and forestry goals, but believes that health of the industry will always be the principal constraint on policy-makers.

At this point, Baskerville withdraws into the role of technical advisor, using computer-generated models to set out a number of alternative futures for the forest. However, he does make one more suggestion as to how the forest management option might become more influential. Noting that forest management is becoming a public issue, he welcomes it: "This is a GOOD sign." He recognizes that his fellow foresters may be ambivalent towards greater public input, but he argues that problems arise only because the public is ignorant about forestry and that this ignorance is compounded by distorted media reporting, especially on environmental issues. In support of his claim, he carried out a content analysis of Maritime newspaper reports about the budworm spray issue. Of 200 articles surveyed, only 32 made explicit truth claims, and, of these, 88 percent were either false or subject to misleading constructions (Baskerville 1976:134-8). In these circumstances, he called for a higher level of public education on forestry matters. In other words, he suggested that foresters appeal over the heads of politicians and business leaders to the electorate, on the condition that the electorate has first been educated to a point where it could understand the force of the foresters' claims.

SEARCH FOR A COMMON POLICY AGAINST THE BUDWORM

The appeal to the electorate recommended by Baskerville has become a major focus of Canadian foresters' efforts to make their voices heard, but it is not the only focus. As the budworm ate its way across eastern Canada, the other provinces, whose forest industries were not at first so seriously threatened by shortfalls, began to fear for future wood supplies and became embroiled in spraying controversies. Industry spokesmen demanded extensive spraying. Loose coalitions of environmentalists, tourist operators, and small private woodlot owners lobbied against spraying with the broad-spectrum chemical insecticides then in use. Foresters attempted to chart a middle course based on establishing professional independence and presenting themselves to governments and the electorate as disinterested experts and guardians of the public forest. In doing so, they had to develop a strategy for influencing the bureaucratic elites who made the decisions. They perceived themselves to be at a disadvantage here compared with the well-established industry lobbies and even with the efforts of environmentalists.

In Ontario, for example, government foresters quickly found themselves in conflict with the pulp and paper industry over the companies' demands that immediate, widespread spraying of budworm-affected areas was necessary to ensure future wood supply. The supervisor of the Ontario Ministry of Natural Resources' (MNR) pest control section was quoted as saying that "industries blow things a little out of proportion at times," pointing out that the companies were demanding the spraying of low value balsam fir and white spruce while they actually intended to continue harvesting the remaining stocks of higher value black spruce.[8] The foresters of the MNR won this conflict, persuading the Ontario government to link spray plans with commitments by the companies to harvest affected stands.

Once a spray plan had been adopted, however, the foresters encountered a more difficult obstacle, public opposition to aerial spraying of chemical insecticides. Speaking at a budworm symposium in 1983, Chief Forester Armson of Ontario echoed Baskerville, lamenting the fact that "the forestry and scientific professions have been in the main inarticulate in the public arena ... they have often countered emotion with logic and jargon, and it doesn't work." As he pointed out, political pressure against the use of registered pesticides in forest management "essentially calls into question our professional competence and judgement in managing the public forest" (Armson 1983:4-5).

In response, foresters redoubled their public relations efforts and set in motion their second strategy. Through their professional associations, the CIF and the provincial associations of professional foresters, they began a lobbying campaign. In particular, they used their annual conventions to pass resolutions on the integral role of pesticides in forest management. These resolutions were sent to federal and provincial ministers. The ensuing correspondence was published in their professional journal. Resolution 81-3 of the CIF's 1981 Halifax conference affirmed the forestry profession's commitment to the use of chemical pesticides and herbicides. In their published replies, the resource ministers generally welcomed the resolution, but at the same time stressed their perception of a public demand for alternatives (CIF 1982). At their 1982 CCREM meeting, the ministers set up a task force on pesticides which was directed to speed up the registration of high priority substances, including alternatives to chemicals. This ambivalent response, and the growing saliency of the budworm spray issue, prompted the CIF to reaffirm its policy in 1983 and to arrange a meeting with the federal environment minister (then responsible for forestry) at which the CIF and representatives of provincial associations presented position papers on the use of chemicals. Together, they called for "leadership" from the federal government (CIF 1983).

The original strategy, the appeal to public opinion favored by Baskerville, was not neglected either. Prompted by submissions from the CIF and from the federal Canadian Forestry Service (CFS), royal commissions held to consider the future of forestry in Newfoundland (1981) and Nova Scotia (1984) endorsed the use of chemical pesticides against the budworm. In addition, they both came out in favor of spending money to promote greater public awareness of forestry issues. The Nova Scotia report endorsed forestry courses in high schools, and proposed a press officer who could rebut media distortion of forestry matters. Giving the presidential address to the CIF, Reed (1984:102) warned that "there is no challenge today that is more serious and more potent for disaster to forestry" than public opposition to the use of chemical pesticides and herbicides. In his view, such opposition is a case of intimidation by interested minorities which could only be successfully countered by a program to make the public aware of the rigorous registration procedures and the record of safe use.

Both of the foresters' strategies came under strain in the 1980s with the development of the biological insecticide *Bacillus thuringiensis* (Bt) for use against the budworm. From the foresters' point of view, Bt was clearly more expensive and less effective than chemical alternatives, and demands for its use were perceived as another challenge to the professional authority of the forester. The CFS consistently advised against Bt use in its submission to commissions and inquiries (Environment Canada 1981a), and foresters in the Ontario MNR agreed. However, provincial governments came under increasing pressure from environmentalists to use Bt, and politicians saw Bt sprays as an acceptable compromise between chemical spraying and no spraying.

As far back as 1976, small woodlot owners in Quebec had demanded the use of Bt if spraying had to be conducted, prompting one of Quebec's most respected budworm researchers to bemoan the "emotional response" to pollution and environmental protection issues (Blais 1976:60). The Quebec government eventually opted for Bt in 1985 against the advice of its own foresters. Foresters at the Ontario MNR feared a similar decision and were particularly active in appealing to public opinion once spraying decisions had been taken. Officials of the MNR mounted a major public relations campaign, distributing a booklet (Ontario 1985) which explained the extent of the outbreak and the relative merits of the different sprays. In a series of open houses held in the proposed spray areas they polled visitors, releasing figures showing overwhelming support for chemical sprays.[9] In spite of this effort, the Ontario government followed Quebec's lead in overruling its own foresters and carried out Bt-only aerial spraying in 1986. It has proposed a similar plan for 1987.

Faced with this failure, both strategies have been re-examined. In 1983, J.R. Carrow, then a senior forester in the New Brunswick Department of Natural Resources, saw the possibility of a strategy based on Bt. He agreed that, on purely scientific grounds, Bt was inferior to chemicals,[10] but "while many in the forestry community bemoan the irrational and emotional criticism of forestry use of pesticides," foresters must face the fact that they do not have public support on this issue. What Carrow saw was the possible role of Bt in establishing professional foresters' control over the public forest: "We either develop the capacity to protect with acceptable techniques, or we lose the option to protect a significant portion of the forest" (New Brunswick 1983:3). In 1986, the CIF presented a new brief on pesticides and herbicides to federal and provincial forestry ministers which, while sharply criticizing the confusion caused when governments refuse to allow the use of properly registered substances, calls for more research to "develop alternatives to conventional chemical insecticides for the control of insect pests, with special attention to microbial agents, parasites and predators, and pheromonones" (CIF 1986:261). In the published correspondence, most forestry ministers seized eagerly on this reference to alternatives to chemicals.

Nonetheless, if some foresters see the public acceptance of Bt as an opportunity to be grasped, others remain resentful. Armson, who has suffered more than most, told the 1986 National Forest Congress that decisions not to use registered chemicals against the budworm by "political fiat" had created uncertainty in the forest community: "No one disputes the right to such a decree, but that its basis is such that it does little to establish any credibility with the forest managers of the same jursidiction is crucial" (Armson 1986:381). His presentation contained additional references to media distortion of forestry issues.

DISCUSSION

The issue of budworm protection has brought the political concerns of Canadian foresters into sharp focus. The Canadian forest tenure system ensures that government decisions will be unusually important for the future of commercial forestry. If the foresters' account of events is to be believed, the cozy relationship between industry and government responsible for bringing about the wood supply crisis is now complicated by the inability or unwillingness of governments to stand up to the loose coalition of interest groups gathered together under the environmentalist label. Foresters responded to this perception of events with the two strategies described in the preceding section. First, they tried to combat media "distortion" and to influence public opinion directly through educational programs. Second, they attempted to achieve a higher political profile for the forestry profession through lobbying. Judged by the continuing dissatisfaction among foresters over government decisions concerning the use of chemical insecticides, neither strategy has been an unqualified success.

Underlying each of these strategies is a particular conception of power and the political process. The one-dimensional conception of power is evident in foresters' understanding of spraying decisions as contests between groups and individuals out of which emerge clearly defined winners and losers. The focus is on an *overt* conflict in which government foresters make recommendations, are overruled, and end up losing credibility. Opposition to the use of chemicals is perceived as based on ignorance, encouraged and perpetuated by self-interested minorities. Analogously, an economist might explain the continued use of an inferior product as the result of false advertising. This perspective sees the solution as better education of the electorate. All being well, they will respond by recognizing their general interest in a healthy commercial forest protected against insects with the best available technology.

The second strategy, lobbying activity by professional associations, is best understood as a response to a two-dimensional conception of power, involving both *overt* and *covert* conflict. Foresters claimed that forest management generally, and an integrated forest management approach to the budworm specifically, had simply failed to appear on the Canadian political agenda. They complained that in spite of their repeated warnings nothing was being done about the impending wood supply crisis and the budworm's part in accelerating it. The direction of their lobbying efforts confirms this perception of organizational inefficiency in government. Their demands for federal leadership to solve jurisdictional problems, their successful pressure on CCREM to create a task force to speed up pesticide registration, and their demands for more money to be spent on research and development are all classic solutions to perceived "bureaucratic disorganization" (Alford and Friedland 1985).

Most significant, however, is the possibility that some of these responses imply a three-dimensional understanding of power and conflict. Certainly, Baskerville's analysis of the constraints on policy-makers was a step in this direction, but Baskerville was apparently unwilling to thoroughly work through his own implications. If it is true that the most important constraint on spray decisions is an economic one, and an "industrial forest policy" conflicts with a "forest management policy," then the industrial forest policy will have a privileged place in decision-makers' calculations. Resolving the conflict in this way is an example of the exercise of *latent* power in which a deeply entrenched institutional practice, the commercial exploitation of natural resources, makes one policy seem the obvious solution. Not until that practice itself can be seen as contributing to the problem, causing both market failure and bureaucratic disorganization by "weighting" a particular interest, can a different kind of solution be entertained.

The considerable accomplishment of Canadian foresters is to have pushed at least some way in this direction. The 1986 National Forest Congress involving politicians, corporate and union leaders, and foresters from industry, government and the universities was significant for the extent to which almost everyone paid lip-service to the goals of forest management. Here is an example of what American political scientist Hugh Heclo has called an "issue network," a group of policy-watchers sharing a common language within which problems are identified and solutions generated (Heclo 1978). The group transcends traditional boundaries between governmental and nongovernmental organizations and, if successful, sets the agenda for policy discussions in their area. Similar networks can, no doubt, be identified in other areas of natural resource management. What makes them distinctive is their shared commitment to the discourse of management. Natural resources are seen as a management problem. The main beneficiaries of such networks are management professionals who have a monopoly on the training and expertise necessary to formulate and implement management solutions.

In this respect, the Canadian forestry example is especially significant because of the perception, however inarticulate or opaquely expressed, that a forest management policy contradicts an industrial forest policy. Can the issue network survive the latent, structural power of industrial forestry? Three areas of future research look promising. First, continuing ambivalence exists within the forestry profession toward public concern over the use of chemicals in forest management. The development of Bt has depoliticized the pesticide issue for the moment. The next overt conflict will be on the herbicide issue, and there are already signs that the foresters' strategy of blaming public ignorance and media malice needs rethinking.[11]   Second, the foresters' lobbying effort has been largely directed toward putting forest management issues on the policy-making agenda. Despite their defeats on chemical spraying, they have been successful in this agenda-setting effort through the creation of an issue network. At the level of covert conflict the focus will now shift to *implementation*. Compared with other countries, Canada remains relatively undersupplied with foresters, and those who are available often have difficulty finding appropriate employment for their skills.[12]

Finally, and most important of all, is the extent to which forest management can continue to operate as an "exclusionary discourse," defining its own problems and generating its own solutions. The strength of latent power is such that actors rarely perceive its operation, but forestry professor Kenneth Hearnden has already been moved to object to the "indiscriminate figurative uses to which [forest management] has been put in the realm of public relations to describe the operations of the forest industry" (Mackay 1985:148). Here, institutionally dominant values are already beginning to coopt the discourse of forest management.

The ability of forestry professionals to respond to these challenges will depend, in part, on their ability to articulate and become more familiar with their own assumptions about power and politics. As in other resource areas, the study of policy will have to be recognized as an integral part of a professional education in resource management.

NOTES

1. Following Lortie (1982), "forester" and "professional forester" are used throughout to mean a university graduate in forestry, forest engineering or forest sciences.

2. See Dahl's classic (1961) study of politics in New Haven.

3. Most often cited is Crenson's (1971) study of the failure of an Indiana steel community to enact clean air legislation.

4. The three-dimensional conception of power is analyzed in Lukes (1974). An example is Alford's (1975) study of the role of the medical profession in health-care politics.

5. According to recent estimates, land classed as Not Satisfactorily Restocked (NSR) increased from 5 million hectares in 1960 to 22 million hectares in 1981 (Honer and Bickerstaff 1985).

6. Of an estimated 44 million cubic meters of merchantable timber lost to insects annually, the spruce budworm is responsible for 35 million cubic meters (Toovey 1986: 29).

7. Between 1949 and 1983, 16,000 tons of five different insecticides had been sprayed on New Brunswick forests (Irving and Webb 1985).

8. Quoted in news story, "Timberland facing ruin from outbreak of budworm," *Globe and Mail*, August 3, 1984.

9. Cited in news story "Ontario didn't heed opinions on forest sprays, industry says," Toronto *Star*, February 14, 1986.

10. Early problems with the formulation and application of Bt seems to have been overcome, but it remains true that, compared with chemicals that kill on contact, Bt allows the budworm to continue feeding after ingesting a lethal dose (New Brunswick 1983).

11. Armson's (1986) attack on media distortion received a very negative response during the ensuing panel discussion.

12. Canada has approximately one forester per 50,000 hectares of productive forest, compared with one per 15,000 hectares in the United States, Norway and Sweden (Lortie 1982).

REFERENCES

Alford, R. 1975. *Health Care Politics*. Chicago: Chicago University Press.

Alford R. and R. Friedland. 1985. *Powers of Theory*. Cambridge: Cambridge University Press.

Armson, K. 1983. "Why Are We Here?" In *The Spruce Budworm Problem in Ontario--Real or Imaginary?* Sault Saint Marie, Ontario: Canada-Ontario Joint Forestry Research Committee. 1-5.

_____ 1986. "Chemicals and Our Forests." *Forestry Chronicle* 62:379-382.

Baskerville, G.L. 1975. "Spruce Budworm. The Answer is Forest Management: Or Is It?" *Forestry Chronicle* 51:157-160.

_____ 1976. *Report of the Task Force for Evaluation of Spruce Budworm Control Alternatives*. New Brunswick: Prime Minister's Office.

Bellyea, R.M., C.A. Miller, G.L. Baskerville, E.G. Dettala, K.B. Marshall, and I.W. Varty. 1975. "The Spruce Budworm." *Forestry Chronicle* 51:135-160.

Blais, J.R. 1974. "The Policy of Keeping Trees Alive Via Spray Operations May Hasten the Recurrence of Spruce Budworm Outbreaks." *Forestry Chronicle* 50:19-21.

_____ 1976. "Can Bacillus Thuringiensis Replace Chemical Insecticides in the Control of the Spruce Budworm?" *Forestry Chronicle* 52:57-60.

Canadian Forest Congress. 1980. *The Forest Imperative*. Toronto: Ontario Science Centre.

Canadian Institute of Forestry (CIF). 1982. "Resolution on the Use of Pesticides." *Forestry Chronicle* 58:4-5.

_____ 1983. "Policy Statements on the Use of Chemical Pesticides in Forestry." *Forestry Chronicle* 59:288.

_____ 1984. "A Case for Improved Forest Management in Canada. Brief to the Macdonald Commission." *Forestry Chronicle* 60:29-33.

_____ 1986. "Pesticides for Forest Management. A New Technology Gap." *Forestry Chronicle* 62:266-270.

Crenson, M. 1971. *The Unpolitics of Air Pollution.* Baltimore: Johns Hopkins University Press.

Dahl, R.A. 1961. *Who Governs?* New Haven: Yale University Press.

Environment Canada. 1981a. *Review of the Spruce Budworm Outbreak In Newfoundland.* Canadian Forestry Service Submission to the Newfoundland Royal Commission on Forest Protection and Management. Saint John's, Newfoundland: Environment Canada.

_____ 1981b. *Critical Choices in the Management of the Forestry Sector.* Technical Report. Ottawa: Environment Canada.

_____ 1982. *Policy Statement: A Framework for Forest Renewal.* Ottawa: Environment Canada.

Heclo, H. 1978. "Issue Networks and the Executive Establishment." In Anthony King (ed.), *The New American Political System.* Washington: American Enterprise Institute. 87-124.

Honer, T.G. and A. Bickerstaff. 1985. *Canada's Forest Area and the Wood Volume Balance 1977-81.* Victoria, B.C.: Canadian Forestry Service.

Irving, H.J. and F.E. Webb. 1985. "Questions of Safety in Aerial Application of Chemical Against Spruce Budworm in New Brunswick." *Canadian Forest Industries* 105:41-49.

Lortie, M. 1982. *Evaluation of Future Canadian Requirements for Professional Foresters.* Toronto: Canadian Forestry Advisory Council.

Lukes, S. 1974. *Power. A Radical View.* London: Macmillan.

Macdonald, D.S. 1985. *Royal Commission on the Economic Union and Development Prospects for Canada*. Report of The Macdonald Commission. Ottawa: Minister of Supply and Services.

Mackay, D. 1985. *Heritage Lost: The Crisis in Canada's Forests*. Toronto: Macmillan.

Marchak, P. 1983. *Green Gold: The Forest Industry in B.C.* Vancouver: University of British Columbia Press.

New Brunswick. 1983. *B.T. and the Spruce Budworm*. Fredericton: Department of Natural Resources.

Ontario. 1985. *In Answer to Your Concerns About Aerial Spraying in Northern Ontario Forests*. Toronto: Ministry of Natural Resources.

Reed, F.L.C. 1978. *Forest Management in Canada*. Forest Management Institute Information Report, FMR-X-102.

_____ 1984. "A Check Up for the Professional Forester." *Forestry Chronicle* 60:101-103.

_____ 1986. "Wood Supply. A Growing Concern." *Forestry Chronicle* 62:335-338.

Swift, J. 1983. *Cut and Run: The Assault on Canada's Forests*. Toronto: Between the Lines.

Toovey, J.W. 1986. "Forest Management in Canada." *Canadian Forest Industries* 106(5): B27-32.

14

FOREST PLANNING: LEARNING WITH PEOPLE

Margaret A. Shannon
*College of Environmental Science
and Forestry
State University of New York, Syracuse*

Few ideas permeate American society more thoroughly than our belief in rational action. Our cultural understanding of individuals, organizations, economic activity, and government policy all presume a strong relationship between information and choice. An equal, if not more important value of our democratic society, is the ideal of allowing citizens to participate in choices that affect them. Attempts to realize this ideal have generated traditional concerns both about effective representation and mechanisms of direct participation, such as the referendum (McConnell 1966). Rationality and participation are usually presented as separate and conflicting normative theories (Rein 1976), and as two sources of legitimacy for public choices (Mashaw 1983).

However, while politics and rationality may seem on the surface to be contradictory modes of choice, recent efforts to increase public participation in administrative processes have not necessarily led to a decline in rationality, as some observers expected (Krutilla and Haigh 1978, Sax 1973). Instead, rationality may actually be strengthened by citizen participation (Shannon 1985). Once good information becomes public and known to all participants in the decision process, it is difficult to ignore.

This article describes how legal requirements which formalized land management planning at the national forest level within the United States Forest Service (USFS) evolved in ways to legitimate both rationality and public participation. How formal organizations respond to competing visions of legitimate action in their daily business tells us about processes of organizational change and how democracy and administration can work together (Krieger 1986). The story of forest planning extends beyond the service itself to the nature of the social environment and to how processes requiring collective action are dependent upon the development of shared understandings (Klosterman 1980, Selznick 1949). The following three sections establish the organizational, historical, and cultural context for forest planning. A fourth section presents results of a field study on six western forests. A fifth section focuses discussion on the roles of the forest supervisor and the local social environment in the development of forest plans. A final section considers the future of forest planning.

AGENCY CULTURE, SCIENTIFIC MANAGEMENT AND PUBLIC PARTICIPATION

Public administration consists of a set of shared ideas, values, and practices--a culture--as well as tangible organizations and functional roles (Brown 1978, Meyer and Rowan 1977). People alter culture continuously; given new situations, people invent culture. As Becker (1982:520) notes, new collective understandings arise within the context of social action:

> A group finds itself sharing a common situation and common problems...members of the group experiment with possible solutions.... In the course of collective discussion, the members of the group arrive at a definition of the situation, its problems and possibilities, and develop a consensus as to the most appropriate and efficient ways of behaving.

Solutions, however, are only partially determined by the nature of the problem. They are also influenced by the available cultural repertoire of familiar solutions, differences in the ability of individuals or groups to influence the nature of collective discussions, and happenstance occurrences (Meidinger 1987).

Approaching forest planning from the viewpoint of culture focuses our attention on the interplay between ideas and practices that bring about change. A brief review of the milieu of ideas influencing public administration helps us better grasp those ideas which oriented USFS officials to their role as public agents (Ladd 1970).

Public agencies pervade most areas of life in modern society. The development of large, formal organizations drew heavily on popular ideas of scientific management (Burrell and Morgan 1979). In principle, such organizations can dissect complex social problems into simple segments that individuals can manage; the management of the whole can be achieved by the aggregation of individual actions. However, to sustain and coordinate such complex patterns of collective action, participants must share perceptions of the problem and the possible solutions.

A central rationale for applying scientific management to public agencies was efficiency (Hays 1959). Scientific management and efficiency formed the basis of a model positing public administrators as politically detached, well-trained professionals drawing on neutral information (not direct political influence) to make decisions in the public interest.

In response to the tremendous expansion of the administrative state in the 1940s, concern developed, primarily among lawyers, over the problem of controlling the administrators. Realization that unelected bureaucrats were formulating significant social policies led to calls for accountability and review of decisions (Boyer 1983). In 1946, the demands for procedural control over certain types of administrative decisions led to the enactment of the Administrative Procedures Act. For the most part, this law affected only actions defined as administrative rule making or adjudication. By implication, that left other types of administrative actions open to more informal processes and accountable at best to the "arbitrary and capricious" standard (Gellhorn and Boyer 1982). Although the Act did specify procedures, the general norm of broad, loosely reviewed administrative discretion remained.

In the 1960s and 1970s, previously excluded interests and groups demanded and received increased participation in formal and informal agency processes (Krause 1968). Requirements for increased participation were accompanied by ever-widening definitions of what constituted formal actions of rule making and adjudication. Courts began to specify what factors adjudicatory processes must consider (U.S. Court of Appeals 1971) and who should be permitted to review administrative decisions (U.S. District Court 1972). Citizen participation as an ideology grew out of pluralist political theory which gained significant social currency as public agencies touched more of people's lives, and as the diversity of interests affected by "rule bound" decisions became evident (Stewart 1975). The broader the scope of administration and the greater the public awareness of its effects, the greater was the distrust of the ability of public agents to make decisions in the best interest of either affected individuals or the "public interest" (Klosterman 1980, Lowi 1969).

The environmental protection and natural resource management statutes of the 1970s were strongly influenced by this atmosphere of distrust. As a group, these statutes incorporated both traditional ideas of efficiency and new norms of citizen participation (Coggins and Wilkinson 1981, Rodgers 1977, Schoenbaum 1985). They demonstrated a continued faith in the potential for good process to lead to good decisions. Yet, they also relied ever more heavily on express moral goals for environmental quality and prescriptive standards for governing substantive outcomes.

Legislative control over administrative decisions was thus strengthened by (1) specifying procedural requirements; (2) relying on formal administrative records (of both scientific analyses and citizen views) for justifying decisions; (3) restricting discretion by prescriptive substantive requirements; (4) including citizen participants not only as sources of public views, but also as co-formulators and enforcers of appropriate agency policies.

FORMAL PLANNING COMES TO THE FOREST SERVICE

The United States Forest Service, established in 1905 as the administrator of the National Forest Reserves, is one of several federal land management agencies.[1] In theory, the purpose of bureaucratic organization is to centralize policy making at the top of a "pyramid" of lines of formal communication. Authority to implement that policy devolves to the field level. In contrast, the Forest Service operates as a decentralized bureaucracy. Authority delegated to district-level district rangers and forest supervisors is substantial. (Indeed, the existing process for appealing a forest officer's decision pertains to decisions made at the field level of the organization.) In his classic study of the USFS, Herbert Kaufman (1960) found that although the organization showed a vast internal system of record keeping and review, the real mechanism for ensuring consistency across forests was identification of forest officers with agency ideology. Thus, to view the agency as merely a bureaucracy vastly oversimplifies it.

Despite mechanisms to ensure that local actions will be consistent with broad policy, local decisions and policies reflect the professional training and values of the line officer, the local situation (both biophysical and socioeconomic), and culture. Broad policy and local decisions are "loosely coupled." To be legitimate, decisions must fall within boundaries derived from legislative mandates, internal rules and regulations, and agency culture. However, these boundaries cannot fully determine any particular outcome.

Thus, because the USFS grants substantial authority to field officers, attempts to influence local decisions by changing national policy might successfully be resisted. Respect for the power of local commitments led to the USFS practice of the frequent transfer of field officers.

In the late 1960s and early 1970s the Forest Service faced challenges from the rapidly growing cadre of environmentalists. Where historically national forest management was hardly local news, suddenly both national and local voices criticized conventional practices as out of step with current values. The "crisis of legitimacy" (Lowi 1969) facing other administrative services now extended in full force to the agency (Coggins and Wilkinson 1981). The net effect of this well-known story was new statuatory guidelines for policy formation, implementation and budgeting (LeMaster 1984). These new requirements were imposed primarily by the Forest and Rangeland Renewable Resources Planning Act of 1974 (RPA) and its significant amendment in 1976 by the Natural Forest Management Act (NFMA). These Acts prescribe complex planning processes designed to make local decisions conform with national policy.

The above statutes envisioned a rational, comprehensive planning process--in vogue at the time--extending from a national assessment of all renewable natural resources and a national program for Forest Service management to integrated management plans at the local forest level. Although planning had long been an important activity of the Forest Service, it had been an informal process for attaining internal accountability (Wilkinson and Anderson 1985). Now formal planning processes as well as methods for rational assessment of alternatives are specified by regulations which are further elaborated in the *Forest Service Manual* (USFS n.d.) and *Handbooks* (NEPA in FSM 1950, NFMA in FSM 1920).

Forest planning incorporates both rational and participatory images of how public decisions should be made. The steps of the forest planning process follow the general model of rational-comprehensive planning. Early and frequent public participation is required throughout the planning process, and extends into the implementation and monitoring of the plan.

Initially, the Forest Service simply tried to blend forest planning into its existing planning routines by broadening the geographic scope of its Unit Plans and by integrating its functional, resource specific plans into one huge process. A complex computer model (FORPLAN) for considering resource management potentials given different demands and constraints was developed to look at everything at once. Viewed as a highly structured and rational process it seemed for a while that forest planning had successfully formalized ongoing routines in agency operation.

However, when in 1979 the first draft of the Lolo National Forest Plan (Missoula, Montana) appeared, the timber industry, long accustomed to exclusive informal access to the national leadership of the agency, realized that forest plans would shape local policy. Fearful of losing informal influence in affecting national policy, the industry association prepared a massive critique of the Lolo Forest Plan.

The forest planning process also was addressed by the courts. A California court ruled that wilderness evaluations in the national Roadless Area and Review Process (RARE II) had not considered an adequate range of alternatives for protecting the qualities of wilderness (U.S. Court of Appeals

1982). Evaluating the wilderness values of roadless lands was to be part of the forest planning process. After approximately one year, during which the agency re-thought its approach to forest planning, forest plans again surfaced for public review in 1983. These plans were clear evidence that both the USFS and the public had developed new understandings of forest planning which went far beyond the idea of a technical process for rational-comprehensive analysis.

CREATING A CULTURE FOR FOREST PLANNING

> Technical knowledge would be viewed as only one rather uncertain input into a situation that also requires commonsense, ethical insight, and a great deal of conversation with those affected before a policy can be formulated or a decision made. The important point is that technical knowledge does not necessitate anything. Decisions and commitments must emerge from the practical context of communicative action. (Bellah 1983:57)

In practice, blending the normative ideals of rational analysis and citizen participation provides plenty of creative opportunities for agencies to reframe historical commitments and to evaluate missions and practices (Selznick 1957, Benveniste 1972). Forest planning illustrates how participatory and technical-rational modes of administrative decision making can be merged into a coherent process.

For all the apparent specification of forest planning in both the NFMA Regulations and the *Forest Service Manual* and *Handbooks*, just how the processes would work in practice could not be envisioned fully in advance (Majone and Wildavsky 1978). Here, I outline an ideal model of how forest planning was expected to merge technical competency with responsive communication.

Ideally, forest planning is a communication process between the Forest Service and the participating public. The dialogue focuses on potentially available resources on the forest, and current policy. The issue-driven model of planning emerged first in the National Environmental Policy Act "scoping" process. By regulation forest planning begins with public identification of issues and seeks to resolve those issues.

Current planning efforts are constrained by historical use and management of forests. Thus, planning issues reflect both task commitments and new values. After assessing the implications of the current management direction, the agency constructs alternative courses of action. Evaluation of the alternative management directions is much like hypotheses testing: If this mix of management policies and practices is chosen, then these consequences will follow. The public, after seeing what changes in policy direction and management practices follow from their concerns, respond by refining their issues and values.

Next, decision criteria for comparative evaluation of the alternatives are specified by the agency. Out of this evaluation emerges a proposed management direction--the draft forest plan. The public then comments on the draft plan. Incorporating some comments and formally responding to all, the USFS produces the final plan which will govern the management of the forest for about a decade unless something changes significantly. Out of the public dialogue and choice process evolves a set of mutually understood rules governing local forest decision making. The Record of Decision documents the reasons that account for choices in the plan.

Thus, as an ideal, forest planning melds public participation with technical analysis to produce a plan acceptable to the agency and the public. By incorporating citizen participation in agency decision making, forest planning changed the social environment of the agency (Child 1972). Forest planning processes are now at the forefront of agency attention. With planning process evolution, the public and the agency are gradually coming to better understand both their own and other's perspectives.

EMERGING NORMS FOR A RESPONSIVE MANAGEMENT STYLE

Carl Friedrich (1974:420) describes a "responsible administrator" as one who is responsive to two dominant factors--technical knowledge and popular sentiment. This section will address how on some forests the tension between the demands of participatory planning and technical competence has opened the way for the development of a responsive management style (Nonet and Selznick 1978). In a responsive management style, the public participates in the culture-creating role of forest planning through a process of public deliberation. Managers who run their forests using a responsive style of management are likely to develop forest plans which effectively blend the requirements of participation and technical analysis. Such plans imply that the agency and the public share an understanding of the role and purpose of national forest management. Such shared understandings can be termed "local culture."

During the fall of 1984, I studied six western forests and interviewed both agency staff and local citizens. Five factors emerged as strongly related to the type of local culture and norms of forest planning likely to develop on a particular national forest (Shannon 1985). In order of importance, the five factors are as follows:

1. Management style of the forest supervisor

2. Relationship of decision-making personnel on the forest
   to the planning process

3. Social environment of the local communities involved in
   the planning process

4. Organization of the forest staff.

5. Presence of individuals in the agency and public who
   grasp the essential qualites and value of public
   dialogue

The study showed that, consistent with the norm of substantial independence of the national forests, staff organization and management style remain primarily the prerogative of the forest supervisor.

This real decentralization meant that the response of forest staff to planning was importantly constrained by the nature of the local social environment. However, how particular forest supervisors responded to forest planning depended as much on the supervisors' own ideas of how actions should be constrained as it did on actual external forces (cf., March and Olsen 1976). This point is critical to those concerned with organizational innovation, showing that legislation does not guarantee decision-makers will take advantage of opportunities to innovate.

Of the five factors listed above, two are especially critical to emergence of a responsive management culture on a forest: internal management style of the supervisor, and the nature of the local social environment.

Management Style of the Forest Supervisor
The pivotal factor in whether a forest developed a responsive management style was the recognition by the forest supervisor that the public viewed narrowly defined, technical decision making as inconsistent with the kinds of decisions public agencies make. Responsive supervisors recognized that the forest plan had to emerge from discussions with the public, address the political issues currently or potentially relevent to political representatives, and yet be soundly based in the scientific information necessary to make professional judgments about uncertain outcomes. Although often confused

and overwhelmed by this seemingly impossible task, these supervisors reached out to their staff and to their social and political communities in seeking ways to work together (cf., Duncan 1972).

A few examples illustrate the abstract concept of "responsive management style." On several forests, the line officers, recognizing the critical role of the plan in determining their management choices, formed the core of the "interdisciplinary team responsible for formulating the plan." Sometimes they did the actual content analysis of the public comments. As a style of internal management, the forest supervisors encouraged ongoing, open discussions among the forest staff of what the public meant by an issue, as well as the implications of the scientific data on that issue. Constant debate and dialogue among the staff later opened the way for staff acceptance of different interpretations of the issues and data by members of the public.

On one forest, the results of the FORPLAN analysis were hung on huge acetate overlays on the wall of the planning team's room. Nearby were maps drawn by the public of how and where they used the forest, and where they would like to see certain types of management. Constant discussions took place in front of this wall as resource specialists debated among themselves the meaning of this information. When the public comments came back from review workshops, the staff often recognized in them many of the debates they too had struggled with. Their responses to the public's comments were both genuine, as they had the same questions, and substantive, in that those indeed were the issues being addressed by the planning process.

On another forest, the forest supervisor, planning officer and resources officer went to every public meeting held by the district rangers on their district. On this forest the management team also served as the interdisciplinary team responsible for planning. This meant that the district rangers were responsible for working with their staffs in "scoping" the public issues and then generating district alternatives in response to public issues. When it came time to put together forest-wide alternatives, the management team met, in their role as the planning team, to merge the issues and resource availabilities present on their very different kinds of districts. The result was a geographically cohesive plan based on the management of difference.

Of particular pride to the supervisor was the actual design and organization of the forest plan document. Each management section was geographically organized so that any staff member, even a seasonal specialist, could put the relevant portion in a "backpocket or the glove compartment of the truck" and refer to it easily. The forest-wide management standards and guidelines were contained in one section designed for easy reference. With its color coding, the plan functioned not as an abstract document but as a daily tool. This result can be squarely attributed to the commitment of management to the success of the plan.

The management style of the supervisor generally set the tone for both internal and external relationships. On forests where more authoritarian management styles characterized the organization of the forest staff, the potential creativity of the staff was usually blocked. On these forests, the understanding of the role of the public in forest planning was limited to the supervisor's views, even when his views were not shared by the staff.

On the forests studied, how the forest supervisor treated the staff was directly correlated to how he viewed the role of the public. If the forest supervisor encouraged open staff discussion and cast his own role as facilitator of good debate, then that forest was likely to conduct extensive public involvement workshops, or consensus groups, or organize other ways for groups to discuss forest management. The melding of public deliberation with technical data was accomplished in these cases by the content of the public discussion. Public participation extended into the scope and content of policy and programs; thus, the public's role was not limited to that of external commentator, as it was on some forests. However, technical analysts faced a challenge of effectively communicating the meaning and implications of scientific information. Whereas on some forests the role of the public as reviewer could be justified by presuming a lack of technical sophistication, responsive forests presumed that the technical information could inform public debate.

To highlight the difference, on one forest the district staff was not involved at all in the planning process and indeed saw nothing until the draft plan was issued. The planning staff on the forest was a separate staff and had put the plan together entirely as a staff function. The supervisor expected no problems in implementation because he expected the rangers to follow that plan just as they had followed other plans. For the supervisor, forest planning was a technical exercise. However, this forest did have a complicated social environment characterized by high long-term unemployment and by threats from the timber industry of further layoffs if the forest did not give them what they wanted. Because they were not part of the forest planning process, the district staff could not help alleviate the public uncertainty as to what changes the plan might bring. As a result, the forest, viewed as insensitive to local needs, subject to unholy bargains with powerful interests, or run by unresponsive bureaucrats, grew ever more defensive and the public became polarized. While certainly the ultimate polarization of the community cannot be attributed solely to the management style of the forest supervisor, in this instance his management style exacerbated and intensified existing fears, rather than providing a forum for potential community action in coming to terms with the new economic environment.

Local Social Environment

The second important factor in the development of a responsive management culture was the presence of a diverse social environment where a broad range of social values found local expression (Terreberry 1968). The more diverse the environment, the more likely an effective dialogue between the public and the forest staff. While this factor often supported understanding between members of the public as well as by the forest staff, it did not protect some forests from still being perceived as adversaries or the communities from becoming polarized (Shannon 1985).

Most forests had both formal and informal opportunites to work with organized public groups. For example, on one forest the local "movers and shakers" had long met together to discuss issues of community policy and development. The forest supervisor joined this group as their permanent "invited guest." Because of a strict norm of confidentiality, this group could provide the supervisor with the opportunity to informally discuss pending decisions or problems.

This general arrangement seems quite similar to traditional norms of agency participation in various community groups and service clubs (Kaufman 1960). Indeed, on one forest, the previous forest supervisor had tried to organize the staff to ensure that someone belonged to each of the relevant local groups. His stated purpose was twofold: to communicate informally about forest management with the community and to keep tabs on community or group views.

Most forests found they had to create the social linkages among community members in order to have effective public dialogue on forest planning. Several supervisors noted that often those people who came to public workshops or participated in consensus groups admitted to having never met many of their neighbors before. Even more pertinent, these individuals told the agency personnel that as a result of the public discussions, they now had a much greater appreciation of the real needs and constraints on other members of the community. The conflicts did not go away, but greater empathy among the members of the public and between the agency and the public did seem to result from these discussions.

Several forests organized "consensus groups" to seek, through greater mutual understanding, ways to manage the forest. It must be noted that two such forests were deeply embroiled in divisive public disagreements over general visions of the nature of a national forest. These divisions are local microcosms of the national controversy over the role of the national forests as timber producers. It appeared in this initial analysis that the presence of these consensus groups forced the political interest groups as well as local community members to negotiate with each other, rather than putting pressure on the agency to meet demands individually.

It is important to reiterate that the above organizational changes were also influenced by the presence of particular individuals with foresight, leadership, and the ability to communicate with both scientists and citizens. These individuals invariably had prior experiences that prepared them for this task. A few notable examples follow: (1) the supervisors had served in one of several locations--New England, Southern California, the late 1970s Lake Tahoe planning process, and job corp programs; (2) they had been exposed to the Management by Objectives process in California in the 1970s; (3) they had encountered complex social environments before and learned how to work within them. Every individual had a different combination of experiences, but these were the patterns that emerged when aggregated.

LOCAL ENVIRONMENTS AND FOREST PLANNING CULTURE

For towns and communities near national forests, the USFS is a part of everyday life. Indeed, in many parts of the western states, the agency preceded towns of any size (Wiebe 1967). In seeking to bring the principles of conservation and forest management to the national forests, agency professionals often worked with the local people to educate them about the principles and objectives of the Forest Service and to elicit their support of agency programs (Starbuck 1975). As the history of the agency attests, conservation and scientific forest management were progressive but not populist movements (Pisani 1985). Rather, consistent with progressive public agencies, the purpose of the agency was to help meet societal goals both by changing the public's behavior, and by implementing the agenda of conservation and management.

Because of the powerful legitimating authority of scientific and professional expertise, the Forest Service enjoyed substantial autonomy from outside political control during its first half century (Coggins and Wilkinson 1981, Wilkinson and Anderson 1985). It was not until the late 1960s that deference to expertise and professionalism was superceded by concerns for the degree to which agency purposes fit with changing resource protection and management values. While informal communication both at the local level and in the "halls of power" had always characterized the relationship between the Forest Service and its social or political environment, new requirements for public participation formalized this relationship and included expectations for change (Karr 1983).

Traditionally, the public communicated with the agency in two general ways. Local people went to district offices for information or to discuss particular issues regarding their use of the forest. Timber or livestock association representatives (and other similar interests) or resource interest groups tried to influence the policies guiding local management. In either instance, the communication was between the agency and the public.

What appears to have emerged on responsive forests is a community of natural resource interests which provides the forum for discussion of forest planning. Imagine a wheel with many spokes. In the old pattern of communication, the agency was the hub and the interests, the spokes, each communicated directly to it. What now seems to describe the communication patterns on these forests is a wheel where all the interests and the agency are arrayed in a circle and discussion occurs among all participants--the spokes now crisscross between all parties and there is not a clearly defined hub. For organized interest groups accustomed to using personal influence to shape policy, this new arrangement displaces their exclusive access. For the agency, this new arrangement provides some new opportunities for political compromise and negotiation. For newly organized and small local interest groups, these relationships provide an opportunity to rapidly enter and substantially affect the discussions regarding forest policies.

The social environment of forest management was, until recently, an institutionalized pattern of relationships among a known set of actors. Now, broad public participation in forest planning has created new social groups and interests and promises to create more (Schattschneider 1975). The kinds of information and how it was presented also affected how interests coalesced. As the nature and implications of the choices to be made became clearly framed, new connections arose among members of the public (Berger 1976).

This development will be important in the future evolution of forest planning. Most techniques for public participation reflect the assumptions of pluralist political theory that interests merely exist and that adequate representation is the problem (Stewart 1975). Similarly, the requirement for measuring costs and benefits of alternative programs relies on a premise that resource values can be derived from the existing preferences of claimants and users. But to the extent that social interests and resource values are created by the planning process, they cannot be specified in advance. To the extent that relationships among the members of the resource community exist, resource interests and values will be socially constructed in this forum (cf., Berger and Luckman 1967). It follows that conventional assumptions about preference structures and interest theory may need re-examination (Landy and Plotkin 1982).

DISCUSSION

Over a decade ago, Norman Wengert (1976) observed that citizen participation seemed to be a "practice in search of a theory." Today, a new theory of governance is emerging which emphasizes public deliberation in forest planning (cf., Reich 1985). In addition, new relationships between the public and an agency are also developing in relation to programs in other agencies, such as the Environmental Protection Agency (Boyer and Meidinger 1986).

The story of forest planning can be usefully told from many vantage points. This article stresses that our cultural understanding of the USFS, its professional pride and spirit, and its role within the social environment all contribute to natural resource management (Morgan 1986). It is these shared assumptions that are currently being changed, at least on a number of forests.

In several western locales, the source of intra-organizational diffusion for innovations in planning or public participation methods was often the public itself.[2] Because individuals, associations and interest groups are usually affected by several forests, those involved in forest planning "keep track of" and participate in a number of forest planning efforts. To the extent that one forest moves in a responsive direction, this experience affects how the participating public views the planning process of other forests. Further study of the public's role as participants in forest planning may illuminate more fully their "diffusion-innovation" function.

Forest planning provides a political administrative forum for public deliberation over public policy. In order for such collective decision making to be possible, the participants must create and share a set of ideas and norms which serve to define the process and their roles in it. This article has described some of the recent developments in management style on several national forests as part of this culture-creating process.

John McGuire, chief of the USFS when NFMA was passed, termed the planning efforts envisioned by RPA and NFMA as "an experiment in land management" (McGuire 1982). The purpose of experiments is to facilitate learning. Although once viewed as a rule-bound bureaucracy, the USFS is adapting to changing values. Accordingly, learning with people is a part of forest planning.

ACKNOWLEDGMENTS

This paper benefitted from a study the author conducted for the Director of Land Management Planning, USFS, Washington D.C. during the fall of 1984. Other studies for the Forest Service and service to the agency in various capacities since 1970 also contributed to my understanding of the policy process. This paper, however, reflects only the views of the author. I would like to gratefully acknowledge the helpful comments and editing of Richard P. Gale, Susan Stiles Gale, and Errol Meidinger.

NOTES

1. Readers are encouraged to study the many excellent accounts of the USFS in natural resource management (Culhane 1981, Dana 1956, Dana and Fairfax 1980, Ise 1920, Kaufman 1960, Robinson 1975, Steen 1976).

2. In 1979, I interviewed nearly all of the forest supervisors in one western region just prior to their involvement in forest planning. It was already evident then that the changed political role of the public was affecting how supervisors viewed their local community, the national interest groups, and politicians who directly influenced their decisions. "Trying to get a plan or project to fly" concerned all of them as they worried over the political volatility of the social environment. One of the most important developments in forest planning has been the degree to which the public both shapes and becomes involved in forest policies. None of the supervisors I interviewed really anticipated this.

REFERENCES

Becker, H.S. 1982. "Culture: A Sociological View." *The Yale Review* 71:513-27.

Bellah, R.N. 1983. "Social Science as Practical Reason." In D. Callahan and B. Jennings (eds.), *Ethics, the Social Sciences, and Policy Analysis.* New York: Plenum Press. 37-64.

Benveniste, G. 1972. *The Politics of Expertise.* Berkeley: Glendessary Press.

Berger, P.L. 1976. "In Praise of Particularity: The Concept of Mediating Structures." *The Review of Politics* 38:399-410.

Berger, P.L. and T. Luckmann. 1967. *The Social Creation of Reality: A Treatise in the Sociology of Knowledge.* New York: Doubleday.

Boyer, B. 1983. "Fifty Years of Regulatory Reform in the United States." Paper prepared for the Conference on Regulation in Britain, Trinity College, Oxford.

Boyer, B. and E. Meidinger. 1986. "Privitizing Regulatory Enforcement: A Preliminary Assessment of Citizen Suits Under   Federal Environmental Laws." *Buffalo Law Review* 34:834-965.

Brown, R.H.   1978.   "Bureaucracy as Praxis: Toward a Political Phenomenology of Formal Organizations." *Administrative Science Quarterly* 23:365-82.

Burrell, G. and G. Morgan.   1979.   *Sociological Paradigms and Organizational Analysis: Elements of the Sociology of Corporate Life.* London: Heinemann.

Child, J. 1972. "Organizational Structure, Environment and Performance: The Role of Strategic Choice." *Sociology* 6:1-22.

Coggins, G.C. and C. F. Wilkinson. 1981. *Federal Public Land and Resources Law.* New York: Foundation Press.

Culhane, P.J. 1981. *Public Lands Politics: Interest Group Influence on the Forest Service and the Bureau of Land Management.* Baltimore: John Hopkins University Press.

Dana, S.T. 1956. *Forest and Range Policy: Its Development in the United States.* New York: McGraw-Hill.

Dana, S.T. and S.K. Fairfax. 1980 *Forest and Range Policy: Its Development in the United States*, Second Edition. New York: McGraw-Hill.

Duncan, R.B. 1972. "Characteristics of Organizational Environments and Perceived Environmental Uncertainty." *Administrative Science Quarterly* 17:313-27.

Friedrich, C.J. 1974. "Public Policy and the Nature of Administrative Responsibility." In A.A. Altschuler (ed.), *The Politics of Federal Bureaucracy.* New York: Dodd, Mead. 414-425.

Gellhorn, E. and B. Boyer. 1982. *Administrative Law and Process.* St. Paul: West Publishing Company (Nutshell Series).

Hays, S.P. 1974 [1959]. *Conservation and the Gospel of Efficiency: The Progressive Conservation Movement, 1890-1920.* Cambridge: Harvard University Press.

Ise, J. 1920. *The United States Forest Policy.* New Haven: Yale University Press.

Karr, R. 1983. *Forests for the People: Case Study of the Rare II Decision.* Unpublished Ph.D. Dissertation, University of Montana.

Kaufman, H. 1960. *The Forest Ranger: A Study in Administrative Behavior.* Baltimore: John Hopkins University Press.

Klosterman, R.E. 1980. "A Public Interest Criterion." American Planning Association Journal 46:323-33.

Krause, E.A. 1968. "Functions of a Bureaucratic Ideology: Citizen Participation." *Social Problems* 16:129-143.

Krieger, M.H. 1986. "Big Decisions and a Culture of Decisionmaking." *Journal of Policy Analysis and Management* 5:779-97.

Krutilla, J.V. and J.A. Haigh. 1978. "An Integrated Approach to National Forest Management." *Environmental Law* 8:373-415.

Ladd, J. 1970. "Morality and the Ideal of Rationality in Formal Organizations." *Monist* 54:488-516.

Landy, M.K. and H.A. Plotkin. 1982. "Limits of the Market Metaphor." *Society* 19:8-17.

LeMaster, D.C. 1984. *Decade of Change: The Remaking of Forest Service Statutory Authority During the 1970s.* Westport, CT: Greenwood Press.

Lowi, T.J. 1969. *The End of Liberalism: Ideology, Policy and the Crisis of Public Authority.* New York: W.W. Norton.

Majone, G. and A. Wildavsky. 1978. "Implementation as Evolution." *Policy Studies Review Annual* 2:101-117.

March, J.G. and J.P. Olsen. 1976. "Organizational Learning and the Ambiguity of the Past." In J.G. March and J. P. Olsen (eds.), *Ambiguity and Choice in Organizations.* Norway: Universitetsforlaget. 54-67.

Mashaw, J.L. 1983. *Bureaucratic Justice: Managing Social Security Disability Claims.* New Haven, CT: Yale University Press.

McConnell, G. 1966. *Private Power and American Democracy.* New York: Alfred A. Knopf.

McGuire, J.R. 1982. "The National Forests: An Experiment in Land Management." *Journal of Forest History* 26:84-91.

Meidinger, E.E. 1987. "Regulatory Culture." *Law and Policy* 9:forthcoming.

Meyer, J.W. and B. Rowan. 1977. "Institutionalized Organizations: Formal Structure as Myth and Ceremony." *American Journal of Sociology* 83:340-63.

Morgan, G. 1986. *Images of Organization.* Beverly Hills: Sage.

Nonet, P. and P. Selznick. 1978. *Law and Society in Transition: Toward Responsive Law.* New York: Harper and Row.

Pisani, D.J. 1985. "Forests and Conservation, 1865-1890." *The Journal of American History* 72:340-59.

Reich, R.B. 1985. "Public Administration and Public Deliberation: An Interpretive Essay." *The Yale Law Journal* 94:1617-1641.

Rein, M. 1976. *Social Science and Public Policy.* England: Penguin.

Robinson, G.O. 1975. *The Forest Service: A Study in Public Land Management.* Baltimore: Johns Hopkins University Press.

Rodgers, W.H. 1977. *Handbook on Environmental Law.* St. Paul, MN: West Publishing Co.

Sax, J.L. 1973. "The (Unhappy) Truth About NEPA." *Oklahoma Law Review* 26:239-248.

Schattschneider, E.E. 1975. *The Semisovereign People: A Realist's View of Democracy in America.* Hinsdale, IL: Dryden Press.

Schoenbaum, T.J. 1985. *Environmental Policy Law.* New York: Foundation Press.

Selznick, P. 1966 [1949]. *TVA and the Grass Roots: A Study in the Sociology of Formal Organizations.* New York: Harper and Row.

_____ 1957. "The Definition of Mission and Role." In P. Selznick, *Leadership in Administration.* New York: Harper and Row. 65-89.

Shannon, M.A. 1985. "Assessing Communication Effectiveness in Developing Forest Plans and EIS Documents." Report to the Director, Land Management Planning, U.S. Forest Service, Washington, D.C. (August).

Starbuck, W.H. 1975. "Organizations and Their Environments." In M. Dunnette (ed.), *Handbook of Industrial and Organizational Psychology.* Chicago: Rand-McNally. 1069-1121.

Steen, H.K. 1976. *The U.S. Forest Service: A History*. Seattle: University of Washington Press.

Stewart, R. B. 1975. "The Reformation of American Administrative Law." *Harvard Law Review* 88:1667-1813.

Terreberry, S. 1968. "The Evolution of Organizational Environments." *Administrative Science Quarterly* 12:590-613.

U.S. Court of Appeals. 1982. California vs. Block, 690 F. 2d 753 (9th Cir. 1982). Affirmed decision in California vs. Bergland, 483 F. Supp. 465 (E.D. Cal. 1980).

_____ 1971. Scenic Hudson Preservation Conference vs. Federal Power Commission, 453 F. 2d 463 (2d Cir. 1971), cert. Denied, 407 U.S. 926 1972).

U.S. District Court. 1972. "Mineral King"--Sierra Club vs. Morton, 405 U.S. 727 (1972).

U.S. Forest Service (USFS). *Forest Service Mannual*. Washington, D.C.: Department of Agriculture.

Wengert, N. 1976. "Citizen Participation: Practice in Search of a Theory." *Natural Resources Journal* 16:23-40.

Wiebe, R.H. 1967. *The Search for Order 1877-1920*. New York: Hill and Wang.

Wilkinson, C.F. and H.M. Anderson. 1985. "Land and Resource Planning in the National Forests." *Oregon Law Review* 64(1 and 2).

PROFILES OF THE AUTHORS

Stanley K. Brickler is Associate Professor in the School of Renewable Natural Resources at the University of Arizona. He holds a bachelors and a masters degree in zoology and natural resource management from Southern Illinois University. His doctorate is in natural resource management from Colorado State University. A member of the University of Arizona faculty since 1970, he has organized and directed research and teaching programs in water quality, wildland recreation management, and resource planning.

Perry J. Brown is Professor of Recreation Behavior and Department Head in Resource Recreation Management, and Director of Forestry International Programs at Oregon State University. His research focuses on recreationist behavior and on social inputs to natural resource management. He has published in the *Journal of Leisure Research, Leisure Sciences, Wildlife Society Bulletin, Fisheries, Journal of Environmental Education, Journal of Forestry* and *Transactions of the North American Wildlife and Natural Resources Conference,* among others.

Tommy L. Brown is a Senior Research Associate in the Department of Natural Resources at Cornell University. He is the leader of the Human Dimensions Research Unit, which focuses on socioeconomic aspects of resource issues and problems. Under his direction since 1973, this unit has carried out some 75 studies dealing with fish, wildlife, and forest management; outdoor recreation; and tourism under sponsorship of numerous state and federal agencies.

C. Hobson Bryan is Professor and Chairman of the Department of Sociology, University of Alabama. His research interests include social implications of natural resource issues and environment/resource policy. From 1979-1981 he served as the National Program Leader for Social Impact Assessment with the U.S. Forest Service, and in 1984 he was awarded a Fulbright Senior Research Fellowship to New Zealand to study natural resource and social impact assessment issues in that country.

Daniel J. Decker is a Senior Extension Associate in the Department of Natural Resources at Cornell University. Since joining the Human Dimensions Research Unit in 1976, he has conducted, directed, or been a consultant on over 50 studies dealing with the human behavioral aspects of resource management, primarily focusing on wildlife issues. His current responsibilities include human dimensions research, wildlife extension programming, and Cornell Cooperative Extension administration.

Stephen R. Dennis is an Assistant Professor in the Department of Recreation and Parks Management at California State University, Chico. He holds a Ph.D. in renewable natural resources studies from the University of Arizona. His scholarly interests concern natural resource policy and citizen involvement in policy formation, and systems delivering outdoor recreation opportunities on public lands.

Donald R. Field is Senior Scientist in the National Park Service and Professor in the College of Forestry at Oregon State University. His Ph.D. degree in rural sociology was earned at Penn State University. His current work focuses on the study of recreation areas as human ecological systems and the study of rural communitites, parks and forests as an integrated regional resource system. He is the co-author along with N.H. Cheek and R.J. Burdge of *Leisure and Recreation Places*, co-editor with J.C. Barron and B.F. Long of *Water and Community Development*, and co-editor with G. Machlis of *On Interpretation*.

Richard P. Gale is Professor of Sociology at the University of Oregon. In addition, he is Affiliate Professor of Marine Studies at the University of Washington. His specialities are environmental and natural resource sociology. He has published in *Sociological Perspectives, North American Journal of Fisheries Management, Fisheries, Journal of Forestry, Environment and Behavior*, and *Natural Resources Journal*, among others. He served as a sociologist with the U.S. Forest Service and the National Marine Fisheries Service, and has been a consultant to other resource agencies. He has held offices in the Environmental Sociology Section, American Sociological Society.

Robert Graham, as Assistant Professor in Recreation and Leisure Studies at the University of Waterloo, has research interests in protected area planning and management and marine conservation. He has been involved with the planning and implementation of several projects for Environment Canada, Parks which focus on managing the tension between the resource and users. Jon Lien of the Whale Research Institute and he recently edited *Marine Conservation: Challenge and Promise*.

Darryll R. Johnson is a Research Sociologist and Project Leader, Social Sciences Program, National Park Service, College of Forest Resources, University of Washington. He has bachelor and master degrees in sociology from South Dakota State University and has finished all but the dissertation in a doctoral program in forest sociology at the University of Washington. His current research interests include applied sociology in natural resource settings and depreciatory behavior.

George F. Mattfeld is an Environmental Management Specialist with the Bureau of Wildlife, NYS Department of Environmental Conservation, where since 1978 he has held various administrative positions, including among his responsibilities coordination of contract research with the Human Dimensions Research Unit, Cornell University. Previously, he has held research positions with the University of Michigan and SUNY-CESF. His research involvement has led to numerous published articles on ecology and management of white-tailed deer and, recently, human dimensions of wildlife management.

Marc L. Miller is Associate Professor of Marine Studies and Adjunct Associate Professor of Anthropology at the University of Washington. In addition, he holds a guest appointment as Associate Professor of Sociology at the University of Oregon. His research focuses on modern work, recreation, tourism, and natural resource management. He has published in over a dozen academic journals including the *Coastal Zone Management Journal, North American Journal of Fisheries Management, Ocean Development, International Law, Leisure Sciences, and Human Organization, Urban Life, and Annals of Tourism Research.*

Steven D. Moore is Research Associate in the School of Renewable Natural Resources at the University of Arizona. He is currently pursuing a doctoral degree. He holds a masters degree in business administration from the University of Illinois and a bachelors degree in biology from Southern Illinois University. At the University of Arizona, Moore has been involved in resource management planning for military lands and is currently conducting research on sociological aspects of wildland recreation.

Per W. Nilsen has conducted research for Environment Canada, Parks' Visitor Services Plan for Point Pelee National Park. As a graduate student, his thesis research addressed Parks' Visitor Activity Management Process and northern protected areas. He has also worked as a visitor services planner at Wood Buffalo National Park in the Northwest Territories. His research interests include northern national parks, service marketing and planning.

Robert J. Payne is Assistant Professor in the Department of Geography, Wilfrid Laurier University, Waterloo, Ontario, Canada. His main research interests center on parks and protected areas, resource management and person-environment fit. His contribution in this volume is based on collaborative work for Environement Canada, Parks on visitor management and national park planning.

David Peerla has taught sociology and forestry at Lakehead University, Ontario, Canada, and has been involved in research projects on single-industry towns and natural resource management in Northern Ontario. He is currently a doctoral candidate in sociology at the University of California-Santa Cruz, where he is studying Canadian forest policy.

Jeremy Rayner was educated at the universities of Cambridge, Durham and British Columbia, and is Assistant Professor of Political Studies at Lakehead University, Ontario, Canada. He is the author of several articles on political language and political ideologies. He is currently developing a research project on professionalization in Canadian forestry and its impact on Canadian politics.

Herbert W. Schroeder attended the University of Arizona from 1969 to 1980, where he received a bachelors degree in mathematics, a masters degree in psychology, and a Ph.D. in environmental psychology. Since 1980 he has worked for the USDA Forest Service, North Central Forest Experiment Station in Chicago. His research concerns public perceptions, preferences, and behavior in urban forest recreation sites.

Margaret A. Shannon is Assistant Professor of Forest Policy at State University of New York, Syracuse. She has also worked as a private consultant. Her research interests broadly concern natural resource sociology and law, and wildland resource science. She has published in *Western Wildlands* and in *Proceedings: Society of American Foresters Annual Meeting*.

C. Nick Taylor is a Research Officer at the Centre for Resource Management, Lincoln College, New Zealand. His training has been in sociology, anthropology and resource management (Ph.D. University of Canterbury, 1981). His research in rural sociology, rural development and social impact assessment has focused on the social effects of New Zealand agricultural aid projects in the South Pacific, coal development, and the sociology of resource communities.

Erik Val is a graduate in geography from the Universities of Waterloo and McGill, with a specialization in resource management. He has undertaken socio-economic research related to native people and northern development, commercial fisheries and petroleum development, and national park planning and management. He is currently the Head of Socio-Economic Research for the Ontario Region of Environment Canada, Parks in Cornwall, Ontario.

Joanne Vining holds a Ph.D. in environmental psychology from the University of Arizona. She is Assistant Professor of Environmental Psychology in the Institute for Environmental Studies and Department of Psychology at the University of Illinois. In addition to her work on emotional and affective processes in environmental preferences, judgments and decisions, she is presently studying the perception of risks associated with environmental hazards, and developing means for assessing amenity resource values.

Lambert N. Wenner is Group Leader for Social Impact Analysis for the U.S. Forest Service. From 1978-1982 he was a minerals impact specialist with the agency. From 1963-1978 he held faculty positions at the universities of Idaho and Maryland, and at other institutions. Wenner has a Ph.D. in social science from Syracuse University. He is the author of over 20 journal articles and federal publications on education, community life, and social aspects of resource management.

INDEX